Julian Mott
Anne Leeming
Edited by Helen Williams

information & communication technology

for AQA A2 Level

second edition

Hodder Murray
A MEMBER OF THE HODDER HEADLINE GROUP

In order to access teacher support materials for this book, please go to www.ict4aqa.co.uk and register your teacher details online. We will then contact your centre to verify the information provided is accurate and send you a password that will provide you with access to the site. It is important that you provide a valid e-mail address when submitting your details.

NB Old Spec

O/P

1/2 SS

The Publishers would like to thank the following for permission to reproduce copyright material:

Photo credits
Cover TEK Image/Science Photo Library; **p.27** educationphotos.co.uk/walmsley; **p.103** Ace Stock Limited/Alamy; **p.142** Anne Leeming; **p.174** Steve Connolly; **p.175** © Royalty-Free/Corbis; **p.180** Mark Scheuern/Alamy; **p.199** Stock Connection Distribution/Alamy.

Acknowledgements
p.62 Amazon.co.uk; **p.63** Sainsbury.co.uk; **p.123** Pass Training (www.pass.co.uk); **p.125** Freeskills.com; **p.127** Screenshot reprinted with permission of Microsoft® Corporation © 2001 MousePointer Manuals Ltd.; **p.236** Copyright © 2003–2005 McAfee, Inc., 535 Oakmead Parkway, Sunnyvale, California 94085. All rights reserved.

All AQA material is reproduced by permission of the Assessment and Qualifications Alliance.

Orders: please contact Bookpoint Ltd, 130 Milton Park, Abingdon, Oxon OX14 4SB. Telephone: (44) 01235 827720. Fax: (44) 01235 400454. Lines are open from 9.00–5.00, Monday to Saturday, with a 24-hour message answering service. Visit our website at www.hoddereducation.co.uk.

Examination support and mark schemes can be found on the AQA website www.aqa.org.uk/qual/gceasa/inf_assess.html

First published in 2003 by
Hodder Murray, an imprint of Hodder Education,
a member of the Hodder Headline Group
338 Euston Road
London NW1 3BH

This Second Edition first published 2006

Impression number	5 4 3 2
Year	2010 2009 2008 2007

Typeset in 11/14pt Stone Informal for Hodder by Pantek Arts Ltd, Maidstone, Kent
Printed and bound in Italy

A catalogue record for this title is available from the British Library

ISBN 13: 9780 340 907269

Contents

1 Organisational structure

What is an organisation?

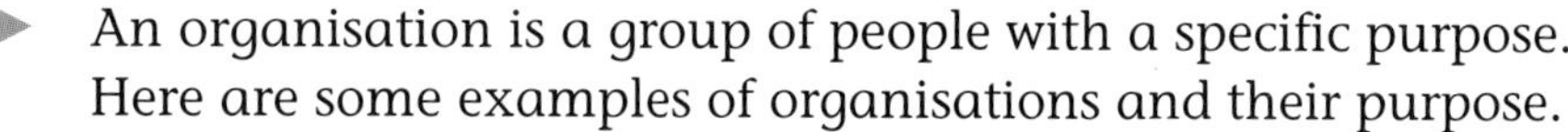

An organisation is a group of people with a specific purpose. Here are some examples of organisations and their purpose.

Organisation	Purpose
A multinational oil company	to make a profit
A government pensions department	to pay pensions to pensioners
A bowls club	to arrange and play bowls matches
A college	to educate students

The purpose of an organisation, whether it is big or small, will determine how it operates.

Roles within an organisation

Individuals within an organisation will have defined roles. Activities and tasks are allocated according to these roles, enabling the organisation to take advantage of specialisms and skills.

The allocation of tasks is called **division of labour**.

By specialising, individuals can develop knowledge and expertise in a particular group of tasks. The larger the organisation, the more likely specialisation is to occur.

For example, in a two-person business, the individuals concerned may share all the tasks. In a very large company, there would be separate staff who specialise in accounts, personnel, marketing, sales, etc.

Organisational structure

All organisations must have some structure. The structure determines who is responsible to whom. This can be shown in an organisational chart like the one shown in figure 1.1. The four telesales assistants are all responsible to Sheila Burnside.

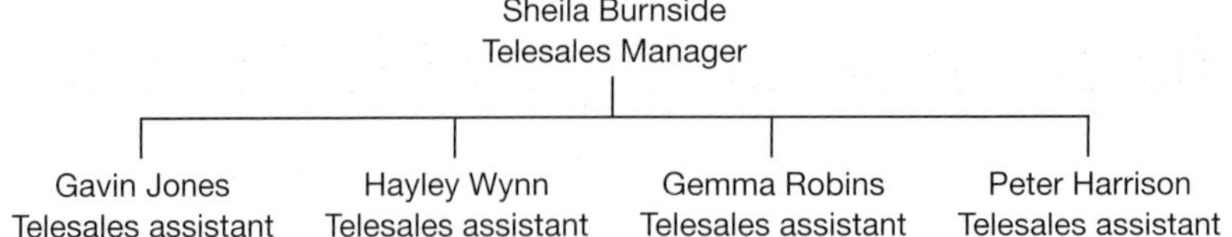

Figure 1.1 Example of an organisational structure

This is only part of the organisational chart for the whole business. Sheila Burnside is responsible to the Marketing Manager. The Marketing Manager is responsible to the Marketing Director and so on.

At the top of the organisational chart is the Managing Director or the person who has ultimate responsibility for the organisation. This could be the chief executive or the owner.

The organisational structure will:

- determine to whom an individual is answerable
- determine who can make what type of decision
- enable managers to co-ordinate, control and monitor the activities of their staff.

Span of control

The **span of control** is the number of employees who are directly supervised by one person. In figure 1.1, Sheila Burnside's span of control is the four telesales assistants.

Too wide a span of control leads to a lack of control and is inefficient. Too narrow a span wastes staff.

The nature of the roles of the staff being supervised will help to determine the appropriate span of control in any particular circumstance. A supervisor of supermarket checkout operators would be able to sustain a larger span of control than a personnel manager. The checkout operators are all carrying out the same, fairly straightforward, tasks whilst a personnel manager's subordinates would have a range of spheres of work such as recruitment, industrial relations and remuneration.

The span of control should be clear in the organisational structure.

Chain of command

The **chain of command** is the path through the levels of management, from the managing director downwards. Instructions go down the line of authority. Problems are referred up the lines to a higher level. Long lines of communication mean messages can be distorted and take time to reach their destination.

The chain of command should also be clear in the organisational structure.

The pyramid or hierarchical structure

The pyramid or hierarchical structure is the traditional shape of an organisational structure in a large business. It is common in large public limited companies, the military and the civil service.

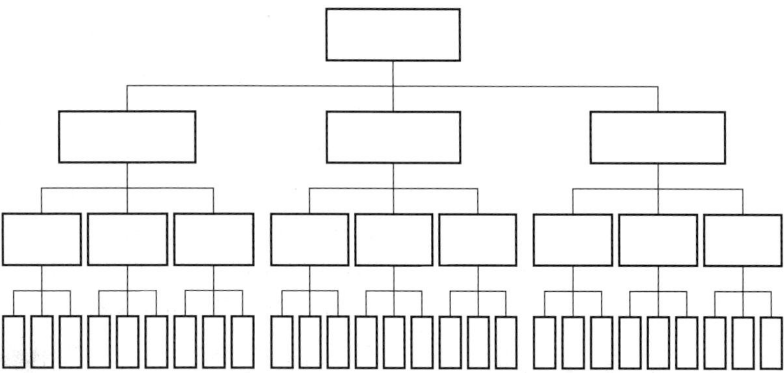

Figure 1.2 The pyramid or hierarchical structure

Roles are clearly defined within a large number of layers, each responsible to the layer above.

At the top of the pyramid is the managing director or chief executive who is responsible for the success or failure of the organisation. Each manager has a relatively small span of control. The chain of command down from the managing director is long.

This hierarchical structure is suitable for large organisations with centralised decision making by the strategic staff.

Problems with the hierarchical structure

- Organisations with a hierarchical structure are likely to be slow to change as important decisions have to be referred all the way up the line.
- Decisions take a long time to be made and take even longer to implement.
- Senior staff can be very remote from the lower levels of the structure.

The horizontal or flat structure

An alternative structure is the horizontal structure (see figure 1.3). In a flat structure there are fewer layers, but the spans of control are much wider. As a result, problems being referred up the line can be resolved more quickly.

As more people are directly answerable to the managing director, the power to make decisions for themselves may need to be delegated. Parts of the organisation may tend to operate independently of the other parts but are still under the umbrella control of senior management.

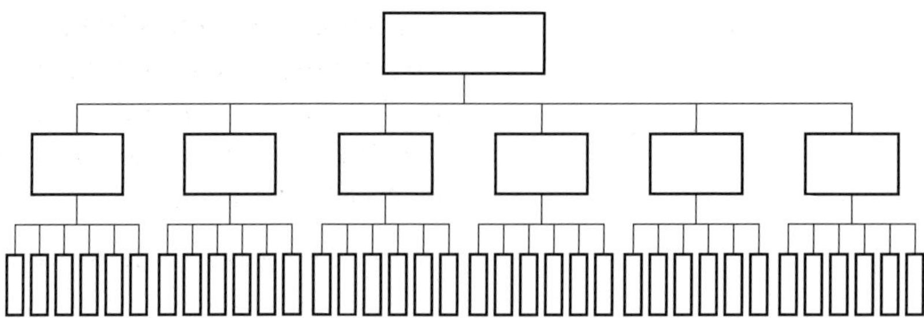

Figure 1.3 The horizontal or flat structure

Employees have more responsibility which often leads to better motivation. It is more likely that employees can contribute more to decision making as there is better communication between staff working at different levels.

Problems with the flat structure

- As departments are specialised, different departments may have little to do with each other, which can lead to poor communication across the organisation.
- Managers can be responsible for several departments so their role is not always clear. They can be responsible for areas beyond their own expertise.
- Control of top management could be weakened as they may have too wide a span of control. They may need to delegate more frequently.
- Fewer levels will usually mean that there are fewer prospects of promotion.

The flat structure is becoming more popular. It gives considerable independence to different units which means that these units can make decisions and change more rapidly. Hierarchical organisations are *static* – changing the way the organisation operates is difficult.

Flat organisations, on the other hand, tend to be more *dynamic* which means that they are more flexible and open to change.

The levels of an organisation's structure

There are generally three levels of personnel in a business organisation, although there may be considerably more layers.

The **strategic** level is the highest level. This consists of senior management, responsible for long-term planning and major decision making. The board of directors and the chief executive make decisions at the strategic level. This might include whether to:

- open a new factory
- move production to a new location possibly overseas
- start to produce a completely new product.

The **tactical** level is the next level. This consists of middle management who are, for example, in charge of one particular department or area of the business. Examples would be a training manager in a factory or a head of department in a school. The tactical decisions they might make include:

- what training courses to offer to staff
- timetable issues such as who should teach which class
- what teaching materials such as text books to buy.

The **operational** level is the lowest level. This consists of the workforce who are making the product, taking sales orders, keeping the accounts, and so on.

Remember: Operational staff may be very well qualified. A surgeon in a hospital, a teacher in a school, an airline pilot are examples of operational staff.

Note*: These three levels of organisation,* ***strategic****,* ***tactical*** *and* ***operational*** *are referred to many times in ICT4. Make sure that you learn them well.*

How has the development of ICT affected organisational structure?

The introduction of Information Technology has tended to lead to flatter organisational structures. One reason is that the introduction of ICT and the pace of hardware and software development means that frequent change is inevitable and businesses must be dynamic to cope with the change.

ICT systems provide better information on staff performance, thus enabling managers to monitor more people and cope more easily with a wider span of control, a feature of flatter organisational structures.

Some jobs at lower levels may disappear altogether, such as typists in the typing pool as a result of the growth of word processing. New, direct methods of data entry reduce the number of clerical staff needed.

All these changes have resulted in the reduction of the number of levels in an organisation.

Over the last twenty years, the jobs of middle managers have been eroded. Contributory causes include the developments in ICT and communications. These have enabled information to be produced, in a form suitable for the strategic managers, directly from the operational level. This removes the need for manipulation and interpretation by middle managers.

Many decisions that used to be taken by middle managers are now taken by computer-based systems. For example, decisions regarding granting of loans to bank customers and stock ordering in supermarkets can all be made by computer-based systems. Increasingly, operational staff can work without needing as much direct middle management involvement.

SUMMARY

Organisations can be structured in a number of ways.

They can have:

- **a hierarchical structure or**
- **a flat structure.**

Hierarchical structures can be rigid and decision-making can be slow. Flat structures can be flexible and autonomous.

There are three main levels of hierarchy in an organisation:

- **strategic**
- **tactical**
- **operational.**

New technologies have affected the organisational structures of many businesses, leading to flatter structures.

ICT has altered the way in which decisions are made by providing information at all levels of the organisation's structure. Decisions can be based on this information.

Chapter 1 Questions

1 Information is communicated at three levels within an organisation. State these **three** levels. (3)

ICT4 January 2003

2 A message has to pass from the chief executive of a company to all the operational staff.

a) Is the message likely to get through more quickly if the company has a hierarchical structure or a flat structure? (1)

b) Explain your answer to part (a). (2)

3 Companies rely on their information systems to provide good quality information. Identify **three** different categories of users of information systems, and state the level at which they operate. (6)

ICT4 June 2003

4 A small company with a rigid hierarchical structure is planning to introduce a computer system. State **four** concerns a director may have on the effect on the structure of the company. (4)

5 For each of the following types of organisation, suggest decisions which would be made at the (a) strategic, (b) tactical and (c) operational level.

a) a multinational bank

b) a retail chain of shoe shops

c) a school or college

d) a car manufacturer. (12)

6 The Apex Insurance Company has a hierarchical structure. Instructions from managers to subordinates are normally given verbally, face-to-face. The company is thinking of investing in an internal e-mail system. Other than the fact that messages arrive more quickly, explain how internal e-mail may speed up communications at Apex. (6)

7 A company with a hierarchical structure is considering making a whole tier of middle management redundant and adopting a flatter structure. Give **two** advantages and **two** disadvantages of this action in the table provided.

Advantages	Disadvantages
1	1
2	2

(4)

8 Explain why it is necessary to have an organisational structure in a business. (2)

2 Information systems and organisations

Data processing systems and information systems

A **data processing system** is a computer system that deals with the routine, day-to-day transactions of an organisation. They carry out repetitive, routine business activities such as the production of invoices or stock control. Such systems are usually involved in large quantities of electronic data capture. These transactions will be at an operational level, for example: recording the loan of books from a library; producing bills for an electricity company or making seat bookings for a cinema.

An **information system** is a system that processes data in a way that improves performance; it should produce information that can be used to help in decision making and provide support for management. The decisions are likely to be at a tactical level or a strategic level. Often this data comes from the data processing system. An example of an information system is a sales information system that summarises overall sales in a number of ways, perhaps showing the total sales by product, region or by salesman.

Examples of data processing and information systems

Data processing system	Operational purpose	Information system	Examples of decisions to be made
Online airline booking system.	Reserving seats for passengers, producing tickets, boarding cards and passenger lists.	The system can provide the airline with the percentage of seats sold.	Whether to continue the service. Whether to put on extra planes for a popular service.
A company payroll system.	Calculating wages and salaries, printing pay slips, conducting money transfers.	The system can provide the company with attendance records and the total wage bill, each broken down by department.	Whether the company can afford to employ more staff or pay them more. Whether to take action over sickness levels.
A school or college timetable system.	Allocating students to classes and printing individual timetables.	The system can provide the school management with summaries of class sizes, staff work load and room utilisation.	Whether to split large classes. Whether to cut unpopular classes. Whether more staff and rooms are needed.

In each of the three examples shown in the table above, decisions have to be made. These decisions can be based on information provided by the information system. Use of an information system is likely to lead to more informed decisions, better decision making and more transparent decision making (the reasons for the decision will be clearer).

Activity 1

Copy the grid below and fill in the empty boxes.

Data processing system	Operational purpose	Information system	Examples of decisions to be made
Stock control			
Supermarket POS	Data on items sold acquired through scanning bar codes is used to calculate customers' bills. Loyalty points are calculated and assigned to the customer through the use of a loyalty card.		
Telephone billing system			
Examination board mark recording system for A level examinations			

The use of ICT-based information techniques has speeded up the data collection process. Large amounts of data can be processed and analysed, and the information generated can be communicated very quickly. Electronic links improve communications and reduce the need for paper. Decision making can be speeded up.

However, more information may not necessarily lead to better decision making. Too much information may lead to information overload. Information must be at a suitable level of detail. An **exception report** is one which, instead of listing information about every item, lists information only on those items that meet certain conditions. The manager can immediately see where action may need to be taken without having to wade through huge amounts of data.

In a school or college an exception report that shows details only of those students whose attendance has been less than 90% over a period could be produced so that students who had a poor attendance record could be swiftly followed up. The exception report would be of more use in highlighting students with problems than a list showing the attendance of every student for the same period. Most students would have an attendance rate >90% and so a list showing the attendance of all students would be very long; the reader would have to search through to find out those who attendance was <90%. Exception reports could also be used by an airline. For example, a list of flights with an unusually low or exceptionally high number of seats sold could be produced which would focus attention on issues that needed to be addressed.

Information may be presented as a summary or in a graphical or tabular form.

Management Information Systems

A **Management Information System (MIS)** uses operational-level data to provide management-level information. The data can come from both internal and external sources and is combined and often presented in an easy-to-read format such as tables or graphs. The information is used by managers at different levels of the organisation to make effective decisions or plan appropriately.

An MIS aims to provide a manager with all the information needed to make decisions associated with the job as effectively as possible.

The use of such systems has increased as a result of the rapid growth in the use of database systems. An MIS is usually based on data from one or more databases and allows managers at different levels to access information that is appropriate and in an easily understandable form.

Example of an MIS

The manager of a chocolate factory needs to decide the number and types of bars to be made in a particular week. The following information would help him make this decision:

- the number of each type currently in stock
- outstanding orders still to be delivered
- the sales of each type last week
- the sales of each type this time last year.

This information could be created from the data collected as part of the day-to-day operational data processing system.

The sales manager for the same company will require information on products sold rather than products produced. He will need to be able to compare the performances of different members of the sales force. Information on the products' market share and the nature and performance of a rival manufacturer's products will be needed by the manager so that he can make decisions on which product to promote and on the size and nature of any advertising campaign. Such information is **external**.

Management Information Systems provide information to be used by managers at a strategic or tactical level.

The information is often grouped but the MIS allows the manager to 'drill down' and get the information in more detail, if required.

Strategic information

Strategic information is used by senior managers such as directors and the chief executive in a business, head teacher and governors in a school, or directors of a charity. Long-term planning is a key function at this level of management and most decisions made will reflect this. An overview of the operation of the whole organisation is required so that an assessment can be made of how well objectives are being met. Actual costs and profits need to be compared with forecasts for all sections of the business. An MIS can produce projections and predictions based on current data, both internal and external, that relate to the business.

The nature of strategic management means that the information that is required at this level can be very varied both in content and in timing. There will be a need for some regular reporting, but depending on the decision to be made, other, 'one-off', information may be needed. External sources will often play a major role at this level.

For example, a company that produces and sells ice cream and other associated products has six factories located in different parts of the United Kingdom. The senior management may wish to close down one factory to reduce costs. This would be a strategic decision and the management would need a wide range of information. An example of internal information would be the increase in labour costs at each factory. External information would include the present site value of each factory.

Most Management Information Systems will provide summary statistical information suitable for senior management. Often, however, such summarising hides crucial detail. The need for such detail would be impossible to predict as it depends on specific circumstances. This lack of appropriate detail could result in incorrect decisions.

A form of MIS called an Executive Information System (EIS) provides aggregated information for senior managers. Usually an EIS will have an extremely user-friendly, graphical interface. If the manager wishes to learn more about some information that is displayed, he can display the information in more detail by clicking on a point on the screen, a **hot spot**. Such a system would bring together information from a range of internal and external sources.

For example, a senior manager is reviewing company expenditure over the past year, comparing it with the estimated budget. This information is displayed in a graphical form. She then notices that one department is well over budget and decides to investigate further. A click of the mouse button on the appropriate figure results in the details of the budget and expenditure of the department in question being displayed. It appears that the overspend is greatest in the raw materials' expenditure, so our manager clicks on this figure to reveal that prices are as estimated but the department has purchased more raw materials than planned. The manager can investigate sales and stock levels to find out whether these extra purchases were necessary.

Activity 2

The Principal of a college is reviewing the A level results.

- Describe the information that she would need and the form in which it should be presented to her.

Unfortunately, the college pass rate is lower than expected.

- Explain how an EIS could be used to investigate the finding.

Tactical information

Middle managers, typically department heads, have roles that are tactical. Such a manager would be responsible for a certain section of a business and would be responsible to a senior manager. She would be likely to have a number of operational managers reporting to her. In some organisations, such a manager could be responsible for a sales region, a specific factory or group of shops. In another organisation, a middle manager could be in charge of training, customer accounting or ICT Services.

Much of the information needed by such managers relates directly to the performance of the organisation and is used for monitoring and controlling purposes. An example would be sales figures for each of the company's sales representatives. Regular reports to assist making tactical decisions are common at this level in a variety of forms: tabular, graphical and pictorial. The information is usually prepared on a routine basis, perhaps weekly or monthly. A factory manager of an ice cream company might consider running an extra shift during the summer months. Such a decision would be based on tactical information.

Exception reports, for example, a list of all sales figures which fall below their target level, provide managers with a powerful tool in establishing areas for further investigation. Successful decision making at this level often depends upon accurate forecasting, for example, cash flow forecasts.

Operational information

Operational managers are closely involved at the productive end of the operation. A supervisor may oversee the workforce on a particular production line. He may need to work out rotas and rest breaks, monitor the rate of production, ensure that hold-ups due to machine failure or delay in the arrival of spare parts are minimised and ensure that the quality of the finished product is maintained within acceptable levels.

The information system could provide him with details of his employees' working hours as well as current stock levels which would help in his decision making.

Nowadays, many operational decisions, such as when to reorder stock, are made automatically by the computer software. The reordering can itself be initiated automatically.

Simple lists and charts will play a major part in operational information. Such a list could be produced by sorting the transaction data that has been processed as part of the normal data processing function.

At the operational level, information is characterised by a high level of detail. For example, in a shoe shop chain, the local shop manager might require a daily, itemised list of all shoes sold, sorted into types, styles and quantities. The regional manager (tactical level) would require a weekly or monthly summary report showing the total sales for each shop in a region. At a strategic level, the marketing manager might wish to forecast sales trends over the next few years.

Activity 3

A Head of Department in a school has to order new text books for the incoming AS level ICT class. Another part of his role is to see all students who are not progressing well on the course so that he can offer advice and provide them with appropriate support.

- What information could the Management Information System provide him with that will help him carry out the above tasks?

Worked exam question

1 A large chain of supermarkets makes use of data processing systems and information systems.

a) With the use of suitable examples, identify the difference between a *data processing system* and an *information system*. (4)

b) Describe, with an example of each, the role of an information system in decision making for the following levels of supermarket management:

i) tactical

ii) strategic. (4)

c) Give an example of how a data processing operation in a supermarket might provide data for a company-wide information system. (2)

ICT4 June 2002

EXAMINER'S GUIDANCE

It is important in a question that sets a scenario (in this case a chain of supermarkets) that any examples you give relate to the scenario.

Part (a) is fairly straightforward. Essentially you need to define each type of system so that the difference is evident. For each definition there is one mark and for each example a further mark.

The definitions could be: A data processing system is involved in repetitive and routine business activities; an information system uses data collected to improve performance and decision making by management.

Look back at your responses in Activity 1 and list some data processing and some information systems likely to be needed within a chain of supermarkets.

Data processing system	Information system

Now put one of each of these together with the definitions to create a full answer.

SAMPLE ANSWER

A data processing system is involved in repetitive and routine business activities such as stock control whereas an information system uses data collected to improve performance and decision making by management. An example of an information system would be a sales information system.

EXAMINER'S GUIDANCE

Part (b) is testing whether you can highlight the difference between relatively short term decisions and longer term ones. As the company is made up of a chain of supermarkets, the tactical decision making will take place locally at an individual supermarket and the strategic decision making will take place centrally at head office.

SAMPLE ANSWER

At a tactical level, the information system needs to provide information that allows short term decisions to be made at a local supermarket.

EXAMINER'S GUIDANCE

Fill in some ideas for examples that relate to the scenario.

Tactical	Strategic
Staff rosters	Where to locate new stores

Now put together a full answer; the definition for strategic level should take the same form as the one given above for the tactical level.

Part (c) is demanding an answer given in the supermarket context. The first mark will be given for indicating how the output from a data processing system is used by an MIS; the second mark is dependent on the first.

First come up with some ideas of the ways that data input into a data processing system can be used in an information system (look back at Activity 1). Then put them together into an answer.

SAMPLE ANSWER

A suitable answer could be:

The data from the POS system is processed (1) to show who buys what goods, at which location and at what time of day (1)

or

The data from the loyalty card system is processed (1) into information that can be presented in a way that enables management to make strategic decisions (1).

EXAMINER'S GUIDANCE

A key term in each answer is ***processed****.*

case study 1
MIS – West Yorkshire Police

West Yorkshire Police are the fourth largest metropolitan force in England and Wales with 8000 employees, police and support staff. With the introduction of the Government's Best Value regime, the force needed to use ICT for more efficient ways of working and to deliver better value for money.

Police overtime payments were the largest devolved part of the budget. Information given to the divisions about the amount of overtime worked was completely out of date by the time it was sent out.

West Yorkshire Police were looking for a system that gave them better financial budgeting and could deliver management information.

The new system records how many hours each police officer has worked and exports the data directly into the payroll system. It includes an MIS which is able to provide information to managers about which division, which group and which week the overtime is worked in. As a result it is much easier to monitor spending.

- Which information is used at an operational level?
- Which information is used at a tactical level?
- Think up some examples of decisions that could be made based on the tactical information provided.

Success or failure of a Management Information System

In spite of many technical advances and the investment of huge amounts of money, time and effort, many Management Information Systems have not fulfilled their promise and have failed to provide the management with the information that they need. Most such systems involve complex and extensive software and are very often designed specifically for the users.

An MIS is likely to be designed and developed by a specialist team which could be from within the organisation or from a software house. The team members will have to work very closely with the managers who will be using the new system; it is crucial that everyone involved in the project knows exactly what is wanted.

A successful MIS will be well used by the management of the organisation, being seen as a real benefit to the user; it will be easy and quick to use.

There are many factors that will affect whether or not an MIS is successful. The following factors could contribute to the failure of an MIS within an organisation.

Inadequate analysis

It is important that the ICT experts spend adequate time getting to know the information needs of the managers. This can only be achieved once a thorough understanding of the organisation has been gained and a detailed analysis made of the system. A poor analysis will lead to an incomplete understanding of what is required; the MIS that is then developed on the basis of this analysis is unlikely to meet the needs of the organisation and will not be used.

It is important to follow a life-cycle methodology in a standard way to allow effective analysis, design and testing thus making sure that no important steps are missed.

Lack of management involvement in design

It is vital that the management is involved with the design of the system. They are to be the users and it is therefore crucial that any system meets their real needs. The managers involved need to be at the appropriate level in the organisation.

Emphasis on the computer system

A poor system will be produced if there is too much emphasis on the computer system and inadequate attention given to the whole system and the data flow throughout the organisation. The system should be designed around the information needs of the managers rather than be based upon what the computer can easily produce.

Concentration on low-level data processing

Many Management Information Systems have failed to provide adequate information as too much emphasis has been placed on the lower level data processing applications. Information is not provided in the right level of detail to enable managers to make the correct decision quickly. Information should be produced in an easily understandable form that is accessible to the manager. The manager should not have to carry out calculations on data to acquire the information that he needs.

Lack of management knowledge of ICT systems

The management will need to have an up-to-date knowledge of current ICT systems and their capabilities. They will need to be able to make informed decisions and not be blinded by the ICT experts' knowledge and use of jargon.

Inappropriate/excessive management demands

An inadequate knowledge of the capabilities of current technology may result in management making inappropriate or excessive demands from the system. When the system inevitably fails to meet their high expectations they will be disillusioned and may well not then use the system. Strong communication links with management can make impossible demands less likely and can lead to appropriate compromises being agreed for any particular requirement.

Lack of teamwork

Inadequate teamwork can lead to the chain breaking at its weakest link. Unless colleagues cooperate some work can be left undone, other work may be repeated. A successful implementation depends upon an effective and balanced team, with everyone working together on appropriate tasks, well controlled by good leadership. (See Chapter 12 for more detail on effective teams).

Lack of professional standards

A lack of professional standards can lead to missed deadlines and a system that does not function as was intended. Without standards, different team members may be unclear of exactly which tasks their colleagues have completed and whether all aspects have been covered. Testing might not be carried out sufficiently thoroughly.

When professional standards are employed in a project, all team members know what processes and procedures to use during development. All stages of the project development are carried out using agreed methods that everyone works to; everyone will produce documentation in the same format; testing will be carried out in a standard way. See Chapter 12 for more detail of the use of professional standards.

Use of project management methodology should ensure that the project manager is able to monitor progress, particularly checking whether the project is within budget and on schedule. In this way a robust MIS will be implemented appropriately and on time.

All systems need clear documentation that is easy for the user to follow. Incomplete documentation will frustrate the user and could prevent the new MIS from being fully used.

case study 2

▶ Passport to nowhere

'Teething problems' with a new computer system at Britain's Passport Agency led to a backlog of over half a million would-be holidaymakers waiting for their passports.

The problem was made worse by changes in the regulations requiring all children to have their own passport and by a 20 per cent increase in applications for passports. Offices were taking nearly 40 working days to process an application, compared to a target of ten days.

Queues formed outside passport offices. In Glasgow the first people started queuing one night at midnight. By 9.30 a.m. over 1000 people were waiting in the rain.

The new system was installed by the German company Siemens at a cost of £230 million. Siemens said: 'It is misleading to suggest that the delays experienced by the public are primarily caused by failures in ICT systems. It is clear that the application demand has exceeded Home Office forecasts.'

The new computer systems were installed first at offices in Liverpool and Newport. This was where the biggest backlogs occurred. Reports suggested that the need to install the whole system before the end of the year meant that the new system had not been fully tested.

So what went wrong?

Many reasons were given for the Passport Agency's difficulties in issuing passports.

- The new ruling that children had to have their own passports undoubtedly made the problem worse. This obviously meant there would be an increase in the number of passports required and the number of passport applications. Was this taken into account in staffing levels and in the original hardware specification?
- The new computer system went online at the start of the summer – the Passport Agency's busiest time.
- The rush to introduce the complete new system meant that full testing had not been carried out.
- The new system was piloted at two offices. There was inadequate integration with existing systems and procedures

What lessons can be learned from this case study?

SUMMARY

- **A data processing system carries out the day to day operational activities of an organisation.**
- **An information system provides information for the user that can be used in decision making.**
- **A Management Information System (MIS) provides information in appropriate forms for managers. It converts data from internal and external sources into information. This is communicated in an appropriate form to managers at different levels to enable them to make effective decisions.**
- **Decisions can take place at different levels within an organisation: strategic, tactical and operational. The level of detail, form and type of information needed is different at each management level.**
- **Not all MISs are implemented successfully. Factors influencing success or failure include:**
  - **inadequate analysis**
  - **lack of management involvement in design**
  - **emphasis on the computer system**
  - **concentration on low-level data processing**
  - **lack of management knowledge of ICT systems and their capabilities**
  - **inappropriate/excessive management demands**
  - **lack of team work**
  - **lack of professional standards.**

Chapter 2 Questions

1 **a)** What is meant by a 'data processing system'? (2)
b) Give an example of a data processing system. (1)
c) What is meant by an 'information system'? (2)
d) Give an example of an information system. (1)
e) Explain how a data processing system differs from an information system. (4)

2 Describe what is meant by the following terms, and give an example of each:
a) internal information (3)
b) external information. (3)

3 A travel agency with outlets throughout the north of England decides to implement a Management Information System (MIS).
a) Describe what is meant by the term Management Information System (MIS). (3)
b) Explain how the travel agency might benefit from having an MIS. (3)
Many Management Information Systems fail to deliver what is expected of them. One factor that can lead to such a failure is a lack of the use of professional standards in the development of the system.
c) i. Explain what is meant by the term professional standards. (2)
ii. Describe why the lack of professional standards might lead to failure. (2)
d) Describe **three** other factors, other than the lack of professional standards, that might cause an MIS to fail. (6)

4 A hotel chain has 30 hotels in the UK. The management is planning to install a new data processing and information system.
a) Describe **two** functions likely to be included in the data processing system. (4)
b) Describe **two** functions likely to be included in the information system. (4)
c) Give an example of information that could be provided by the system and explain why it would be of use in strategic decision making. (3)
d) Give an example of information that could be provided by the system and explain why it would be of use in operational decision making. (3)

5 A chain of supermarkets uses a number of linked data processing and management information systems, including a point-of-sale system, a stock control system and a management sales information system. Outputs from these systems are aimed at different levels of user.
a) State the level of information needed for each of the following types of user:
i. supermarket stock-checker (1)
ii. manager of the fresh food department in one store (1)
iii. company executive officer, based at head office. (1)
(One word answers are acceptable for this part of the question.)

ICT4 June 2004

6 Chipton School has recently expanded and opened a sixth form. A new Head Teacher has been appointed and she has decided to install a new Management Information System (MIS).
Discuss the implications of installing this new system paying attention to the following:
- what types of information the Management Information System would provide
- ways in which information provided could be used in a range of decision making at different levels within the school
- the factors that should be taken into account to ensure that the new system is implemented successfully.

(The quality of Written Communication will be assessed in your answer.) (20)

7 Management's understanding and involvement can play an important part in the introduction of a Management Information System (MIS). Give **three** actions that managers could take to increase the chances of an MIS being successful.
For each action state how it would help to ensure success. (6)

ICT4 June 2005

3 The development and life cycle of an information system

The system life cycle

The process of introducing a new information system is called the 'system life cycle'. The old system may be a manual system or a computer-based system.

As the term *cycle* implies, producing a new information system is not a one-off exercise involving a few months of activity. A system, once developed, will need maintenance and eventually will be seen as inadequate to meet the users' needs so a new system will then need to be developed, and so on.

Why do we need a new system?

An information system might need replacing for a number of reasons.

The technology used might have become outdated

New technology may offer a more efficient solution or one that offers additional functions, enabling the organisation to be more competitive.

For example, a new system may have wireless connectivity using palmtop computers that can access the computer system remotely.

Of course it is not necessary to replace a system just because a new one has been developed. A company may think it best to stick with an old system if a new one would be prohibitively expensive or cause too much disruption.

Changes in the organisation

The organisation of a business may change, changing the requirements for the information system. This might happen for a number of reasons: the organisation might be expanding, restructuring, merging with, or taking over, another company or diversifying into new areas of activity. (See Case Study 1)

Changes in the demands of the users

What was acceptable to the user when a system was installed might not be a few years later. Users become increasingly sophisticated in their understanding of ICT and consequently are more demanding in how they expect a system to perform. (See Case Study 2)

case study 1
▶ GT Morgan

Leicestershire based shopfitters GT Morgan employ 70 staff and have a turnover of £10 million. GT Morgan used a computerised financial and estimating system.

However, with the business expanding, demands for more quotations increased and the number of staff increased. The computer system was six years old; originally designed for six people it was now serving eight users and was too slow.

GT Morgan invested in a ten-user computer system to replace the old system. It was possible to convert all the data from the old system and install it on the new system.

The new system is faster and the software is more reliable. The new system also provides features which were not available on the old system, such as management reports and the ability to compare estimated quotations with real bills of quantity.

case study 2
▶ Chip and pin cards

In October 2003 banks and credit card companies announced that they would be changing to a new Chip and Pin method for payment from January 2005. Purchasers would have to type in a secret four figure 'PIN' number.

This was an attempt to reduce credit card fraud which was running at over £500 million a year. A similar system in France had seen an 80 per cent reduction in plastic card fraud.

The changeover involved issuing more than 76 million new chip and pin cards to over 36 million people. Over 600,000 tills had to be upgraded in shops and staff had to be trained.

Within a month of the introduction of chip and pin, almost two-thirds of the public had used the chip and pin method. Of the people questioned, 83 per cent said the experience had been 'positive' but nearly a quarter of them said they found it hard to remember their PIN number.

Stages in the system life cycle

Formal methods in the development of information systems

The purchase and installation of a new computer system is likely to be expensive and take some time. It is vital for the organisation that the new system:

- is introduced smoothly
- does not exceed the agreed budget
- does not exceed time deadlines
- is fully working.

As the introduction of the new system is vital to the success of the organisation, formal methods for developing an information system have been developed to try to ensure the new system is a success.

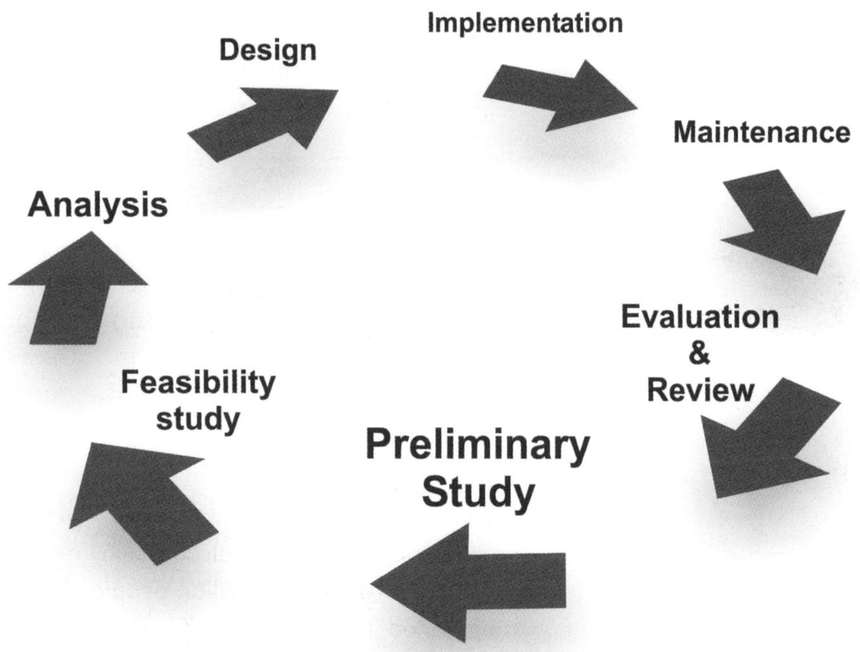

Figure 3.1 The traditional system life cycle

The stages of introducing a new system that have traditionally been used are shown in figure 3.1 The system is a cycle because no system lasts for ever, and after a period of time, the cycle will start again with a new study into the feasibility of a new system.

Although the life cycle goes through a number of stages, a particular stage is often repeated a number of times. For example, when the design stage is apparently complete the prospective users or developers may highlight problems that require the stage to be repeated.

Preliminary study

This is a brief study to look at whether or not a new system is needed. The managers will initiate the study if they feel that the present system is not functioning well or that a new system might lead to improvements in productivity or quality.

Feasibility study

This study looks at the existing system and possible alternatives, including a new system or upgrading the old one. The study should consider:

- Technical feasibility: 'Will the new system work?'
- Economic feasibility: 'Will it save us money?'
- Legal feasibility: 'Does it break the law?'
- Operational feasibility: 'Will it really solve the problem?'
- Schedule: 'Can it be built in time to produce benefits?'

Looking at these five factors is sometimes referred to as **TELOS** after the five initial letters.

The study will include a formal report for the management of the company, who will then decide whether to give approval to continue. If approval is given, the management will decide on a budget for the new system.

Systems analysis

Once approval has been given to go ahead, the next stage is the systems analysis carried out by a systems analyst. This involves investigating the requirements of the users.

This will involve analysing existing documents, looking at issues such as who uses them, how often they are used, how is the data collected, who the documents are sent to and what they do with them.

It will also involve sending questionnaires to staff, interviews and direct observation. The systems analyst will use formal graphical and tabular methods to represent the current system. Data flow diagrams (DFDs) may be drawn up as well as a number of charts showing how data will be organised.

The systems analysts use the information that they have found to produce a set of deliverables for the new system which are agreed with the users. They form a contract between the developers and users.

It is important to agree and write down these deliverables because:

- they will specify the content of the new system
- they will ensure that the work is produced to agreed standards
- they will specify exactly what the users' requirements are
- they will specify what documents will be provided.

Agreeing the deliverables before the work starts will prevent arguments later.

The deliverables will include:

- system functions
- user interface designs
- provision of existing data
- conversion of existing data
- test plan
- user documentation
- technical documentation
- deliverable timetable.

Design

The design stage for the new system determines how the requirements specification will be implemented. It involves breaking the problem down into smaller sub-problems, designing the fields and tables of the database, input formats, output formats, validation checks and the test plan.

Clear time scales are needed to prevent the project from over running. A project timetable and deadlines for each part of the work will be included in the design. A system specification is drawn up in sufficient detail for the programmers to implement the system.

Implementation

Implementation consists of a number of stages:

Hardware and software development

This is the stage when the system is produced by the development of programs and/or customisation of software packages. Programs are coded, tested and documented. In all but the smallest projects, a team of programmers will be involved. It is vital that the work is monitored very carefully, and that time scales are adhered to. Files will need to be converted into a form suitable for the new system. Hardware must also be installed and thoroughly tested. Installation may require extensive cabling and alteration of buildings.

Testing

Testing is a crucial part of program development. Test data should test that all branches of the program perform to specification. Data should be used to test extreme cases. For example, if a temperature value can be any number in the range 0 to 25, the values 0 and 25 would be the extreme values. Testing should also include invalid data to ensure that it is rejected. (Temperature values of 26, –4 and 56 would be invalid.) When testing, it is crucial that the results produced by the program are compared with expected results. Any discrepancies should be investigated.

Changeover

The changeover to the new system takes place once all the programming is complete and follows a complete systems test. It is possible to test a system before full implementation by using historical data. The output from the new system is compared with that produced by the old system.

It is crucial that all users of the new system should be trained. They will need to have confidence in their ability to use it.

Monitoring

Once a system is in full operation it is monitored to check that it has met the objectives set out in the original specification. Inevitably, changes will need to be made to the systems. These changes are known as **systems maintenance**. Most programming hours are spent on maintaining existing systems rather than in producing new systems.

Evaluation and review

When the implementation of a project is complete, it is necessary to evaluate the success of the project and review its effectiveness. Such evaluation will involve returning to the original objectives and performance criteria to assess how well they have been met.

Evaluation will involve discussions with management and users of the system some time after it has been installed to gather their opinions as to the new system's effectiveness. Other, objective, tests of performance should be made, such as testing that the speed of carrying out different tasks is within the requirement specified. Surveys can be used to find out if information flows are correct and whether or not the information that is delivered is of a high quality (see Chapter 5).

case study 3
A new system at Nissan

Paperwork at Nissan's Sunderland plant had reached such proportions that labour costs were excessive and mailing costs high.

A feasibility study suggested that some of this paperwork could be carried out by computer using EDI (Electronic Data Interchange). This means sending documents such as orders and invoices to suppliers electronically via the Internet, rather than by post.

The analysis involved looking at the old manual system to see how it was carried out and what documents were involved.

A new system was designed cutting out the printed mailings. This saved time in communicating and removed the need for rekeying, reducing errors.

After thorough testing implementation took place, originally with only a few suppliers. The system was then extended to more suppliers, cutting mail to suppliers by over 90 per cent.

- Explain why the old system was replaced.
- What is EDI?
- How would changeover be achieved?

case study 4

▶ An electronic registration system

Figure 3.2 EARS register in use in the classroom

A sixth form college in the south of England decided to install an electronic attendance registration system (EARS) for class attendance. Each teacher has an A4 wallet which holds a specialised computer device. Each device is battery run and linked to the central computer by a wireless network.

The new method of registration was chosen to replace the current, paper-based system. Transmitters were installed and wallets configured during the Easter holidays. For the first half of the summer term, the system was piloted by the Biology and English departments. Some errors and operational problems were sorted out during this pilot run. The rest of the teachers were introduced to the system and trained in its use. ▶

After the half-term break, the system went live throughout the college. However, to ensure that backup would be available in the case of failure, the paper-based system was continued in parallel. Gradually the staff became more confident users, fewer mistakes were made and less support needed. The following September the old paper-based system was abandoned.

- Explore the effects that computer failure of the EARS system could have on the college attendance system.
- Describe three other electronic means of collecting attendance data. Explain the advantages and disadvantages of each method.
- Examine the aspects that would have been considered by the college when undertaking a feasibility study.

Worked exam question

Many commercial organisations already operate using computer-based information systems, yet they often introduce new systems or replace current ones.

a) State three reasons why a feasibility study might recommend the replacement or updating of an existing information system. (3)

b) Describe three factors that should be considered when discussing the introduction of a new information system. (6)

ICT4 June 2002

EXAMINER'S GUIDANCE

Part (a) only says 'state' and there are only three marks. Examples of possible reasons include:

SAMPLE ANSWER

- The current system may no longer be fit for purpose, e.g. it may be too slow.
- Technical developments mean the new system will have more features.
- Changes in business methods may require a new system.

EXAMINER'S GUIDANCE

Part (b) requires description. One mark will be given for stating the factor and the second mark for describing it. Examples of possible answers include:

SAMPLE ANSWER

- Technical issues. The new system must be able to do everything the user wants it to do.
- Economic issues. The new system must provide a cost benefit.
- Legal issues. The new system must be within the law.

SUMMARY

The system life cycle is the series of stages involved in replacing an old system with a new one. The stages are:

- Preliminary study
- Feasibility study – A preliminary investigation to look at the technical, economical, legal, operational and schedule feasibility (TELOS) of the required new system. At the end of this stage the senior management will decide whether or not to give the go-ahead.
- Systems Analysis – An investigation into the current system to find out how it works and what is required from a new system.

  Techniques used to investigate the current system include:
  - interview
  - questionnaire
  - observation
  - detailed study of documents
- Deliverables need to be agreed at this stage such as:
  - a timetable for delivering the new system
  - agreed functions of the new system
  - what documentation must be provided
  - user interface designs
  - how the system will be tested.
- Design – All the elements of the new system are planned:
  - inputs
  - outputs
  - data storage
  - human computer interface
  - test plan

  Clear timescales are needed and deadlines set.
- Implementation and testing – The application is built using an appropriate programming language or software development tools. It is thoroughly tested, using a realistic volume of real data as well as extreme and invalid data. The current system is replaced with the new system. New files have to be created, hardware set up, users trained.
- Monitoring
- Evaluation and Review

Chapter 3 Questions

1 In a system development life cycle, describe the need for:

a) clear timescales (2)

b) agreed deliverables (2)

c) approval to proceed. (2)

ICT4 June 2003

2 During the development life cycle of an information system, there is a need for agreed deliverables, e.g. a test plan with data that is produced at the design stage. Give **two** other examples of such deliverables, stating at which stage of the life cycle each one would be produced. (4)

ICT4 June 2005

3 'Information systems are the life-blood of any organisation.'

Discuss this statement with the aid of examples.

Include in your discussion:

- the role and relevance of an information system to aid decision making
- the development and life cycle of an information system
- factors which lead to the success or failure of an information system.

The quality of Written Communication will be assessed in your answer. (20)

ICT4 June 2004

(Hint: this question relates to topics covered in Chapters 2 and 3).

4 Give **two** reasons why it is necessary to use formal methods in the development of information systems. (4)

5 One of the stages in the development of a new computer system is the feasibility study.

a) Explain the purpose of a feasibility study. (2)

b) What areas should be considered in the feasibility study? (3)

6 Draw a diagram to illustrate the main phases of the traditional system life cycle. (5)

7 A systems analyst has been employed to produce a computer-based system to replace the current manual one in a lending library. Describe **three** methods of investigating the current system; for each method explain what information the analyst would expect to gather. (9)

4 Corporate information systems strategy

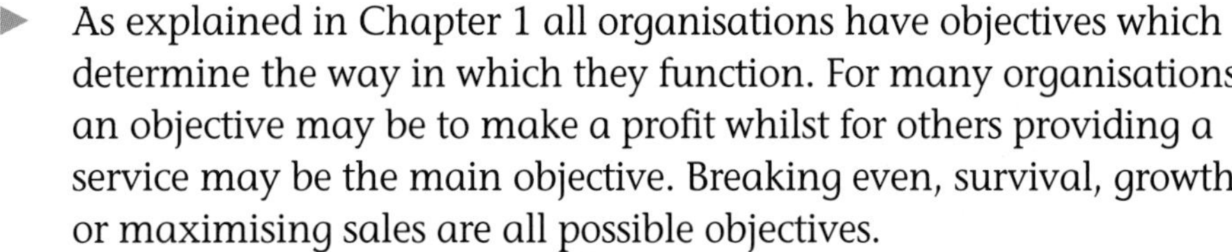

As explained in Chapter 1 all organisations have objectives which determine the way in which they function. For many organisations an objective may be to make a profit whilst for others providing a service may be the main objective. Breaking even, survival, growth or maximising sales are all possible objectives.

Businesses need a strategy to help them to achieve these objectives. The strategy may define what the business will do to become or remain successful. For example, the strategy might plan areas of expansion and anticipate areas of growth.

An organisation needs to establish an information systems strategy so that the information needs of everyone in the organisation can be met.

Factors influencing an information systems strategy within an organisation

Every organisation is different and the information system must be developed to meet its needs. However, such systems need to be strategically planned. Among the factors influencing the choice and design of an information system are:

The objectives of the organisation

The information system is only a means to an end. It exists to support the organisation in pursuit of its objectives. A company manufacturing automotive parts will have different objectives from one selling insurance. This will affect the sort of system required.

The organisational structure of the organisation

The way in which the organisation is structured and the various business functions managed will need to be taken into account. A description of the current departments and how information is used will need to be studied carefully.

The information system needs to provide information to the right person at the right level in the right detail. For example, an organisation which is managed geographically will have regional managers who require reports summarising the performance of all functions within that region. In an organisation that is structured functionally, a production manager would require summaries of the performance at all factories in the organisation.

A formal hierarchical structure will require a method for ensuring information is passed up and down the structure appropriately and in a timely manner.

Information flow within the organisation

The information system should enable good communication within the organisation. The design of the information system must take account of information flow around the organisation. For example, the use of a company wide intranet or e-mail system can be used to get information to all employees quickly and efficiently.

Hardware and software

Any information system must be able to read existing data files. New software must be compatible with old software. To change to another package could cause unnecessary anxiety and require further training. Hardware must be appropriate. In buying new hardware, it is essential that old software and data can be used easily. Continuity is important.

Legal issues

The information system must take account of legal and audit requirements. These will vary from business to business but are likely to involve compliance with legislation such as the Data Protection Act.

Personnel organisation

The system must take account of the personnel and their roles. Differences will depend on who has responsibility for the information system within the organisation; who is responsible for writing the ICT strategy; who is responsible for implementing it and who purchases equipment.

Management style and decision making methods

The nature of the information system will depend on who makes the decisions in the company. It could be the Chief Executive, Managing Director or the Board of Directors. Some organisations make extensive use of committees for decision making. Some delegate decisions to less senior staff.

The resources available

The hardware and technology used and its age and capabilities will be important considerations. Potential for upgrading and compatibility issues will also need to be considered. The current software that is in use within the organisation will also influence the policy. Issues relating to software include the types used, whether generic or bespoke and possible future directions of the company.

Behavioural factors

In any organisation human behavioural issues will determine priorities. The personalities of the people who will use the system, their motivation and ability to adapt to change all have to be taken into account.

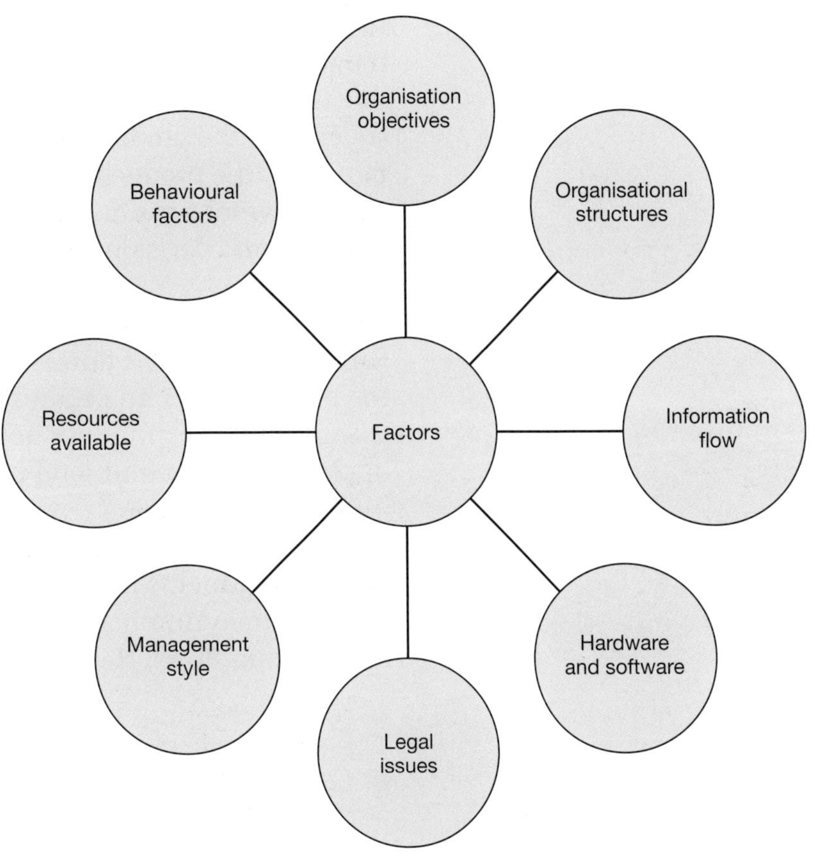

Figure 4.1 Factors influencing an information systems strategy within an organisation

Information flow

Managers need information that is relevant to the task in hand. Good information helps them to plan, to control and to make the right decisions. The better the information, the greater their knowledge of the situation and the better the decision making.

Information flows externally between the organisation and the outside world. For example, a customer might order items from the company. The company might respond by sending an acknowledgement to the customer. These are both examples of external information flow.

Information also flows internally within the organisation. Huge amounts of information can be generated as a result of day-to-day processes. An organisation must establish appropriate methods and routines for communicating information internally. For example, distribution lists will be kept with the names of all people who should receive a certain report when it is produced.

Within the same department, information usually flows up and down the chain of command. It is unusual for information to go up or down more than one level at a time. For example, the production line in a factory breaks down; the production line workers tell the foreman; the foreman tells the production supervisor; the production supervisor tells the production manager; the production manager tells the production director who may make the decision. This may mean that messages get distorted and decisions take a long time.

Formal information flow

Formal information flow is the flow of information created by the procedures of an organisation.

Someone applying for a job would fill in a formal application form and send it to the company. This is formal information flow.

Orders, dispatch notes and invoices are other examples of formal documents involving formal information flow.

There are a number of different formal methods by which information flows. Here are some examples:

- Formal meetings are a common way of disseminating information.
- Internal memos can be sent to individual employees or to a whole section or department.
- Notice boards in common work areas such as corridors, staff rooms or canteens. These are often used for legal requirements such as health and safety regulations and fire notices.
- Presentations to groups of employees to explain why something is going to happen.
- A company intranet is a fast growing development. All policies and other corporate information can be stored so that all employees can access them.

Informal information flow

Of course there are less formal methods of information flow which may be less reliable and less accurate but nevertheless cannot be ignored when looking at information flow within an organisation. Informal information flow is not structured but is naturally arising within the organisation. It can arise from:

- phone calls
- the office grapevine
- stories in the local press and rumours
- personal conversation or observation.

E-mail is an increasingly common way of communicating internally, particularly as e-mails can very easily be sent to a 'global' mailing list of every employee. If e-mail is tied in to proper procedures then it is part of the formal information flow. For example, an agenda for a meeting can be sent by e-mail. However it can easily be used for informal information flow such as 'Has anyone lost any keys?'

When an employee requires some stationery he fills in a form that is sent to the Supplies Department where the data is entered into a system that produces a weekly list of requests. Goods are then distributed and a report sent to the Accounts Department detailing the amounts to be charged to the appropriate departments. This is the formal information flow. When a member of staff needs an item of stationery urgently she phones the Supplies Department with the request. This is an example of informal information flow.

A company information system must support the information flow of the company. For example, if the Marketing Department use information on last month's sales to plan their next campaign, the department manager will require accurate information quickly on which to make decisions.

Information flow and the organisational structure

It is crucial that information arrives at its destination in time to be used. For this to happen, it is vital that the data and information flows within an organisation are carefully planned. These flows will differ between organisations and are dependent upon a number of factors.

The size, type and structure of an organisation will all play a large part. Within a small business the close proximity of employees means that formal systems for sharing information are not always necessary.

Quite different information flows will be required depending on whether the organisational structure is hierarchical or flat. Within a large organisation, with a hierarchical organisational structure, the flow of information needs to be carefully planned. As information normally flows up and down the chain of command, it often has to pass through many levels. This can lead to delays and distortions. If the organisational structure is poorly designed, one person may have to deal with more information than they can cope with. This creates a bottleneck and inevitably other people will be waiting for the information.

The amount of information will affect information flow. Obviously the more information, the longer it can take to process.

The nature of the data will have a major effect on information flow. How and where the data originates is a factor. It could be electronically generated, for example, through Point of Sale (POS) terminals and processed by powerful tools to produce information that is disseminated over a network to managers on their desktop computer. Alternatively, it could have originated from handwritten notes and telephone conversations.

ICT, particularly e-mail, can make information flow more easily. Firstly, it is practically immediate. Secondly, it is easy to send to many recipients, such as every employee, and so can bypass the bottlenecks. Thirdly, it is easy to reply to, or forward, by clicking on one button. This may however lead to information overload. It is too easy to send the message to everybody even if it is not really relevant to them. Users in many organisations complain of e-mail overload where the indiscriminate copying and forwarding of messages has caused an unmanageable volume.

Many large organisations now provide information internally using an intranet enabling employees to share information.

Personnel

The three different levels of an organisation (strategic, tactical and operational) have different information requirements and this will be reflected in the design of a company's information system. The dissemination and distribution of reports to the appropriate people at the appropriate time will be a crucial factor in a system's success. Reports must arrive at the right manager's desk at the time when a decision needs to be made, in a suitable format to be useable.

Operational

ICT was first used at the operational level for data processing. It is still used extensively at this level. A supermarket checkout operator receives operational information, that is, the price of each product as it is barcode scanned and the total price of a customer's purchases.

At a cinema, a person selling tickets will receive a request from a filmgoer for a number of seats to see a particular film at a chosen time. The seller will enter the data relating to the request into a computer and will receive operational information: which, if any, seats are available at the required showing, together with their price.

Tactical

When making decisions, a supermarket manager will not be interested in individual sales. However, she will be interested in sales trends and information on staff performance. Information may be aggregated using an MIS and the manager may have access to a range of graphical displays.

At the cinema, the local manager will be interested in the total sales for the various showings of different films. He can use this information to help make such decisions as whether to show a film for an extra week, move it into a larger or smaller auditorium, or alter the start times of the shows.

Strategic

The supermarket's chief executive will not be interested in individual staff within a store but will want to know which stores are performing well and which are performing badly, which products are no longer popular and which products are increasing in sales. This information will be used when decisions about future strategies are made.

For a cinema chain, the management at head office will be interested in the overall performance of certain films as well as the revenue coming from individual cinemas.

Activity 1

1. For each of the following examples state whether the information is strategic, tactical or operational:
   a) Contents of the managing director's diary for next week.
   b) Details of a car's former owners from the Police National Computer.
   c) Sales figures for a supermarket's 200 stores.
   d) News that George will be off sick today.
   e) 6000 widgets need to be delivered immediately.
2. Copy and complete the table below with your own examples of strategic, tactical or operational information. The examples should be different from those given above.

Strategic	Tactical	Operational

case study 1
Newspaper deliveries

Sharon owns four news shops that deliver newspapers to householders who live in the region. She employs a manager at each shop who deals with paper orders and manages the deliveries which are carried out by a number of paper boys and girls. Customers can make payments, establish new, or modify existing orders in the shop. All people involved need information to make decisions.

- Complete the table below giving the level of information (strategic, tactical or operational) that each of the following users might require for two different examples of information each. You need to supply the second example in each case.

User	Example	Level of information
Sharon	1. Whether or not to open a further shop 2.	
Paper boy or girl	1. List of which papers need to be delivered to which house 2.	
Shop manager	1. Allocation of houses to different paper boys for delivery 2.	

Worked exam question

The owner of an independent driving school, which employs six instructors, decides to get a local software house to write a bespoke package to manage client information, including the booking of lessons, the tracking of progress, and the recording of payments.

a) Identify **two** different potential users of this system. (2)

b) With the aid of examples, describe the different levels of information that each of these two users might require. (6)

ICT4 January 2003

EXAMINER'S GUIDANCE *Part (a) only says 'identify' and there are only two marks. An example of a possible answer is:*

SAMPLE ANSWER Two potential users of this system are the owner of the driving school and the driving instructors.

EXAMINER'S GUIDANCE *Hint: there are 3 marks allocated for your answer for each user in part (b). You will get 1 mark for stating the relevant level of information, 1 for a description of why that is the appropriate level and 1 for an example. Have a go. Don't read the sample answer below until you have tried yourself!*

SAMPLE ANSWER The owner would require strategic information to support him in decision making, e.g. whether or not to employ more instructors.

Now write an answer for another user.

SUMMARY

- **Organisations should have policies on:**

  ICT – A corporate approach to buying equipment ensuring current data can be used.
  Upgrading – compatibility needs to be considered.
- **Issues that affect the Corporate Information Systems Strategy include organisational structure, decision making methods, legal requirements, information flow, hardware and software and behavioural factors.**
- **Information flow can be formal or informal.**
- **Formal information flow is defined by the system with fully documented and agreed procedures stating stages of flow, control, exception handling and the network for distribution.**
- **Informal information flow 'naturally arises' within the organisation via phone calls, personal conversation, meetings or observation.**
- **Information flow is affected by a number of factors. Delays can occur at all stages of flow. Factors include:**
  - **the structure of the organisation**
  - **the size of the organisation**
  - **the geographical structure of the organisation**
  - **how data originates within an organisation**
  - **the form of the information**
  - **the volume of data.**
- **E-mail and intranets can speed up access to information.**
- **Different levels of an organisation need different levels of information.**

Chapter 4 Questions

1 A supermarket cashier scans a bar code on a product. The code is sent to the store's computer. The price and name of the product is sent to the till and printed on the receipt. Details of the sale are immediately stored in a transaction file. Every hour the transaction file is sent to the store's warehouse to update stock levels.

a) What is the source document?

b) What level of information is the code going into the computer?

c) What level of information is contained in the transaction file going to the warehouse? (3)

2 The structure of an organisation can influence the flow of information through it. Explain **two** effects that the structure of an organisation could have on the flow of information. (4)

ICT4 June 2005

3 Managers at the highest, or strategic, levels of an organisation have particular requirements from an information system.

a) Give **one** example of an information system that would be useful to managers at this level, and explain how they would use it. (3)

b) State the **two** other levels of task and/or personnel within an organisation. (2)

ICT4 June 2005

4 Describe **three** factors that can influence an information system within an organisation that should be considered when writing a Corporate Information Systems Strategy. (6)

ICT4 January 2005

5 In an organisation information flow can be *formal* or *informal*.

a) Explain each of the following terms, giving an example of each:

i. Formal information flow (3)

ii. Informal information flow. (3)

b) Information flow can be affected by a number of different factors such as the size of an organisation.

i. Explain why information flow can be affected by the size of an organisation. (2)

ii. Describe **three** other factors that can affect information flow within an organisation. (6)

6 An increasing number of organisations have a Corporate Information Systems Strategy in place.
Discuss the importance of a Corporate Information Systems Strategy including in your answer:

- who should draw up the strategy
- the reasons for having a strategy
- the factors to consider when drawing up the strategy. (20)

The quality of Written Communication will be assessed in your answer.

5 Information

- In the AS ICT course you learned the difference between data and information:
  - Data means recorded raw facts and figures.
  - When data is processed and given a context it becomes information.

Information is a vital tool at all levels of an organisation. However, it is not just a matter of 'the more information the better' – too much information, particularly if much of it is irrelevant to the particular situation, can make it harder to pick out what is important. This is often called *information overload.*

The use of e-mails as a major medium of communication has led to problems in some organisations. Some managers can return to their desks after a few hours away to find dozens of e-mail messages awaiting them. Many will have been sent to them unnecessarily, forwarded by colleagues. Many users click on the 'reply all' option rather than the 'reply' so sending their response to a message to everyone on the circulation list instead of just the originator of the message. Some e-mails that are sent contain trivial or personal messages.

Workers may wonder how they managed before e-mail was introduced. Misuse of e-mail has become so bad in some organisations that management have instigated e-mail free afternoons, when employees are banned from sending internal e-mails.

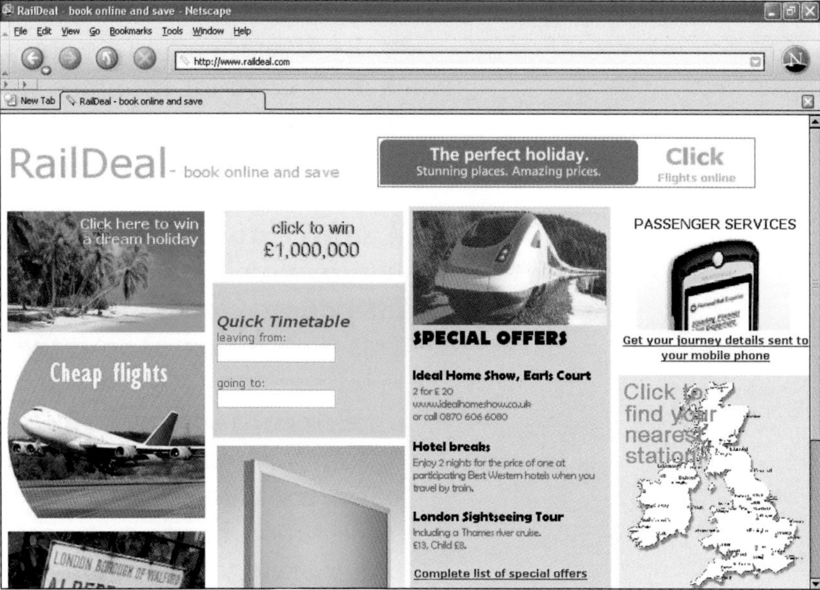

Figure 5.1 I only wanted to find out the train time!

Internet users can often be frustrated when they find it hard to find the exact information they need. It is not unusual to visit a website to find out the time of trains to a particular destination only to be faced with details of special offers, timings of railway maintenance and holiday ideas (as shown in Figure 5.1).

Management information

Managers need information to help them to make decisions such as planning future actions or controlling production. The information must be relevant to the task in hand, and the form in which it should be will be different in different situations.

The type of information needed will depend on a number of factors, including the level of the user in the organisational structure, the actual task being carried out and its urgency.

Classifying information

By putting information into various categories, we may be able to see how useful it could be to an organisation. Information can be classified in many ways including:

- **By Source:** for example, internal, external, primary, secondary.
- **By Nature:** for example, quantitative, qualitative, formal, and informal.
- **By Level:** for example, strategic, tactical, and operational.
- **By Time:** for example, historical, present, future.
- **By Frequency:** for example, continuous (real time), hourly, daily, monthly, and annually.
- **By Use:** for example planning, control, decision making.
- **By Form:** for example, written, aural, visual, sensory.
- **By Type:** for example, detailed, sampled, aggregated.

Sources of information

A **source document** is the original document bringing information into an organisation. When a school calculates attendance figures, the source documents are the registers. This is an **internal source of information**. When a mail order company receives a written order from a customer, this is an **external source of information**.

Both these examples are filled in directly, they are **primary sources of information**. Sometimes the information has to be transferred on to another piece of paper or on to a computer file. These are **secondary sources of information**.

Internal sources of information

Internal information is generated from within the organisation. Its source could be an information system or it may be produced as a by-product of a data processing system. For a more detailed study refer to Chapter 2.

External sources of information

External sources of information are those which are outside an organisation. Businesses may use external surveys and annual reports from other organisations, as well as statistics and research reports. There are many information sources available: newspapers, magazines, radio, television, teletext, local authority departments and government agencies.

The Government publishes a huge amount of statistical information that is publicly available. It is very useful in planning such items as the number of classrooms a school needs, the number of houses that need to be built or the by-pass for a town.

Nature of information

Quantitative and qualitative information

Information can be of two general types: **quantitative** or **qualitative**. Quantitative information is that which can be measured numerically. For example, 3476 cars were sold last week; Mike German's net salary was £1243.44 last month. Quantitative information can easily be presented in numerical or graphical form. A balance sheet or a graph showing sales trends both show quantitative information.

Qualitative information cannot be measured in numerical terms. The different colours that a model of car can be produced in is an example of qualitative information. Qualitative information may have come from data based on value judgements. This is data that is based on a person's opinion. Qualitative information is often harder to present and interpret than quantitative data, but can be just as important to a manager.

case study 1
▶ Ed Black

Ed Black runs his own business. He sets up management training courses for a wide range of organisations. For each course that he runs he gathers information that helps him in the running of his business. He records the number of people attending each course, if the course was full, the number whom he was unable to accommodate, the amount paid by each course member and ▶

client satisfaction with the course together with any comments on how it could be improved.

- Explain how Ed would use each of the items of information he collects.
- Identify the qualitative and the quantitative information that Ed collects.
- Can you suggest any further internal information that would help Ed in the running of his business? Give your reasons.
- Can you suggest any external information that would help Ed in the running of his business? Give your reasons.

Formal and informal information

Formal information is created and disseminated as part of the predetermined procedures of an organisation. For example, someone applying for a job would have to fill in an application form – this is a formal procedure and the information obtained is formal information.

The details of an agenda for a departmental meeting, the minutes of the meeting after it has been held and the distribution list for these documents are all examples of formal information.

Informal information naturally arises within the organisation and is communicated through personal conversations both by face-to-face contact or through telephone conversations. It can also be conveyed in memos or even scribbled notes written on a piece of paper. There is no clearly defined distribution network for informal information.

Activity 1

A school or college will use both formal and informal information. Working in a group of three or four, identify as many examples of information used in your institution and then categorise each as formal or informal. Then highlight those examples that are qualitative information.

Level of information

Strategic information is that which is required at the highest levels to make decisions. A director or chief executive would use strategic information to decide on future policy, for example the decision of a supermarket to offer a banking service. Strategic information is often in the form of a report where information from a number of sources and of a number of types has been brought together.

Tactical information is used by middle managers. For example, a sales manager may need information related to each product and its sales performance so that he can make appropriate decisions on future promotions.

Operational information is required for the day-to-day running of an organisation. An example of operational information is that used by a foreman in a factory to decide on the day's production and staff rotas.

Timing of information

Management information systems attempt to ensure that managers can obtain accurate, relevant information at the right time to improve their decision making. It should provide information about the past (**historic** information about production levels, and so on), the present (that is, **current** production figures, markets, and so on) and the **future** (that is, projected or forecasted profits, and so on).

An example of **historic information** could be last December's sales figures. These would be needed by a toy shop to plan for this Christmas's stock levels. The information in a company's annual report for shareholders will be historic with summaries of sales, expenditure and development in different areas of the company.

Summaries of GCSE and A level results for all schools appear in national newspapers a few weeks after the results are received by the pupils. Such a report is historic information.

An example of **current information:** information from time sheets for this week's wages which have to be paid on Thursday.

An example of **future information:** projected sales figures and population details for an area, helping a company decide whether to open a new store or expand an existing store.

Frequency of information

The use to which information is put determines the frequency of its production.

Real time information is produced immediately when transaction data is processed.

When a shop assistant swipes a customer's credit card to make a sale, he requires feedback from the credit card company's computer about whether the customer has exceeded his credit limit or the card has been reported stolen. This information is needed at once before carrying on with the sale.

When booking a flight at a travel agency, accurate information on availability and cost are needed straight away so that a decision can be made whether or not to book.

Other information is needed at **regular intervals**: perhaps hourly, daily, weekly or monthly. Percentage figures for student attendance in class can be obtained on a weekly basis from an electronic attendance registration system. The amount outstanding on a credit card account is calculated monthly; a statement and request for payment is then sent to the card holder.

case study 2
Sainsbury's

A report in 2004 from consultants Capgemini (http://www.capgemini.com) suggested that almost a quarter of the decisions made by senior UK executives were wrong. One example of a bad decision was at supermarket giant Sainsbury's.

In 2004 Sainsbury's had to scrap a computerised stock system and other IT systems that had cost £260 million. The system was developed to control stock but was found to be flawed. Staff at every store had to update the stock levels on its shelves manually.

The company had spent £3 billion over four years on new technology but this did not stop Sainsbury's falling into third place in the UK grocery market that it once led, behind Tesco and Asda.

Give an example of each of the following and describe how it might have helped Sainsbury's make the right decision:

a) external information
b) historic information
c) future information.

Uses of information

Information helps managers in several ways.

Information is used by a manager to **monitor and control** the work done under his span of control. For example, a sales manager may use the monthly sales figures of different regions as the basis for making changes where individual performances are below target. In a factory producing plastic mouldings for car interiors, the foreman can make technical adjustments to the machinery on the basis of quality control information on faulty goods.

Information can be used for **planning**. For example, a marketing manager, planning the launch of a new product, would use historic sales information on other company products together with their projected sales and costs. External information gathered from consumer surveys would also be valuable in deciding how to market the product, which market sectors it should be aimed at and what price to charge.

Information is a vital tool in the **decision making** process. For example, if a manager has to decide whether or not to continue producing and selling a particular product, he will need a range of information on which to base his decision. Such information would include: the level of sales over a period; the profit from the sales; the projected sales for the future and the performance of similar products.

Activity 2

The case study on pages 43 and 44 referred to Ed Black, who runs his own management training business. Describe what information Ed would need to enable him to plan his next series of courses.

Decision making takes up a large part of the work of a manager. The appropriate information helps the manager make good decisions. It is a management cliché that 'a decision is only as good as the quality of information it is built on'. What makes good information is discussed in detail later in the chapter.

Form of information

Information can be presented in a variety of forms. The intended audience may determine the form that the information takes.

Much business information is **written** – in the form of reports, memos or tables. Most such reports will be produced by computer.

However, for many purposes, a more **visual** representation can convey the same information with more impact; charts, graphs and pictures are often used to convey information more clearly.

Some information is received **aurally**, (by ear), in casual conversations, at meetings or over the telephone. Information can also be obtained through **other senses** such as touch.

Types of information

Aggregated information consists of totals created when detailed information is added together. A manager will not necessarily be interested in sales for every product, but will look at the sales for each department. The sales for each department are aggregated (added).

HATHERLEY HATS UK SALES - 2005							
	Trilby	Boater	Bonnet	Topper	Bowler	Cap	Total
1st Quarter	234	1245	345	734	3456	2421	8435
2nd Quarter	245	1078	356	722	7894	2567	12862
3rd Quarter	256	1076	376	678	5567	2789	10742
4th Quarter	287	1098	386	456	5237	2599	10063
Quarterly Average	255.5	1124.25	365.75	647.5	5538.5	2594	10525.5
Quarterly Total	1022	4497	1463	2590	22154	10376	42102
% of Total Sales	2.43%	10.68%	3.47%	6.15%	52.62%	24.64%	100.00%

Figure 5.2 Report showing aggregated information

Figure 5.2 shows the total number of each type of hat sold by a manufacturer for each three month period during 2005. This information could be used to spot trends in sales of particular hat styles as well as highlighting the most popular models.

More detailed information, such as the time and date of every sale, would not be useful.

Disaggregated information is produced by splitting up grouped data into more detail. This might be useful if a manager wants more information on how successful a particular product is. He can 'drill down' and get the information in more detail. Detailed information like this is most often used at the operational level. The sample list in figure 5.3 shows such a report.

```
Item    : Benylin & Codeine           PC : 1    S.A. POM'S
P. Ref  : BENCO          ( 2)         SC : 1    Vet Drug          BC:
S. Ref  : PD79                        MC : 1    Parke Davis
-----------------------------------------------------------------------------
Pack Cost   : 2.98                    Pack cont. : 300            Ana : 240
Actual Cost : 2.40                    PackDisc   : 15%
-----------------------------------------------------------------------------
Quantity    : 6.00
_____________________________________________________________________________
Item    : Codeine         PC : 1      S.A. POM'S
P. Ref  : CODEN          ( 4)         SC : 1    Vet Drug          BC:
S. Ref  : PD80                        MC : 1    Parke Davis
-----------------------------------------------------------------------------
Pack Cost   : 1.98                    Pack cont. : 400            Ana : 360
Actual Cost : 1.40                    PackDisc   : 15%
-----------------------------------------------------------------------------
Quantity    : 10.00
_____________________________________________________________________________
Item    : Dentalyne       PC : 1      S.A. POM'S
P. Ref  : DENTA          ( 6)         SC : 1    Vet Drug          BC:
S. Ref  : PD81                        MC : 1    Parke Davis
-----------------------------------------------------------------------------
Pack Cost   : 2.56                    Pack cont. : 300            Ana : 240
Actual Cost : 2.20                    PackDisc   : 15%
-----------------------------------------------------------------------------
Quantity    : 6.00
_____________________________________________________________________________
Item    : Myolyne         PC : 1      S.A. POM's
P. Ref  : MYOLE          ( 2)         SC : 1    Vet Drug          BC:
S. Ref  : PD82                        MC : 1    Parke Davis
-----------------------------------------------------------------------------
Pack Cost   : 3.97                    Pack cont. : 600            Ana : 540
Actual Cost : 3.45                    PackDisc   : 15%
-----------------------------------------------------------------------------
Quantity    : 4.00
_____________________________________________________________________________
```

Figure 5.3 Report showing detailed information

Sampled information refers only to selected records, for example, details from just a few of the customers. Reports of this type are often called exception reports. The report shown in figure 5.4 could be used to highlight major customers who may be sent a special offer.

Good decisions require good information. The characteristics of good information are given below.

Orders over £1000 in value				
Order Number	Order Date	Co. Ref	Co. Name	Value
21403	11-Mar	1289	Bradshaw & Son Transport	£4,456.06
21409	12-Mar	1289	Bradshaw & Son Transport	£1,652.00
21405	09-Mar	1414	Garvey Linguistic Services	£1,466.23
21406	11-Mar	2561	ADS	£1,654.56
21410	12-Mar	1414	Carr Associates	£2,489.57
21407	10-Mar	1451	Green Cosmetics	£2,389.89
21408	11-Mar	1290	Joslin International	£1,495.23

Figure 5.4 Report showing sampled data

Internal and external information requirements – an organisation has to produce information for a number of reasons. Most information is used internally but there are certain needs external to the organisation. Examples are company reports to shareholders and product information for customers.

A sixth form college has an MIS that produces information including details of student attendance and performance, exam entries and results. Many internal reports are produced for different personnel that are relevant to their roles. Information is also needed for external use. Together with a prospectus with details of courses, prospective students and their parents often require a summary of the exam results of the previous year giving the number of passes in each grade band for each subject.

Detailed tables of information on all student enrolments and achievements together with a range of other statistics are required by the Learning and Skills Council (LSC) for funding purposes. The information is transmitted electronically.

The college governors require an annual report that summarises the number of students and their achievements in different subject examinations.

Characteristics of good information

Good information is that which is used and which creates value. Experience and research show that good information has numerous qualities. Good information is:

- **relevant** for its purpose
- sufficiently **accurate** for its purpose
- **complete** enough for the problem
- **reliable** – from a source in which the user has confidence
- communicated to the **right person**
- communicated in **time** for its purpose
- that which contains the **right level of detail**
- communicated by an appropriate **channel of communication**
- that which is **understandable** by the user.

Relevant

What is relevant for one manager may not be relevant for another. The user will become frustrated if information in any way contains parts that are irrelevant to the task in hand. A stock report would not be relevant to a human resources manager who is responsible for employees.

Accurate

Information needs to be accurate enough for its intended use. To obtain information that is 100 per cent accurate is usually unrealistic as it is likely to be too expensive to produce on time. The degree of accuracy required depends upon the circumstances. At operational levels information may need to be accurate to the nearest penny, £, kilogram or minute.

A supermarket till receipt, for example, will need to be accurate to the penny. A regional manager comparing the performance of different stores at the end of a month would find information rounded to the nearest £1000 most appropriate.

Complete

If a marketing manager was deciding whether the sale of a particular product should be discontinued, their decision could be impaired if they did not have figures for overseas sales. Ideally all the information needed for a particular decision should be available. However, this rarely happens. In reality, good information is often incomplete, but complete enough to meet the needs of the situation.

From a reliable source

There is no point in producing information if it is not going to be used. Managers will not use information if they do not have confidence that it is likely to be good information. If the source has always been reliable in the past the user is likely to use it.

Communicated to the right person

Each manager has a particular area of work within the organisation and needs to be provided with the necessary information to help them do their job. A retail organisation's managing director does not need detailed information on current stock levels of a particular warehouse but the warehouse manager does.

Timely

Good information is communicated in time for it to be used. If information arrives too late or is out of date by the time it does arrive, then the manager cannot use it when decisions are made. For example, a marketing manager decides to stop selling a particular product whose sales have been dropping over the last few months. When they made their decision they had not received the last month's figures showing a sudden, large growth in sales.

The frequency at which information is produced is important and needs to be driven by the needs of the manager who is using it. A factory manager organising shifts will need daily information on personnel absence; the company's personnel manager will need summary information on absence on a monthly or annual basis.

Detailed

The amount of detail needed in information should be determined by the purpose to which it will be put. More detail than is necessary will confuse the recipient. Too little detail will provide an incomplete picture of the situation. When a regional sales manager is checking the monthly expense claims of salespersons within their region they will require a summary report of monthly totals for each person. The team leaders who check the claim will need a detailed, itemised report of all claims made.

Understandable

Understandability, or putting into context, is what changes data into information. If the information is not understood then it has no meaning and cannot be used. The method and style of the presentation of the information will affect its understandability; for example, the appropriate use of charts and graphs can make complex numeric information more understandable.

case study 3
▶ Poor information

One example of a bad management decision based on poor quality information was the decision to commission a new £456 million computer system for the Child Support Agency (CSA). The system went live in January 2003 – 11 months late and £29 million over budget. The suppliers claimed that the CSA had made more than 2,000 changes to the original specification for the system.

The new system soon proved to be performing more slowly than the old system. This was made worse by the fact that the CSA could not transfer cases from the old system to the new system, which used a different calculation to work out payments.

Observers suggested that the rush to get the project underway meant that the specification was based on inaccurate information. It is often impossible to satisfy the competing demands of speed and accuracy.

Which is more important: speed or accuracy? That depends on the application. In some cases short timescales and fixed deadlines mean that speed is important. But in this case, surely the CSA could have waited until the specification was completely accurate.

Activity 3

Copy the grid given below. For each of the characteristics of good information, give a suitable example that is different from those given in this book.

Characteristic	Example
relevant	
accurate	
complete	
reliable	
communicated to the **right person**	
timely	
detailed	
understandable	

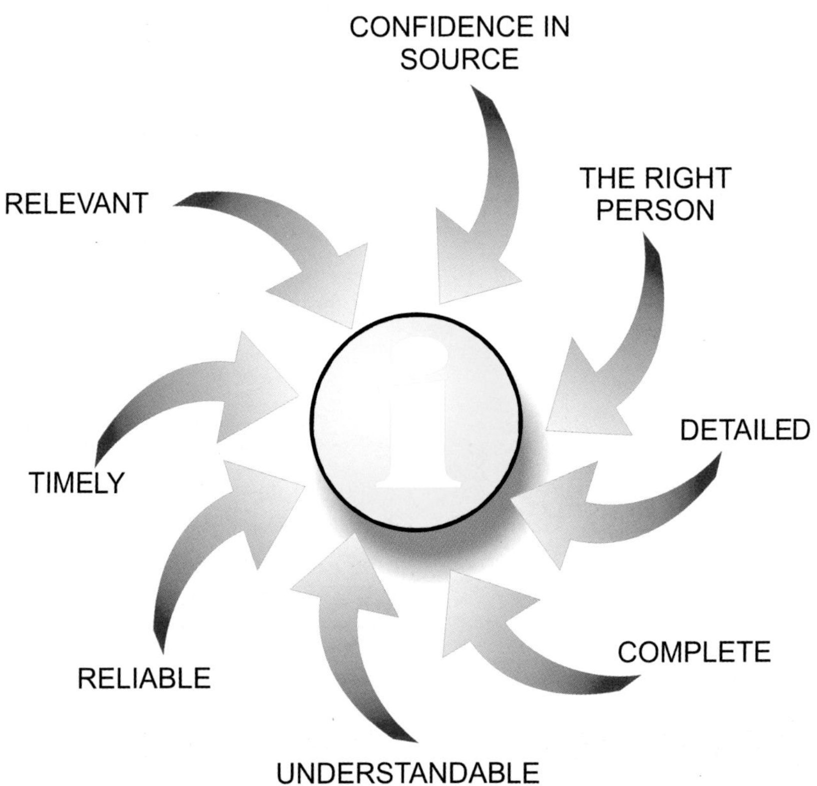

Figure 5.5 Characteristics of good information

case study 4

▶ 'Lennon Provides a Ticket to Ride' adapted from article in Computing 2002

Train services are provided by a number of operators, but ticket sales are made through one system. If you purchase a ticket for a long distance journey that involves several different trains, run by different operators, you do not have to make separate payments for the different stages of the journey, each to a different operator. The allocation of ticket sales and revenue is made by a computer system. A new such rail settlement system, called Lennon, is being installed. The system is designed to allocate revenue generated from ticket sales to the appropriate train operators, as well as providing detailed information about how, when and to whom the tickets were sold.

Lennon will replace a 15-year-old system and will process about 700,000 ticket sales every day. The train companies will be notified of their revenue and presented with sales information the following day. The current system takes up to six weeks and does not have the data analysis facility.

The new system will deliver information that will be used in marketing and promotional activities. It will aid the train companies in their decisions to introduce new ticket types and allow them better understanding of their customer requirements.

- In which ways will Lennon provide better information than the old system?
- What is the purpose of the information that is produced by the system?
- How could information be used in marketing and promotional activities?

Activity 4

Prepare an interview for a manager in a local organisation to find out the information needs for his job.

After you have carried out the interview, list the information categories that are needed and classify each category using the classifications given earlier in the chapter.

Effective presentation of information

For information to be of greatest use it must be presented in a style and form that allows the person for whom it is intended, the audience, to understand it best. Information is not always printed. It could be presented orally or on a visual presentation such as a PowerPoint slide show.

The variety of ways that information can be represented was discussed in ICT for AS level Chapter 17. Great care must be taken over the correct choice of presentation method and style, otherwise the correct message may not be given.

A detailed list of sales, in date order, would not be appropriate for a regional sales manager wishing to review the performance of each of his salespersons over the last month. For him, a summary report showing the total number and total value for each person in a table would be most appropriate.

The breakdown of the annual expenditure of a company, to be included in the annual report for shareholders, would best be presented as a pie chart.

Activity 5

For each of the following, choose the most appropriate method of presentation from the options given. Explain carefully why you made the choice, and why you feel the other options are not appropriate. If you feel an alternative method would be better than the options given, state your reasons.

Information need	Option 1	Option 2	Option 3	Option 4	Option 5
A level results – for class teacher	A table showing the number of each grade in each subject	Text report in alphabetical surname order of all students in all subjects	Text report of students' results ordered by subject	A table showing the percentage of each grade in each subject	A pie chart showing the percentage of each grade in each subject
A level results - for head teacher	A table showing the number of each grade in each subject	Text report in alphabetical surname order of all students in all subjects	Text report of students' results ordered by subject	A table showing the percentage of each grade in each subject	A pie chart showing the percentage of each grade in each subject
A level results – for the governors' report	A table showing the number of each grade in each subject	Text report in alphabetical surname order of all students in all subjects	Text report of students' results ordered by subject	A table showing the percentage of each grade in each subject	A pie chart showing the percentage of each grade in each subject
A level results for the parents of prospective students	A table showing the number of each grade in each subject	Text report in alphabetical surname order of all students in all subjects	Text report of students' results ordered by subject	A table showing the percentage of each grade in each subject	A pie chart showing the percentage of each grade in each subject

Worked exam question

A car showroom has three sales staff who have recorded the following sales of cars:

Salesperson	Week beginning May 4	Week beginning May 11	Week beginning May 18	Week beginning May 25	Week beginning June 2
David Garner	12	18	9	17	5
Sarah Jennings	21	14	19	On holiday	On holiday
Roger Mallinson	13	On holiday	4	2	6

This information is now to be presented to different people:

a) The owner of the car showroom

b) The sales manager

c) The sales staff themselves.

For each of these people suggest, giving reasons, a suitable but different way of presenting this information. Include the format and the content in your answer. (9)

SAMPLE ANSWER There are clearly three marks for each of the stated groups. For each group you must give a format, describe the content and give a reason. Although you must answer in sentences, you can see how the nine marks can be gained from looking at this table.

	Format	Content	Reason
The owner of the car showroom	Information aggregated to show total car sales in a line graph	Total car sales for each week	So the owner can see week by week how well the showroom is performing
The sales manager	A pie chart showing total sales for each salesperson	Total sales for each salesperson	So that the manager can see the relative sales
The sales staff	A table showing their sales	Their own sales week by week	For example, so that they know what commission is due

SUMMARY

Information is necessary to make good decisions.

- **Formal information is created by an organisation's procedures such as filling in an application form.**
- **Informal information arises naturally.**

Information can be classified in a number of ways:

- **By Source: for example, internal, external, primary, secondary.**
- **By Nature: for example, quantitative, qualitative, formal, informal.**
- **By Level: for example, strategic, tactical, operational.**
- **By Time: for example, historical, present, future.**
- **By Frequency: for example, continuous (real time), hourly, daily, monthly, annually.**

- **By Use: for example, planning, control, decision making.**
- **By Form: for example, written, aural, visual, sensory.**
- **By Type: for example, detailed, sampled, aggregated.**

Good information is important in aiding the decision making process.

Good information has the following characteristics:

- **relevant**
- **accurate**
- **complete**
- **reliable**
- **in time**
- **right level of detail**
- **disseminated by an appropriate channel of communication**
- **understandable.**

Chapter 5 Questions

1 Managers want good information and not bad information. Using examples, give **three** reasons why information may be of poor quality. (6)

2 Information can be classified by its level, that is, whether it is strategic, tactical or operational. Using examples, describe **two** other ways of classifying information. (6)

3 The Chief Executive of a business complains that a report he has received contains inaccuracies
'But, sir, you wanted the information in a hurry', is the reply.
Using examples, explain why speed may not be compatible with accuracy. (4)

4 Using examples, distinguish between formal information and informal information. (4)

5 Companies rely on their information systems to provide good quality information.

a) Identify **three** different categories of users of information systems, and state the level at which they operate. (6)

b) Describe **four** characteristics of good information. (8)

ICT4 June 2003

6 A college uses a Management Information System to present examination results to the principal, governors and heads of department.

a) Suggest **two** differences between the information presented to the governors and the information presented to heads of department. (2)

b) A characteristic of good information is that it must be relevant. Use examples to explain what information might be relevant to the Head of the Geography department and what information might not be relevant. (4)

7 For each of the following examples say if the communication is internal or external, and if the information is strategic, tactical or operational; historic, current or future.

a) the managing director's diary for next week

b) details of a car's former owners from the Police National Computer

c) a delivery note when a washing machine is delivered to a customer

d) news that George will be off sick today

e) six thousand widgets need to be delivered immediately. (15)

8 Give **two** examples each of strategic information, tactical information and operational information in a school or college. (6)

9 A company has decided to open a computerised distribution warehouse in the Midlands, handling deliveries for the whole country. Give an example of strategic information, tactical information and operational information needed in setting up the warehouse. (6)

6 Data

As part of the AS ICT course, the different ways in which data can arise was studied. Sometimes this can occur as an automatic by-product of a routine data processing operation. In a supermarket, Point of Sale (POS) terminals are used with barcode scanners to capture data on goods purchased. An itemised bill is produced with a calculated total for the customer. The data collected can also be used for:

- stock control – monitoring and reordering stock
- analysing trends in product sales to make decisions about which products should or should not be sold or promoted
- personnel tracking – keeping a check on the rate at which POS operators work.

Data is very often typed in on a keyboard but it can be collected by other means such as by using computer-readable documents (using OCR, OMR or MICR) or voice recognition.

Translation and transcription

If data is not captured automatically, it may require translation or transcription before entry into the system.

Translation involves taking data that is in one form and turning it into another form that is suitable for data entry into a computer system. Translation may involve the coding of data. For example, an order processing clerk for a clothing mail order company might receive an order for a pink T-shirt, size 12. This would need to be translated into the product code (say C72-543-12) for entry into the online order system.

Transcription is the copying of data. When data originates in paper form the details are entered into a computer system by copying the written data with the use of a keyboard.

Translation and transcription can affect the accuracy of the data as human error can cause mistakes to be made. For example, the order processing clerk could mistype the order as C72-453-12, thus creating an order for a completely different garment.

A series of data controls need to be put in place in order to ensure that the quality of the data is maintained. Such controls are designed to highlight when errors are made so that they can be corrected.

Data can get lost before it is even input, or it might contain errors. The likelihood of errors will depend on the method of processing input data. Any form of human involvement will open up the possibility of error.

When data is being written down or keyed in, a number of categories of potential error can be identified. It is common to get the order of characters (especially numbers) wrong. For example, keying in an account number of 58762 instead of 57862. Here the operator has swapped around the 7 and the 8. This is called a **transpositional** error as the position of the characters has been misread. **Spelling mistakes** are common, especially with data such as a customer's name. Other, less common, mistakes can occur when measurements are being made (for example, reading the current value from an electricity meter dial) or incorrectly coding information from a source document.

In fact, any form of human copying of data, called **transcribing**, is liable to cause mistakes. If the source document is handwritten, it may not be easy to read the handwriting. Whenever data needs to be transcribed or translated into another format before entry into the system there is a risk that the accuracy of the data will be reduced.

Choosing the appropriate method of data entry

A number of factors will be taken into account when a systems analyst is designing the most appropriate method of data capture for a particular system. These will include the nature of the data itself and how it arises, the current state of technological development and the quantity of data to be collected.

The method of data capture chosen will have an impact on both the quantity and quality of the data that can be captured.

When the sale of goods is recorded in a supermarket, the use of keyboard entry would prove slow and could generate many mistakes if the wrong prices were entered. Only the prices are likely to be recorded, so little use could be made of the data other than for producing the customer's bill. The use of a barcode scanner, which reads a code identifying the individual product, would allow a greater quantity of data to be entered in a given time. The data would also be of greater quality. It would be more accurate, as the scope for human mistyping error would not be present and the data could be used by a stock control system as the individual products would be itemised.

When a new car is sold a barcode scanner would not be used to enter data of the sale. The quantity of cars sold in a day is very low compared to the number of items sold in a supermarket! Also considerable detail relating to both the car and the purchaser will need to be recorded. Entry of this data is likely to be made by keyboard.

Collecting data from surveys and questionnaires can provide an organisation with a considerable quantity of useful information. This can inform the planning of future services or products. The data can be captured in a number of ways.

Paper forms could be sent to participants. The completed forms could be read using **Optical Mark Recognition** (OMR) technology which scans the printed form and records whether marks are made in predefined positions on the form. This is most useful if there is a large quantity of forms and most of the responses are in check box format. OMR has a low error rate of around 1%.

Alternatively, the forms could be read using **Optical Character Recognition** (OCR) software with a scanner. An OCR system can convert a page of text into a graphical image which is then converted into text codes such as ASCII. These can be input into a word processing program. Advanced OCR systems can read text in a large variety of fonts but can still have problems interpreting handwritten text.

If there are only a small number of forms it may be most appropriate to enter the data via a **keyboard**. This method has the advantage that a keyboard is likely to be readily available and requires no special preparation for use. However, the problem of transcription errors arises.

If the data can be collected online, the user can enter his responses directly.

A range of different methods can be used for payment of goods or services and each may involve a different method of data capture.

When payment is made in cash, the operator keys the amount tendered into the POS terminal. The amount of change is calculated and, in some systems, the appropriate coins are delivered.

Debit (for example Switch) or credit cards (for example Visa or a store card) make use of Chip and Pin technology. When a purchase is made using this technology the details of the account are read from the embedded chip when the card is placed in the reader. The customer then enters her four digit, secret PIN code to verify that she is the owner of the card.

Payment can also be made by cheque. All the cheques received in a store will be collected together and deposited in a bank, where the data will be read using MICR (magnetic ink character recognition) in batch mode. Many banks are adding OCR (optical character recognition) to their processing systems. The optical systems are currently only to assist the magnetic systems.

case study 1

▶ Use of smart cards at football matches

A new anti-hooligan football smart card scheme has been introduced in Belgium. At first some clubs refused to take part. However, after pressure was put on them by the Belgian Interior Ministry, which included clubs having to pay for extra police for certain games and being fined if there was trouble at matches, all clubs are now committed to the scheme. ▶

A smart card is a small, wallet-sized piece of plastic which contains a microchip. Data can be both read from, and stored in, the card. The Belgian smart card contains 1 Kbyte of memory and can be used as an electronic purse and a loyalty card. An agreement has been made with the oil firm, Fina Belgium, to accept it at their petrol stations.

The smart card also acts as an ID card. Once it is used to purchase a ticket the fan must use the smart card to gain entry to the match. Troublemaking fans can have their card deactivated so that further tickets cannot be bought. A controversial issue which worries civil liberty groups is that police have access to the networked smart card computer scheme which is connected to servers at all clubs. This gives police advance access to the identities of all those who will be attending a game.

1. Name and describe two other data capture methods that could be used for an identity card to allow entry into a sports ground, instead of a smart card.
2. Explain why civil liberty groups might be concerned about the introduction of these cards.
3. Describe two other situations when the use of a smart card would be appropriate.

Activity 1

Fill in the table below.

Application	Data entry method	How used	Advantages
Airport baggage handling	Barcode scanner	Paper labels are attached to luggage with barcodes for destination and changeover airports. Luggage is routed automatically to correct loading bay.	Process much faster as baggage handlers do not have to read labels.
Underground train ticketing	Magnetic stripe reader		
Electricity meter readings			
City Council carrying out travel survey with questionnaire to all house holders	OMR reader		
Identifying newborn babies	Barcode scanner	Newborn babies are tagged with strip around ankle.	
Parcel delivery			Know where package is in transit, faster working at post office.

Online shopping

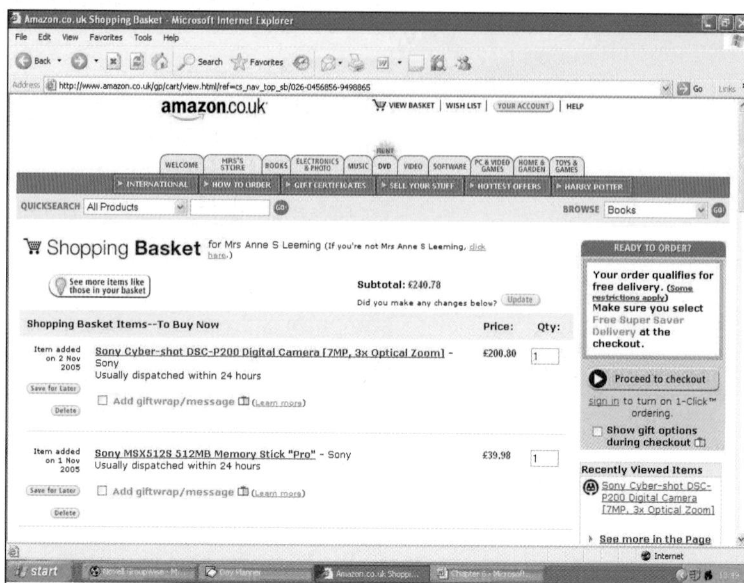

Figure 6.1 Shopping online at amazon.co.uk

There are two main stages in online shopping (or indeed in any form of shopping): selecting the required products and paying for them. The website provides the user with the opportunity of browsing through details of available products and selecting them by adding to a 'shopping basket' or 'cart'. (See figure 6.1).

Once all the goods have been selected the user moves on to a page where details of payment and delivery are collected by the system, 'advance to checkout'. At this stage credit or debit card details are filled in and submitted for payment. Many people are concerned about the security issues raised by purchasing goods online. This is discussed in the section 'control mechanisms' later in the chapter.

Alternatively, a user can print out a form for filling in offline, either by word processor which can later be submitted as an attachment to an e-mail message, or by hand, submitted by non-electronic means (i.e. post with an enclosed cheque).

Many companies' sites such as Tesco hold the details of a customer's previous orders and payment details so that it is easy to reorder the same goods.

Activity 2

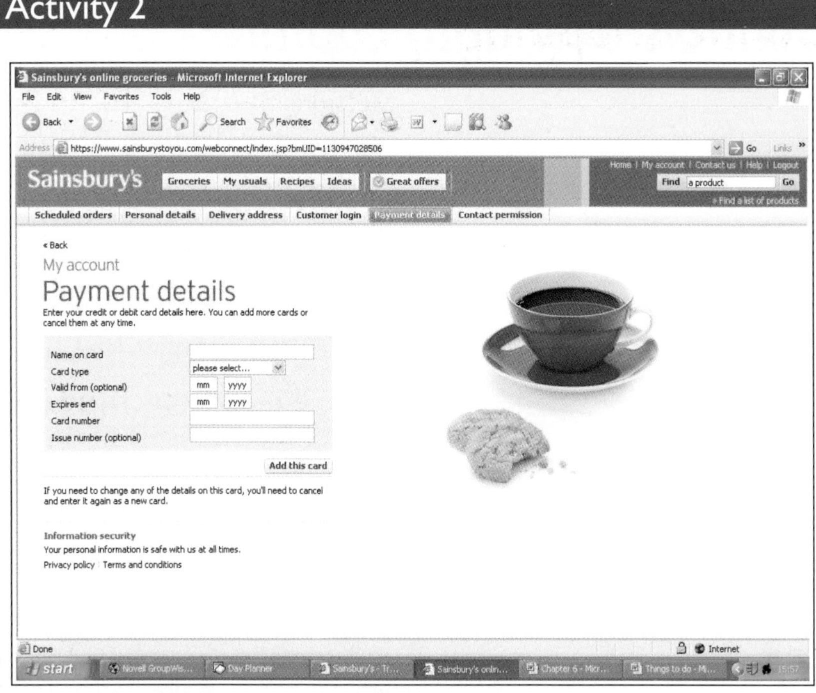

Figure 6.2 Shopping online at sainsbury.co.uk

1. Using a web site such as www.amazon.co.uk, www.sainsbury.co.uk, www.ocado.uk or www.tesco.co.uk, go through the stages of ordering some goods online. (Don't actually carry out the transaction!)
2. Describe the ways in which you could pay for the goods that you wish to purchase.
3. What ICT skills does such a system demand?
4. Carry out a comparison of the supermarket sites, looking at factors such as ease of selecting goods, services offered and the quality of the interface provided. Which site would you prefer to use?
5. Copy and fill in the grid below.

	Site 1	Site 2
Strengths		
Weaknesses		

Controls over data capture

Methods of controlling and checking the accuracy of data are discussed in detail in ICT for AS Chapter 12. **Verification** is used to check that data is entered correctly. The most common method of verification involves typing data into the computer twice. **Validation** is computerised checking that detects any data that is not reasonable or is incomplete.

Control mechanisms

When data is transcribed into a computer system, a number of control mechanisms need to be put in place to ensure that no transaction is missed or lost. When the mode of operation is batch processing, controls are needed to ensure that every batch of data reaches the data entry department and that every transaction within the batch is entered into the system.

Each batch of paper documents is grouped together in a batch and an extra document, the **batch header** is included. This will contain a field, called the **batch total**, for the number of documents in the batch as well as other control totals.

Details of a batch, such as its source, date and time, and an identifying, unique, batch number would be recorded, together with the numbers of transactions in the batch, in a log book at the source of data.

An example of a **control total** for a batch of product sales transactions could be the total value of all the transactions in the batch. The total would have to be worked out manually and added to the batch header before the data is entered. As the transactions are entered the computer program keeps a running total of the value fields from each transaction. When all the transactions in the batch have been entered this total is compared with the one entered on the batch header. If the two values are not the same, an error is reported.

A **hash total** is a particular kind of control total where the sum total has no particular meaning, and is purely carried out for control purposes. An example field that could be used for a hash total is an identity number.

When data is entered interactively as the transaction takes place, fields can be validated as the data is entered. The values in certain fields can be restricted and goods can be chosen from a list of options. **Cross-field validation** can prevent further errors from being collected, for example, by checking that an address is correct for the given postcode.

Fear of fraud

One of the factors that prevents people from purchasing goods online is the worry regarding potential fraud. Companies provide a number of safeguards that should protect the user. They will usually require users to register before any transactions occur. They will then e-mail back an access code to the customer. Thus a person will not be able to make purchases in another person's name. For the same reason, confirmation of any order is sent to a registered user's e-mail address so that if illegal orders are made the user will be made aware, allowing the order to be cancelled. To ensure that this can happen, the seller will need to insist that an e-mail address is provided and check that it actually exists.

Before dispatching goods that are to be paid for electronically, a company is likely to obtain authorisation from the relevant bank or credit company.

Audit mechanisms

When data originates in paper form the documents should be kept as they provide a vital source of information for auditors. An auditor attempts to check that all the recorded transactions are real, that all the transactions that have taken place are recorded and that the correct values are given (see Chapter 8).

When data is captured in other ways then it is important that mechanisms are in place that allow auditors to track the effects of a transaction through a system.

As seen in Chapter 8, an audit trail can provide a history of transactions made. A company selling goods online can make good use of such a trail of transactions. A regular customer can be shown a list of previously chosen goods to make their selection quicker and easier. Amazon provides regular customers with a list of titles of books that might interest them, based on previous purchases.

Worked exam question

Puregreens, a retailer of organic vegetables, has recently launched a marketing website. The e-mail response from the 'contact us' button has been overwhelming, so they are thinking of expanding into selling online.

Discuss the implications of this, paying particular attention to the following:

- methods of data capture that will be available for online or offline payment
- the control and audit issues associated with this method of selling
- the information needs of the management of this system
- the additional information that might be generated.

The quality of Written Communication will be assessed in your answer. (20)

ICT4 January 2003

EXAMINER'S GUIDANCE

This question requires an essay style response and 4 of the 20 available marks will be allocated to the quality of your written communication.

The structure of your answer is laid out for you in the question. Marks will be awarded that relate to each bullet point in the question – so make sure you cover each point and don't just concentrate on one.

First you need to identify the methods of data capture that will be available for online or offline payment. Careful reading of the question reveals that offline payment is included so printing off a form and submitting it by post together with a cheque is an acceptable answer as well as the more obvious filling in of credit or debit card details online and submitting the payment.

*Next you need to discuss the control and audit issues associated with online selling. Points for this section can be found earlier in the chapter, in sections **Control mechanisms** and **Audit mechanisms**.*

Many essay type questions include parts that cover many different sections of the module specification. The material needed to answer the last 2 bullet points is provided in Chapters 4 and 5.

Now have a go...

SUMMARY

- **Data may require** translation **or** transcription **prior to entry into a system. This can affect the accuracy of the data.**
- **The most appropriate method of data capture for a particular system will depend on:**
  - **the nature of the data and how it arises**
  - **the current state of technological development**
  - **the quantity of the data to be collected.**
- **The method of data capture chosen will have an impact on both the quantity and quality of the data.**
- **Verification is used to check that data is entered correctly.**
- **Validation is computerised checking that detects any data that is not reasonable or is incomplete.**
- **Control mechanisms are used to ensure that no transaction is missed or lost. Examples of control mechanisms include:**
  - **batch totals**
  - **control totals**
  - **hash totals.**
- **Audit mechanisms are needed to keep track of data movement as they provide a vital source of information for auditors.**

Chapter 6 Questions

1 A mail order company receives orders for its goods through the post. Control mechanisms can be used to ensure that no orders are lost or the data wrongly entered into the computer system.
Describe **two** control mechanisms that can be used. (6)

2 For each of the following applications state a suitable method for data collection. Justify each choice.
- **a)** Identifying a parcel that is sent overseas
- **b)** The response to a questionnaire
- **c)** The payment of a purchase using a credit card
- **d)** The details of a payment made on the slip provided on a bill from a gas provider. (8)

3 Barcodes are widely used to identify products purchased in a supermarket at a Point of Sale Terminal (POS).
- **a)** Explain why a barcode is an appropriate form of data entry in this application.
- **b)** Sometimes data has to be entered by a different method at a POS. Describe **two** situations when this might happen. (4)
- **c)** Name **three** other applications when a barcode could be used. Justify each choice of application. (6)

7 Management of change 

▶ Change is necessary in life, often due to biological factors such as ageing or parenthood. Organisations change too, often due to external economic circumstances. The introduction or development of an information system within an organisation must lead to change.

This change will not just be about new hardware and software but also about human issues.

Organisations will cope best with change if they prepare for it, plan ahead and avoid potential problems.

Factors to consider when planning for change ◀

Reskilling of employees

The introduction of a new information system is likely to change the nature and content of many jobs associated with the system. Many old skills may become redundant, and employees will need to be taught new skills. In some cases these changes could be relatively minor and simply require a few hours of training. In other cases the changes to the job might be more radical and much training and reassurance will be needed when reskilling staff.

The introduction of information systems can cause a shift from jobs which require basic, manual skills to those that contain a greater component of problem solving. The introduction of networked PCs has resulted in one person performing a much greater range of tasks. The role of many telephonists has been enhanced. Instead of having to pass callers on for help, the telephonist is empowered to answer many questions, for example, concerning availability of stock or product lines through having access to an online database.

Many information systems are designed to be used directly by middle managers who in the past made no use of a computer directly, but would be provided with printed listings appropriate to their needs. For example, when a new information system is introduced, a regional sales manager, who has been sent weekly printouts of the performance of his salesmen, has to learn to access the same information for himself using a networked desktop PC. If he has not made use of a computer before, he may need considerable training.

Attitudes of employees

The change to a new system of working can provoke fear and resistance from employees. There is likely to be a fear of the unknown or an employee may feel that he will not be able to operate the new system. If staff are kept fully informed and up to date about developments and what training they can expect, they are likely to feel more involved and less afraid of what might happen.

Many employees fear that an information system will reduce their status within the organisation. They fear that their importance will be diminished as many of the tasks that are most important in their present role will be taken over by the information system, leaving them with less crucial and more mundane tasks. The introduction of a new database system often brings data together into a central system that was stored in separate departments. Managers are likely to have access directly to much more information, without needing to contact other departments directly.

The tasks required by the new system might even result in a regrading which could pose a threat to an employee's ambitions.

Job satisfaction, an important motivational factor for an employee, can depend on many factors that can be affected by the introduction of a new system. The new system might reduce the range and variety of tasks to be carried out, reduce an employee's interactions with other employees making them more desk bound, reduce the level of decision making and judgment required, or involve an employee with only carrying out part of an operation when before they were involved in all stages. Satisfaction can be reduced when aspects of a job are taken over by an information system, leaving the employee with less interesting, routine tasks to perform.

Organisational structure

The introduction of new information systems can result in major changes within an organisation. Changes in the work done may result in the need to modify the organisational structure. There has been a shift towards flatter, leaner structures as middle management jobs have been eroded. An MIS makes it easier for strategic management to monitor operations more directly. Some decisions, previously taken by middle management can be performed automatically by new systems. An example of such a decision could be the reordering of stock. The clear division between different departments may become reduced as information becomes more widely available.

Major operational changes can result from the adoption of a new system. As POS terminals are installed in shops, stock control, ordering and sales analysis can all be computerised. These changes can result in the need for modifications in the organisation's structure as the traditional structure is no longer appropriate for the new information flow.

Employment patterns and conditions

Some jobs may disappear entirely when a new information system is introduced, leading perhaps to redundancy. Very often the jobs lost are those that require the least skills.

The working hours or the location of work may need to change for some employees. Many computer systems run 24 hours a day and staff are needed to operate and maintain the computers. Shift work may become a necessity and other work patterns may change. Change may also mean having to work in a different location. It may even be necessary to move house. (See Case Study 2.)

The development of communications and ICT has led to a growth in teleworking, the ability for employees to work from home accessing the company's computer system via a network.

Internal procedures

A new information system can lead to changes in the internal procedures of an organisation. The nature of the new system may force the way that things are done to be changed.

A company may invest in a new MIS to provide information to managers to help them make decisions. The manager must change her procedures to ensure that she uses the information appropriately. She must understand the information produced by the MIS and the information must be updated regularly so that decisions are not based on outdated information.

case study 1
▶ Automatic stock reordering at Selfridges

Selfridges was one of the first retailers in Europe to use software that automatically reorders stock.

Previously reordering and delivery was controlled by a manual data entry process that was prone to error and time consuming. The new system uses an electronic catalogue that holds suppliers' details and links with the sales system, reducing the time taken in reordering by 60%.

'Automating will allow employees to move from a wholly clerical function to work that is more exciting and engaging for them,' said a spokesman for the company.

1. What did Selfridges have to do about the reskilling of employees?
2. Why might employees have opposed the changes?
3. Why would the organisational structure have to change?

A company might invest in a new payroll system. The old system was based on batch processing. Any amendments to personal details therefore had to be entered before the payroll program was run. As a result all changes had to be done by the 12th of the month.

The new system allows amendments to be entered more easily and runs more quickly. As a result amendments can be made up until the 24th of each month. The company must change its procedures to ensure that staff are able to make alterations just before the 24th.

Managing change

The key actions in managing change are:

Plan ahead. If change is to be introduced with the minimum of distrust and upheaval, it must be managed. Careful plans need to be worked out well in advance of the implementation of any system. Current work practices and roles should be carefully reviewed. The possibility of redundancy, deskilling or loss of job satisfaction can all lead to resistance. Management should set out to involve the personnel involved, and where appropriate, the trade unions, from the start and communicate fully and frankly with all those who are likely to be affected by changes.

Consult. The management style of the organisation will have an impact on the ease with which change can effectively be introduced. An organisation with an open management style, where employees are used to being consulted and having their views taken into account, may encounter fewer problems.

Explain. Whatever the style, the people who are managing the change must explain the coming changes and inform the workforce throughout the development of the project, including them as much as possible in decisions and allaying their fears.

If the organisation does not explain what is proposed to its employees, then rumours and counter rumours will quickly spread – often suggesting far greater changes than are projected.

The possibility of redundancy, relocation, deskilling or loss of job satisfaction can all lead to resistance. However, it is often possible to achieve necessary manpower reduction through natural wastage over a period of time without the need for enforcing redundancies.

Train. Training and retraining schemes should be set up and personnel should be shown that routine, boring work can be eliminated and job satisfaction maintained or even enhanced.

If employees can be convinced that the changes brought about by the new information system will be advantageous to them they are unlikely to oppose or resist the changes.

Lack of planning

If an organisation fails to plan properly, change will not be smooth and many things can go wrong such as:

- there is insufficient time to install and test the system
- there is a lack of functionality because of a lack of user/ management involvement in the design
- software is not error free due to lack of testing
- there are problems with the changeover
- user/technical documentation is incomplete
- staff are not prepared – they don't know how to operate the new system – lack of training
- staff are demotivated
- the emphasis is on the computer system and not on the information needs of users
- there is a concentration on low level data processing
- there is a lack of standards
- there is a lack of post-implementation maintenance.

Other factors

There are a number of factors that influence how successfully change is managed within an organisation.

- The structure of the organisation and the key roles are crucial. Change may bring about a restructuring which may require the loss of some jobs and substantial changes in others.
- The conditions of service under which the workforce are employed will be an important factor in determining the ease with which change can be undertaken.
- The attitude of both management and the workforce will be influential as well as the overall organisational culture. An organisation, whose management has an open style, where there is mutual trust and support, is less likely to fear or resent change. If the skills needed far outstrip the current skills level of the workforce change will be difficult to bring about.

case study 2
▶ Changing to a new call centre

In May 2005 Scottish train operator *First ScotRail* decided to set up a new customer call centre in Scotland. The call centre at Fort William started operation in August 2005. It is open every day from 7 a.m. to 10 p.m. and created 50 new jobs.

Before this, customers had to ring the department of the company they required such as ticket sales, assistance for disabled travellers or customer relations. Staff in the new call centre use information from the company's ICT system to answer all customer queries. As a result of the change the existing Customer Relations team in Glasgow had to close and staff were transferred to the new call centre.

First ScotRail had to plan ahead, consult, explain and train. For example, they had to plan the location of the call centre, acquire premises and install equipment and plan the changeover.

They would have had to consult with the staff trade unions about the new conditions of service. They would have had to explain to the public about the new service and how to use it and train their staff in how to work in the multi-skilled environment.

1. Suggest two reasons why existing *First ScotRail* staff might not be happy with moving to work at the call centre.
2. Why might the timing of the introduction of the call centre have led to problems?

SUMMARY

The introduction of a new information system will result in change which must be managed.

Factors to consider when planning for change:

- **Re-skilling of employees**
- **Attitudes of employees**
- **Organisational structure**
- **Employment patterns and conditions**
- **Internal procedures**

To prepare for change businesses must:

- **Plan ahead**
- **Consult**
- **Explain**
- **Train**

Employees' concerns might include:

- **Redundancy – loss of job**
- **New work patterns – e.g. moving to a shift system**
- **Relocation – their job moving to another town**
- **Deskilling – current skills no longer being needed**

Chapter 7 Questions

1 A delivery company is introducing a new computer system that is designed to plan deliveries more efficiently than at present. Some members of company staff are concerned about the proposed change.

Describe **three** concerns that the staff might have. (6)

2 A borough council is changing from the traditional system of all staff dealing with telephone enquiries to a call centre system where dedicated staff handle all outside calls.

Describe **four** actions the council must take to ensure a smooth changeover. (8)

3 'Changes must be planned, particularly if a new information system is being introduced.'

State **six** things that could be wrong if a new system is introduced without proper planning. (6)

4 CB Supplies sell stationery to businesses. In the past sales clerks have taken orders over the phone or by letter but they now intend to take orders online over the Internet.

a) Suggest **two** reasons why the clerks might be unhappy with the change. (2)

b) Describe the steps that should be taken to ensure that the new system is introduced successfully. (6)

5 A high school is considering introducing a new registration system where all teachers have a palmtop computer. The register will be stored on the computer and the data can be transmitted wirelessly to the school office.

Describe **four** factors that the school's management team should consider when introducing this change. (8)

6 A bookstore company with fifty shops through the country has found that it is losing sales to online bookstores. The company has decided to close down its twenty least profitable stores and to set up its own Internet bookstore to avoid going out of business.

Discuss the factors that need to be considered in planning and managing these changes. Include in your discussion:

- steps the company will need to take
- staffing issues and employment conditions
- concerns of staff
- internal procedures and organisational structure.

Your answer must be written in the form of an essay. (20)

7 An international bank is considering upgrading its information system. This will involve the installation of a new computer network.

State **four** actions the bank must take to ensure that the changeover does not disrupt the service that the bank provides to customers. (4)

8 Legal aspects

Corporate information systems security policy

If an organisation does not take adequate measures then its operations will be at risk. Potential security threats exist to hardware, software and data and such threats can occur from within or outside an organisation (see Chapter 9).

A company's knowledge and data are probably the most important assets of any organisation. Companies must make sure that the confidentiality, integrity and availability of their data is maintained at all times.

Three key security questions are:

- Who sees the data?
- Has the data been corrupted?
- Can I access data when I need it?

Although there are certainly many external threats to security, such as viruses or illegal access to systems by hackers, many experts think that the greatest security threat to ICT systems comes from people working within an organisation itself. Breaches of security can be caused through incompetence, for example: a failure to encrypt data sent over public networks; networks that are poorly implemented and protected only by simple passwords that are easy to crack; a firewall that stops nothing or protection software that is never updated.

On the other hand, breaches in security could be made on purpose by an employee perhaps because they are unhappy with their job or their boss. Such situations sometimes result in the destruction of vital information. There could be an intent to steal information, either for personal use or for selling to others, perhaps a competitor.

The role of a corporate ICT security policy

The role of a corporate ICT security policy is to lay down the procedures, guidelines and practices necessary to keep hardware, software and data safe from theft, misuse and unauthorised access. An organisation has a responsibility to maintain security measures to ensure that the requirements of the laws relating to ICT are not broken. An ICT security policy is established so that misuse can be prevented, with methods of detection and investigation being put in place.

Disciplinary procedures that will be used if staff are found to be breaking the rules laid down in the policy will be explained.

By enforcing the corporate security policy, organisations can minimise their ICT security risks.

Companies storing personal data are obliged to abide by the Data Protection Act which states that personal information must be kept secret. The company is responsible for ensuring that this data is not divulged and that company staff are aware of the legal requirements.

A corporate ICT security policy aims to:

- prevent misuse
- detect misuse through regular checking
- investigate misuse through the use of monitoring software and audit trails
- prevent unauthorised access
- lay down staff responsibilities in the prevention of misuse
- lay down disciplinary procedures for breaches of security.

A corporate ICT security policy will need to be modified as new systems are introduced and old ones altered. For example, when insurance sellers are issued with laptops for the first time, to take with them when they visit clients, the company's security policy will have to be extended to contain rules to protect the data, the hardware and the software.

The content of a corporate ICT security policy

The introduction of one company's ICT security booklet states: 'The company is in a highly competitive industry in which the loss or unauthorised disclosure of sensitive information could be extremely detrimental to the company. These guidelines have been prepared to ensure that all staff understand the importance of safeguarding company information and the protective measures that need to be taken.'

A security policy is likely first to state the purpose of the policy so that employees reading the policy are aware of why it is needed and the threats to security that could arise.

Staff responsibilities should be drawn up and disciplinary procedures agreed so that any misuse is dealt with. A staff ICT security document is likely to specify who can use company computer systems and to set out the password policy. It will lay down the steps that should be taken to provide protection against viruses and the physical security of computer systems. Rules will be provided to ensure that all computer use is within the law.

Activity 1

A template for a corporate ICT security policy is shown below. Any organisation could use this as a basis for their own policy, customising it to meet the specific needs of their own organisation.

1. The following document outlines guidelines for use of the computing systems and facilities located at or operated by [COMPANY NAME].
2. Use of the computer facilities includes the use of data and/or programs stored on [COMPANY NAME] computing systems, data and/or programs stored on magnetic tape, floppy disk, CD-ROM, or any storage media that is owned and maintained by [COMPANY NAME].
3. The purpose of these guidelines is to ensure that all [COMPANY NAME] users (business users, support personnel, technical users, and management) use the [COMPANY NAME] computing facilities in an effective, efficient, ethical and lawful manner.
4. [COMPANY NAME] accounts are to be used only for the purpose for which they are authorised and are not to be used for non [COMPANY NAME] related activities.
5. Users are responsible for protecting any information used and/or stored on and/or in their [COMPANY NAME] accounts. Consult the [COMPANY NAME] User Guide for guidelines on protecting your account and information using the standard system protection mechanisms.
6. Users shall not attempt to access any data, projects and/or programs contained on [COMPANY NAME] systems for which they do not have authorisation or explicit consent of the owner of the data, project and/or program.
7. Users shall not share their [COMPANY NAME] account(s) with anyone. This includes sharing the password to the account or other means of sharing.
8. Users shall not make unauthorised copies of copyrighted software, except as permitted by law or by the owner of the copyright.
9. Users shall not make copies of system configuration files for their own, unauthorised personal use or to provide to other people and/or users for unauthorised uses.
10. Users shall not purposely engage in activities with the intent to: harass other users, degrade the performance of systems, deprive an authorised [COMPANY NAME] user access to a [COMPANY NAME] resource, obtain extra resources beyond those allocated, circumvent [COMPANY NAME] computer security measures or gain access to a [COMPANY NAME] system for which proper authorisation has not been given.
11. Electronic communication facilities (such as e-mail or Newsgroups) are for authorised [COMPANY NAME] use only. Fraudulent, harassing or obscene messages and/or materials shall not be sent from, to or stored on [COMPANY NAME] systems.
12. Users shall not download, install or run security programs or utilities that could potentially reveal weaknesses in the security of a system. For example, [COMPANY NAME] users shall not run password cracking, key logging, or any other potentially malicious programs on [COMPANY NAME] computing systems.
13. Any non-compliance with these requirements will constitute a security violation and will be reported to the management of [COMPANY NAME]

Activity 1 *continued*

and will result in short-term or permanent loss of access to [COMPANY NAME] computing systems. Serious violations may result in civil or criminal prosecution.

I have read and understand the [COMPANY NAME] security policy and agree to abide by it.

Signature: Date:

1. Define the terms **template** and **user account**.
2. What activities could be referred to in paragraph 4?
3. Draw up a table listing all the actions that a user must **not** take; for each give a clear reason.

Must not....	Reason

4. What sanctions for breaking the rules have been included? Can you include any other possible sanctions?
5. State what you would put into the User Guide for guidelines on protecting your account referred to in paragraph 5 of the policy.
6. Use the template to create an ICT security policy for your school or college. You might need to leave out some conditions, modify others and add further ones of your own.

Methods of improving awareness of corporate ICT security policy

For a security policy to be effective the staff must be fully aware of its contents and it must be enforced. All users, including the most senior employees, must be seen to be keeping to the policy.

Induction training

Many organisations ensure that staff receive a lecture from the security manager on issues of security when they join the organisation as part of an induction training programme for all new employees. They should have the contents of the policy carefully explained to them in an atmosphere that encourages them to ask questions.

The employee is usually given a handbook or leaflet with a copy of the policy to keep and read. They may also be given a CD or DVD that contains further information so that they can refer to the matter at a later time. In addition, every new employee will be expected to sign a copy of the corporate ICT security policy.

Staff access to guidance

However, an introduction to the policy on induction day is unlikely to be enough. Guidance on the policy should be available to staff when it is required. In some organisations a new recruit is not allowed near a computer terminal until they have been successfully tested on the security matters relating to the tasks in their job.

It is vital that employees remember and absorb what is contained within the ICT security policy so that they do not break the rules through ignorance. A number of methods can be used to ensure that all staff are aware of the contents of the ICT security policy and of any changes that have recently been made. An organisation is likely to use a combination of these. The methods include:

- A staff meeting at which the staff of the whole organisation or department can be reminded of security issues or introduced to new aspects.
- Training can be given to individuals through the use of an internal course.
- A leaflet containing the details of the policy in an easy-to-digest form can be distributed to all staff.
- The policy can be made available on the organisation's intranet or through the use of bulletin boards.
- Posters can be displayed throughout the buildings of the organisation to bring the importance of ICT security to the attention of employees.
- E-mails can be sent to ALL staff reminding them of the policy.

In the USA a new interactive training tool has been developed that tests employees' understanding of the organisation's corporate ICT security policy through the use of multiple choice tests. The new employee can only sign the policy when he passes the test.

Marketing security

The Prudential Assurance Company has introduced an education scheme throughout the company to improve its ICT security. Their Head of Information Risk is reported to have said that companies are often too reliant on the technology of firewalls, antivirus software and intrusion detection systems, focusing too much on the technology and not enough on the people issues. 'It is not that the technology isn't working, but it can't legislate for stupidity,' he said.

Different approaches need to be taken to ensure the board and the staff take security seriously. The executives have direct legal responsibilities. If they are forcibly made aware of these they are likely to support security measures to remove any risk of being sent to prison.

case study 1
▸ Employees need training in security

A security company claims that businesses could cut external hacking attacks by 80 per cent by more effective enforcement of security policies among staff. They demonstrated how weak security can be when they carried out a spot survey of 150 people at Victoria Station in London that prompted two-thirds to reveal their network passwords.

Another recent survey found that 75 per cent of staff in the UK have not received any training on the security issues of using e-mail and accessing the Internet at work. Although most were aware of the risk from viruses, few were able to identify or deal with potential threats.

- What are the dangers that come from SPAM (the junk mail of the Internet) and the jokes and other such mail being forwarded by friends?
- Identify other common practices by members of staff that can lead to an ICT security risk.
- Produce a plan for making and keeping the staff at your school or college aware of the ICT security policy.

The Prudential's computer-based training programme is reinforced through posters and beer mats. It is important to use a variety of ways to educate staff; once a year is not sufficient, a more frequent approach has greater effect.

case study 2
▸ MI5 laptop snatched at Paddington

A few years ago, a desperate search was underway for a computer belonging to MI5, which was stolen from an agent at Paddington station. The laptop was believed to contain sensitive information relating to Northern Ireland.

The machine was snatched on the main concourse when the agent left it for a moment to help a group of youths. The security worker chased the thief but lost him in the station crowds.

The Home Office said that the information was highly encrypted and the theft did not pose a risk to national security.

- Explain what is meant by encryption.
- What other security measures could have prevented the thief from accessing vital information?
- What disciplinary measure was likely to have been taken against the agent?

Disciplinary measures

If an employee is discovered to have broken a rule in the corporate ICT security policy, for example, by installing unauthorised software on the organisation's network, they are likely to be subject to one of a number of sanctions.

They are likely to have network usage monitored very carefully and their access rights restricted. They may be given a verbal or a formal written warning. If the offence were of a serious nature, it could lead to suspension or even termination of employment. The employee could face legal action under the Computer Misuse Act.

case study 3
▶ The threat from within

A report from the Institute of Directors (IOD) states that employees are as great a threat to data security as hackers and viruses. Firewalls, facing outside the organisation, are important but to combat internal security attacks, security controls must be imposed on every piece of data within an organisation. The IOD recommends a system that labels every item of data with the people allowed to see it, as it is being created.

The figures on the number of insider-job security breaches are likely to be much lower than the real figure as organisations often keep the occurrences of such breaches to themselves.

- What is meant by the term 'security breach'?
- Why would an organisation be reluctant to make public the rate of insider-job security breaches?
- What other measures could be taken to protect against a security threat from employees?

Audit requirements

An audit is a check. A financial audit is often required by law. An auditor is an independent person whose job is to check the accounts of an organisation to ensure that they comply with all laws and regulations and that no fraud has taken place.

An auditor will check that an organisation has procedures in place that provide protection against the misuse of ICT systems and data. Auditing systems should detect any misuse that has taken place, for example by uncovering anomalies or discrepancies through regular checking. Any misuse must be investigated through the use of such aids as monitoring systems and audit trails (see below).

The auditor needs to be able to access all relevant records within the ICT system, for example, records of customer transactions, orders, payroll details, as well as the overall end of year statement of accounts

To carry out an audit, an auditor will need to examine the data files. However, files on magnetic media such as disk cannot be read as easily as traditional paper ledgers. Old files are not normally kept for more than a few days before being overwritten. The system must be designed with the work of the auditor in mind; records of transactions must be stored. This is known as an **audit trail** (see below).

Audit package

A range of auditing software packages can now be bought which save the auditor a lot of routine work. They enable the auditor to check computer files.

The main facilities of an audit package are:

- verification of file control totals (these are validation totals stored in the file)
- verification of individual balances in records
- verification that all data is present in records
- selection of records for checking, for example, random records, overdue accounts, non-active accounts, payments over a certain value (these values are selected by the auditor)
- analysis of file contents, for example, debts by age, payments by size, stock by value
- comparisons of two files to show up any differences.

Audit trails

An audit trail is an automatic record made of any transactions carried out by a computer system (for example, all updates of files). This may be needed for legal reasons so that auditors can check that the company accounts are accurate.

An audit trail is a means of tracing all activities relating to a piece of information from the time it enters a system to the time that it leaves. An audit trail should provide sufficient information to establish or verify the sequence of events. It enables the effects of any errors in the accounting information to be traced and the causes determined.

For example, if five items of a product are removed from stock, the number in stock stored in the record for that item will be reduced by five. For audit purposes, a record of the transaction that resulted in that reduction must also be stored. This will have fields: stock number to identify the product, the type of transaction (e.g. adding to or removing from stock), the quantity of items and the date and time of the transaction. This ensures that auditing is an integral part of the system.

A further example of an audit trail in use is the Police National Computer. This is used to trace the history of owners of a motor vehicle. Before computerisation, every car was issued with a paper log book which had to be kept by the car owner. The log book had details of all the previous owners of the car recorded in it. The current computer system has been designed to hold the same information so that the names of all past owners can be found on request.

A trail will tell an auditor what exact data was amended, by whom and when.

An audit trail keeps track of:

- what has happened in a system
- who has been using it
- for how long they have been using it
- what person did what with what data.

Problems with online systems

Online systems provide problems for the auditor for a number of reasons. Transaction details can be entered at many points on a WAN. Source documents may not exist; this could occur if an order was made by phone. Controls such as validation and verification may not be used as they may waste time in a time critical system. Very often, immediate processing may make an audit trail impossible.

The auditor must check the software thoroughly. In particular he or she must pay attention to the validation checks made on input data. Careful checks should be made that passwords are used properly and that any suspicious transactions are reported.

The management of an organisation will need to be able to check that its employees are not misusing the organisation's computer network. If an employee is suspected of breaching the company' s corporate ICT security policy then it must be possible to check an audit trail that keeps a record of all activities at network stations. The data items that will need to be recorded whenever a user accesses the network will include:

- user ID – to identify the user
- address of the workstation being used
- date and time of the access and the time spent logged on
- number of login attempts
- applications accessed
- data accessed.

Overheads of maintaining an audit trail

The maintenance of audit trails does not come without a price. Additional computer storage will be needed to hold the extra data of the trail. The need to record data in an audit trail may well slow down transaction processing.

case study 4
▶ An audit trail

Joanna took her car to the local garage for a service. When she collected her car, she was told that the brakes were worn and that two pads had been replaced. Joanna was convinced that there was something seriously wrong with her car's braking system as she could remember paying out to have them repaired on several ▶

occasions. She talked to the manager who was able to view the trail of past transactions relating to Joanna's car and the specific repairs that had been carried out. With this information he was able to assess whether or not there had been an underlying problem with the braking system.

- List the data items that would need to have been kept in order for the audit trail to have been carried out successfully.

Worked exam question

Data must be recorded to enable auditing of ICT systems.

For each of the following examples, state **two** items of data and describe how they may be used in the audit trail of the system:

a) a company's stock control system (3)

b) a company's network security system (3)

ICT4 June 2004

EXAMINER'S GUIDANCE

In each section there are two marks available for stating an item of data and a further mark for stating how it is used. You should avoid giving the same answer in part (a) and part (b)

SAMPLE ANSWER

a) Two items of data recorded in a stock control system are the **Item Code** and **Number of items in stock**.

This is used to monitor stock levels and reorder stock when required.

b) Two items of data recorded in a network security system are the **User ID** and the **Date and Time** of log on.

This can be used to monitor staff for malpractice.

ICT and the law

Legislation

Laws are a major influence constraining the operations of businesses. The procedures within a company must reflect the requirements of the legislation to ensure that all laws are being adhered to. When new legislation is passed, an organisation will need to look at current practice to check that new requirements are being met and, if necessary, modify procedures accordingly.

If a company employee breaks the law while at work, the company is legally responsible as well as the individual, unless it can be proved that the company has done everything reasonable to prevent the employee breaking the law. For example, if an employee discloses personal information and unwittingly breaks the Data Protection Act, the company can be prosecuted.

Several companies have ended up in court because of the actions of their employees. As well as the possibility of a large fine, the company is likely to suffer through bad publicity. Companies must ensure that employees are aware of:

- the law
- what employees must and must not do
- sanctions against employees if they are found to have broken the law.

The requirement of an organisation in ensuring that all its employees are aware of their legal responsibilities includes those laws that relate to ICT, which are:

- The Data Protection Acts of 1984 and 1998
- The Computer Misuse Act 1990
- The Copyright Designs and Patent Act 1988
- The Health and Safety at Work Act 1974 and the EU Health and Safety Directive 87/391.

You will have studied the details of the Acts as part of your ICT AS Level course.

An organisation might need to alter many of its procedures to ensure that the laws are kept. For example, to comply with the Copyright Designs and Patent Act, it might be necessary to prevent individual users from purchasing and installing their own software. Instead all such software purchases should be centralised with the ICT support department so that careful records can be kept to ensure that the correct licences are held for all the software installed on the organisation's computers.

New employees usually undergo an induction course which provides them with a background to the organisation as well as giving specific training about the job. This course should include a discussion of the legal requirements of the post. All employees should be given a handbook which lays out their legal responsibilities. It is useful to provide a list of 'dos and don'ts'.

It is vital that managers take an active role to ensure that legislation is enforced within an organisation. Employees should be reminded of the law through individual memos, public notices posted on walls, and the organisation's intranet. Employees should be expected to sign an agreement that lists the rules and procedures that apply to ensure that the requirements of all relevant legislation are met.

Methods of enforcing and controlling data protection legislation

The Data Protection Act (DPA) was created to provide individuals with rights that protect them against the misuse of personal data held about them. The main aspects of the DPA are that all personal data held should be secure, accurate and should only be used for the purpose for which it was gathered. Individuals have the right to see data kept about them and can demand that errors in the data be corrected.

Every organisation must ensure that they **register all data stores** that fall under the DPA with the Data Protection Commissioner. It should be clearly stated how the data is to be used and to whom it is to be passed on. Enquiries should be made to the Commissioner in any cases of doubt about the need to register personal data. The organisation should draw up a written data protection policy which should make clear what data can be kept and for how long.

In each department a **Data Protection Officer** should be appointed who is responsible for monitoring practices and making sure they are following the requirements of the Act. Procedures need to be set up to allow for the investigation of possible breaches within the department.

The person whose personal data is being stored is referred to as the **data subject** in the DPA. An organisation should make public its privacy policy and the rights of data subjects. They should be made aware of the use to which their personal data is to be put and no unnecessary data should be collected.

No data can be sold to other organisations without the data subject's consent. This is often obtained by adding an opt-out tick box to the form on which the data is being collected – if the subject does not tick the box it is assumed that personal data can be given or sold to other organisations.

Data collection methods should be designed to ensure that the **data stored is accurate** and methods need to be put in place to ensure that accuracy is maintained. Systems often fall down in this respect: the initial data collection is accurate but subsequent changes to the data are not recorded systematically. It is most important that a systems analyst takes data protection requirements fully into account at the design stage of any new system. The **intended 'life'** of data should be established and procedures put in place to ensure that the data is destroyed when this time has expired.

Procedures need to be in place within the organisation to allow the data subject to **access the information** stored about them. The facilities to make corrections if errors are found must be in place.

It is important that all **employees are aware** of rulings of the Act and of their responsibilities. An organisation must use a variety of methods to remind all staff of their responsibilities in keeping data private. Matters of data protection should be included in the organisation's security policy where the responsibilities and liabilities of employees should be highlighted. Every employee should be expected to sign a copy of the policy on joining the organisation.

Each employee should only be given access to the data that they require to carry out the tasks as laid out in their job description. This should be reflected in the access level assigned to them.

An individual should be responsible within a work area for ensuring that data security and privacy is maintained; this could be the Data Protection Officer himself, or it could be delegated to another manager. Spot checks could be made to ensure that the Act is being complied with and staff should be reminded of the need for care and compliance on a regular basis.

The employee's code of practice should state that they should not create their own individual databases, perhaps on their own workstation, that contain personal data without telling the organisation's Data Protection Officer who will register the database with the Commissioner.

Data should be **protected** through the use of password protection, physical security methods, firewalls and encryption.

However, such protection by itself will not be enough. Careful **operational procedures** need to be set up to ensure that personal data is not disclosed to unauthorised people. Employees need to be trained not to disclose personal information, either in person or over the telephone, without carrying out careful checks that the person they are speaking to is permitted to be given the information. Paper copies of data that have been printed out must always be stored in a secure place out of sight of prying eyes.

Disciplinary procedures, that will be used when an employee breaches their code of practice, need to be in place within the organisation.

case study 5

M&S admits to being in breach of Data Protection Act for 15 years

Based on article by Sylvia Pennington

Some years ago, Marks & Spencer was forced to tighten its procedures for dealing with its charge card holders after learning it had been acting in breach of the Data Protection Act for almost 15 years.

The company will now only disclose information relating to charge card accounts to the primary account holder, who is legally liable for paying the bill. In the past, supplementary card holders who are authorised to charge goods to another person's account but are not responsible for paying the bill, were given access to this data and were allowed to alter personal details, such as mailing addresses.

This could constitute a breach of the eighth data protection principle, which calls for organisations to take steps to prevent unauthorised access to personal data.

A Marks & Spencer spokesman stated that the retailer had been acting in breach of the original DPA since it was passed in 1984, but added that it was unlikely to be alone in this regard.

Marks & Spencer had always sought to both comply with legislation and meet customers' requirements, a second spokesman added. An account holder whose details were altered by a supplementary card holder could allege that the store was in breach of this principle if problems arose afterwards, the spokesman said. He added that stores needed to juggle their desire to be customer friendly with the requirement to protect customers' personal data.

- What steps would Marks & Spencer have to take to keep within the DPA?

Activity 2

- Prepare a slide show to present to employees in an organisation showing how the DPA affects them. You should include all the measures that they should be taking to ensure that they comply with the DPA in their work.
- Find three examples of data collection where personal data is collected. For each example describe how the data subject is informed of their rights under the DPA.
- Explore the website www.dataprotection.gov.uk

Methods of enforcing and controlling the Computer Misuse Act

This act aims to protect computer users against malicious vandalism and information theft. Hacking and knowingly spreading computer viruses were made crimes under the Act which aims to secure computer material against unauthorised access and modification.

An organisation needs to make its employees aware of the Act and to establish procedures that will make it difficult for employees to break the law.

Employees should be banned from using external disks, USB memory sticks and other removable storage media on the organisation's computers. They should not be allowed to install any software of their own on to their workstation. It is important that software downloaded from the Internet is included in this ban. Such a rule can be enforced by spot checks of the hard disks of employees to detect any unauthorised software and backed up with appropriate disciplinary action if an employee is found to have broken the rules.

Dividing up a job so that no one individual has access to all parts of the system is necessary so that no employee is put in a position where they can carry out a fraud. Some banks insist that key staff take a minimum of two weeks of their annual leave at one time to make it harder for them to sustain a fraud.

Methods of enforcing and controlling the Copyright Designs and Patent Act 1988

Copyright laws protect the intellectual rights of authors, composers and artists. They also apply to computer software. When you buy software you do not buy the program, only the right to use it under the terms of the licence. It is illegal to copy or use software without having obtained the appropriate licence.

Every organisation needs to take positive steps to establish procedures that will ensure that the Copyright Designs and Patent Act is not being broken. No software should be used without the appropriate licences being in place. Particular care needs to be taken when LANs are used as sufficient licences for the number of users must have been obtained. The use of software should be monitored; it is possible to buy network software that will keep track of the number of users of a particular piece of software and limit the number of concurrent users to the number of licences held. Once the licensed number of users are accessing a piece of software, other users will be denied access to the software.

Software should only be installed with permission. **Spot checks** can be made to check that employees have not installed programs illegally. If unauthorised software is found on a user's workstation it should be removed immediately and appropriate disciplinary measures taken. Laptop computers should be collected in by the ICT department on a regular basis and checks made to ensure that the software installed has been correctly authorised. Employees should not be allowed to copy software for unlicensed home use. Disciplinary action should be taken if they are found to be doing so.

Software purchasing and control should be **centralised**. All requests for software should be made to one person or team who has the responsibility for ordering and overseeing the installation of the software. They will be able to ensure that all installed software is correctly licensed. An **inventory** should be kept that holds details of all software that is installed on computers within the organisation and the licences that are held. Such centralisation also allows reliable, known suppliers to be used and makes the checking that no unauthorised software has been installed a relatively straightforward matter.

What is unauthorised software in an organisation?

It could be:

- software that has been installed without the permission of the network manager
- software that does not have the necessary licence
- software that is authorised, but has had its source code changed without permission
- software personally owned by the employee
- software that is not standard within the organisation
- software downloaded from the Internet
- pirated software
- software that might affect the network security.

Regular and systematic audits should be taken to ensure that the central inventory holds a correct record of software installation.

Software theft

Software theft can be divided into two categories: piracy and counterfeiting. **Piracy** occurs when more copies of software are made than the number of licences purchased. Many users do not realise that it is illegal and can sometimes do this unwittingly. **Counterfeiting** is when software is illegally copied for sale to other users. Often counterfeit software comes without manuals, user guides or tutorials. The software cannot be registered, so there is no technical support or upgrade service available. An added problem for users is that such software carries a high risk of carrying a virus.

Methods of enforcing and controlling health and safety legislation

Organisations must maintain a healthy and safe environment for work. The role of a **health and safety officer**, who checks that the appropriate laws are complied with, must be established. The safety officer should review health and safety issues. A safety committee, with representatives from all parts of the organisation, should discuss safety matters on a regular basis. Management should encourage and give recognition to a trade union health and safety representative who could act on and report the concerns of colleagues. Such representatives should be given a very thorough training.

It is the management's responsibility to ensure that **risk assessments** are carried out on a regular basis.

All staff need to be reminded regularly of the importance of health and safety issues. Posters can be displayed which show potential hazards and precautions to be taken. A health and safety policy should be produced and a copy given to all staff. Regular **training** should be undertaken to inform and remind employees of potential health and safety hazards when working with computers, especially VDUs, and their responsibilities in preventing them.

Regular **inspections** of workstations should be carried out both against health and safety criteria such as VDU emissions and electrical safety. Procedures must be in place to replace faulty equipment in a timely manner. Inspection of workstations should also take place against ergonomic criteria such as seat positioning, sight levels and the use of wrist supports, and any deficiencies should be followed up.

In workplaces where mistakes can be life threatening, such as oil refineries, **safety incentive schemes** are often introduced. In one such scheme, the team or location with the best safety record each year is rewarded with a bonus payment.

When installing a new computer or designing the layout for a new office, it is important that space guidelines are complied with. Care should be taken to make sure that equipment and furniture are used that are **ergonomically** designed for the required use.

For employees who are using a computer for most of their working day, there needs to be a clear understanding that appropriate breaks are built-in and facilities for refreshment and relaxation away from the computer should be provided.

An organisation should establish a policy that specifies the human–computer interface (HCI) requirements for software design that should be adhered to whenever new systems are developed.

case study 6

▶ Computer-based training for health and safety

A large multinational retail company had problems keeping its in-store employees up to date with health and safety issues. The company did not employ dedicated trainers for its stores; the responsibility for keeping staff up to date fell on the store managers.

Most employees were given a thorough and appropriate induction training programme when they first joined the store, but ongoing and refresher training was more haphazard.

To get around this problem, an online computer-based training package was devised that staff could use at times convenient to them. A log of employee use was maintained centrally that recorded both access to the system by individuals together with details of their performance while working through the material. In this way employees could be reminded when they needed a refresher.

- In what ways would the computer-based training ensure that the company met its obligations for staff training in health and safety?

SUMMARY

- **An organisation needs to have a corporate ICT security policy. Its aim would be:**
  - **to prevent misuse from occurring**
  - **to enable any misuse that did occur to be detected and investigated**
  - **to lay down procedures that should prevent misuse**
  - **to establish disciplinary procedures to be used when an employee has been found committing an act of misuse.**
- **Many ICT applications are subject to audit. The auditor needs to be familiar with data-processing techniques.**
- **An audit trail is an automatic record made of any transactions carried out by a computer system (for example, all updates of files). This may be needed for legal reasons so that auditors can check that the company accounts are accurate.**
- **An organisation has a responsibility to ensure that all its employees are aware of laws relating to ICT and their responsibilities under these laws, which in particular are:**
  - **Data Protection Acts 1984 and 1998**
  - **Computer Misuse Act 1990**
  - **Copyright Designs and Patent Act 1988**
  - **Health and Safety at Work Act 1974**
  - **EU Health and Safety Directive 87/391.**
- **Methods of enforcing and controlling data protection within an organisation include:**
  - **appointing a Data Protection Officer to monitor systems and establish procedures to follow up possible breaches**
  - **establishing security methods such as firewalls, the use of passwords and data encryption**
  - **the code of practice having a clause stating that employees should not build up their own databases of personal data**
  - **using a variety of methods to educate all staff of their responsibilities in keeping data private**
  - **establishing and circulating disciplinary measures that will be undertaken if an employee does not comply with the DPA.**

- **Methods of enforcing and controlling software misuse within an organisation include:**
  - **banning employees from installing unauthorised, unlicensed software**
  - **banning employees from copying software for unlicensed home use**
  - **separating duties between more than one employee so that no one person does the complete job**
  - **centrally controlling the purchase and maintenance of all software licences**
  - **carrying out spot checks, as well as regular audits, to ensure that no unauthorised software is stored on individual computers**
  - **disciplining employees who break the rules.**
- **Methods of enforcing and controlling health and safety legislation within an organisation include:**
  - **appointing a safety officer**
  - **regularly inspecting workstations against health and safety criteria**
  - **regularly inspecting workstations against ergonomic criteria**
  - **carrying out regular staff training regarding health and safety legislation with respect to computer use**
  - **ensuring that all software used is appropriately designed**
  - **establishing procedures that ensure that faulty equipment is replaced in a timely manner**
  - **producing memos, leaflets and/or posters to advise on good health and safety practice**
  - **establishing disciplinary procedures to use when health and safety rules are breached.**

Chapter 8 Questions

1 A medical practice has installed a new information system that links patient records and prescriptions to the financial systems of the practice. The financial records must be secure against fraud as they are used to claim money from the Health Authority.

a) Describe **four** factors that should be included in an ICT security policy for the practice. (8)

b) Describe **one** measure the practice could take to show that their records were accurate. (2)

c) Describe **three** criteria that could be used to select a disaster contingency plan to recover from a breakdown of this system. (6)

ICT4 June 2002

(See Chapter 9 for more information on disaster contingency plans)

2 a) Explain the meaning of the term 'audit trail' as used for an information system. (2)

b) Describe the use of an audit trail for a particular application. (3)

3 Describe **four** methods that an organisation can use to ensure that health and safety legislation is enforced within the organisation. (8)

4 Current data protection legislation lays down the requirements that an organisation must follow in relation to the personal data relating to customers and employees that it holds. Staff training is one method of raising awareness of the legislation.

a) Describe **three** ways in which the training could be provided. (6)

b) Describe **three** further methods, other than training, that an organisation should use to ensure that the requirements of data protection legislation are met. (6)

5 Organisations that make use of Information Technology, and use ICT systems, have to ensure that they comply with the relevant legislation currently in place.

Discuss the implications of complying with such legislation on the operation of an organisation, showing how these may impact on the procedures used by the organisation.

Your discussion should cover:

- data protection legislation
- software copyright and licensing legislation
- computer misuse legislation
- health and safety legislation.

The quality of Written Communication will be assessed in your answer. (20)

ICT4 January 2004

9 Disaster recovery management

► Commercial ICT users must recognise the potential threats to their information systems, plan to avoid disasters which lead to loss of data and have contingency plans to enable recovery of any lost data to take place.

The corporate consequences of system failure

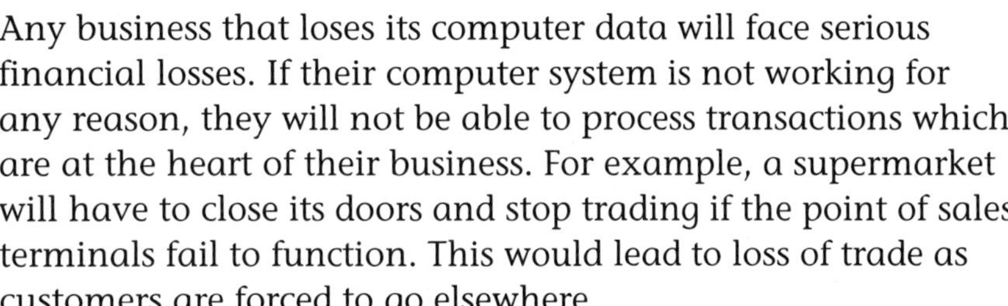

Any business that loses its computer data will face serious financial losses. If their computer system is not working for any reason, they will not be able to process transactions which are at the heart of their business. For example, a supermarket will have to close its doors and stop trading if the point of sales terminals fail to function. This would lead to loss of trade as customers are forced to go elsewhere.

Serious, extensive or repeated failure is likely to lead to a company being forced to stop trading. Customers will lose confidence in the business and its image will be adversely affected. Any disruption to customers will lead to the loss of goodwill, resulting in the loss of both existing trade on a permanent basis and potential new business. A high proportion of businesses never recover from serious failure to their information systems.

It is vital that businesses plan to avoid data loss and have a disaster recovery plan, sometimes called a contingency plan or a business continuity plan.

case study 1
► The scale of the problem (taken from an article in Computing magazine)

Almost a fifth of European organisations have no disaster recovery plan, and many of those that do would find them ineffective in an emergency. Research shows that 45% of organisations have not tested their disaster recovery plan in the last twelve months. Figures show that some organisations put out of action by a disaster can lose more than $1 million per hour – a bank could lose $250,000 per minute if systems are lost. An estimated 40% of companies that suffer a disaster will cease to be around within five years.

1. Why do you think so many disaster recovery plans prove to be ineffective?
2. Why do you think so many organisations fail to test their disaster recovery plans?

Potential threats to information systems

The threats to an information system are far ranging. Some of the major threats are described below.

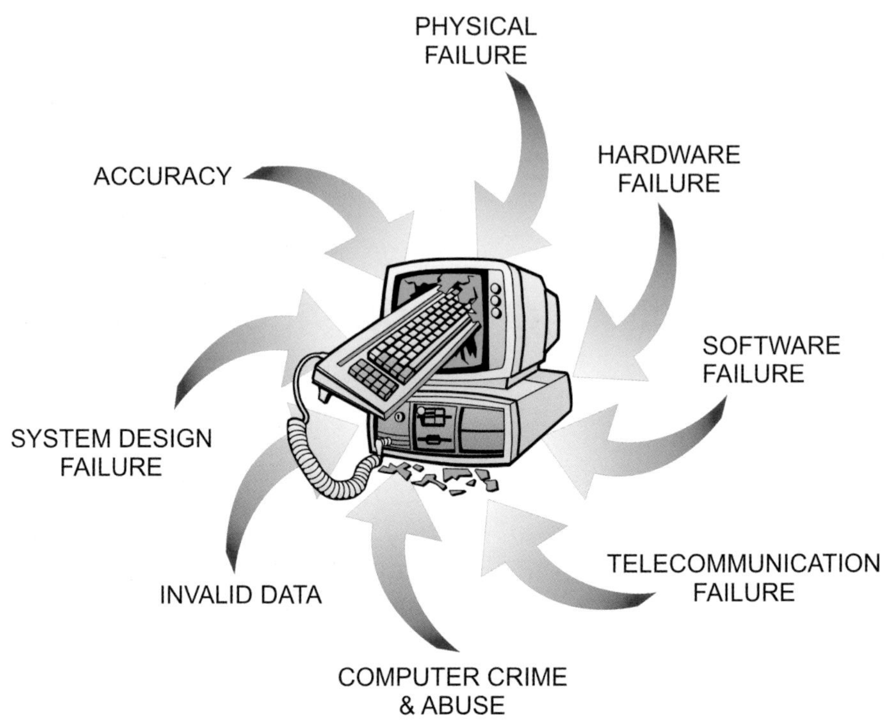

Figure 9.1 Threats to an information system

Physical failure

Physical disasters caused by events such as fire, floods or earthquakes may be relatively rare, but when they do occur they can be devastating. The threat of terrorist attack has increased over the last few years and has to be taken seriously by all organisations. Less dramatic damage can be caused to cables whilst building works are being carried out, or even by spilling a cup of coffee on a stand-alone computer.

As well as equipment, files containing vital data could be destroyed by such disasters. Without far-sighted disaster planning, many businesses would be unable to recover from the data loss. Many organisations employ specialist disaster recovery companies to manage their plans.

Hardware failure

Hardware failure is a major cause of system breakdown. Failure can arise from processor failure or disk head crash. Computers are dependent upon a constant supply of electricity. The failure of one hardware component can cause the whole system to crash. The growth in networks and distributed systems have in some ways made disaster recovery easier as it is possible for alternative sites to take over the functions of a site which has a hardware failure. On the other hand, as sites become more dependent upon each other, a failure at one location could cause universal shut down.

Software failure

Software can contain errors which are only noticed when a particular combination of unusual events occur. Such bugs may not be detected in testing and can lead to system breakdown. They can be hard to locate and put right and cause considerable damage to data as well as a delay in processing. Software can fail because it is unsuitable for the task, such as if the volume of data used in a system grows too large for the system to cope with.

Telecommunication failure

As the use of telecommunications networks has grown, the potential for breakdown has increased. Causes of such failure include faulty cables or a gateway that is non-functioning, thus denying access from a LAN to the WAN or the corruption of data as it is transmitted.

Computer crime and abuse

Data is very vulnerable to illegal access such as hacking. The company's ICT security policy should state exactly how to prevent problems occurring and what to do if they do occur. Viruses can alter the way that programs function and lead to breakdown.

Wireless network hotspots may be subjected to abuse. If data sent by wireless network is not encrypted it may be intercepted and read by a third party.

Invalid data

Data can be invalid either due to user error on entry or through corruption that has gone uncorrected. Such errors can be copied from one backup version to the next without the corrupt data being detected.

System design failure

Many failures arise as a result of poor system design which failed to build in appropriate measures to deal with all situations. Very often exceptional situations, or combinations of data, are missed by the designer.

Risk analysis

Risk analysis plays an important part in counteracting potential threats to ICT systems. It involves:

a) identifying each element of an information system
b) placing a value on that element
c) identifying any threats to that element and
d) assessing the likelihood (or probability) of such threats occurring.

The organisation should then take counter measures to protect data which are appropriate to the risk.

For example, a very tall building in an area with a high incidence of thunder storms may be very likely to be struck by lightning. A lightning strike would probably damage electrical equipment including computer systems. Installing a lightning conductor would be an appropriate counter measure. It may not be appropriate in a low building.

Businesses should consider the potential threats to the data, the vulnerability of the data and the value of the data to the business.

Risk analysis compares the vulnerability to threats and the cost of the potential losses with the cost of possible counter measures.

Every situation is unique. Managers may have statistical data on power failures, crime levels, and so on when making decisions but the value of the data to the organisation will vary. Risks (see figure 9.2) are calculated using:

- the likelihood of it occurring
- the seriousness if they do occur.

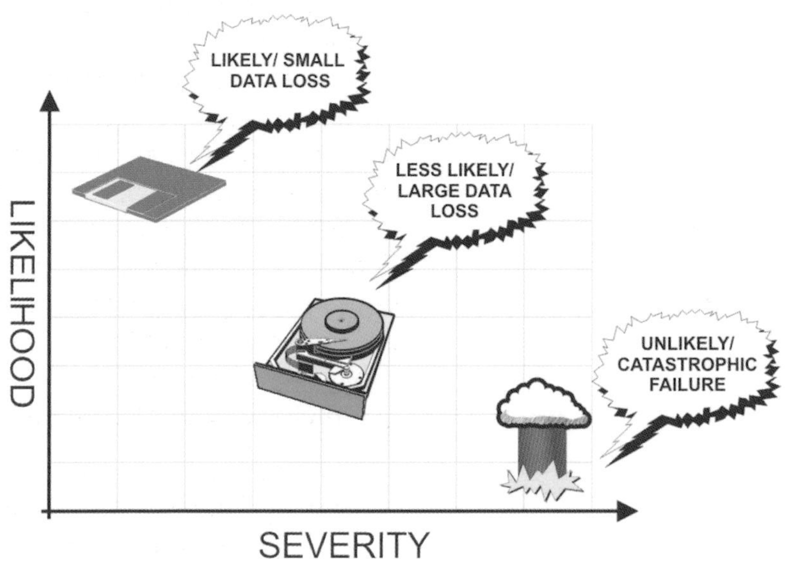

Figure 9.2 Categorising risks

Where a particular system lies on the graph will influence the type of measures put in place.

The criteria likely to be used in selecting appropriate measures are:

- the cost of measures to protect against and recover from failure
- the potential cost of the loss of data
- the statistical likelihood of the problem occurring
- the inconvenience to staff – security measures are useless if everyone bypasses them.

case study 2
▶ Risk analysis

A manufacturer has calculated that if a physical disaster such as a fire occurred at his computer facility and data was lost, the loss of trade could be around £1,000,000.

He uses a software package that provides a checklist of all recognised dangers for different types of installation. The software suggests that the probability of a physical disaster at this sort of building over 10 years is 1 in 50 or 0.02. The software calculates that it would be worth spending up to 0.02 times £1,000,000 or £20,000 to protect the data, for example by investing in a magnetic tape based backup system.

Disaster avoidance

There is much that can go wrong when using an ICT based system, and it is important that any potential problems are identified before they occur. Some failures in a system can be avoided.

The use of **fault tolerant computer systems** provides protection against hardware failure. A fault tolerant computer has extra hardware such as memory chips, processors and disk storage in parallel. Special software routines or built-in self-checking logic detects any hardware failures and automatically switches to the backup device. Some systems automatically call in the maintenance engineers. Faulty parts can be removed and repaired without disruption to the running of the system.

Other methods of avoiding disaster include the following:

- The chances of damage from fire can be reduced by having detectors in the computer room with CO_2 extinguishers available and using fireproof safes for disks and backup tapes.

- The chances of flooding can be minimised by placing the computer room on the upper floor of the building.
- The chances of loss of power supplies can be reduced by installing an uninterruptible power supply and a standby generator.
- The chances of malicious damage to the system can be reduced by having strict physical security methods, such as swipe card controlled access. Strict codes of conduct need to be enforced to protect data. For example, many companies ban the use of floppy disks as they are easily lost and data stored on them is easily accessed.
- The chances of hacking and associated problems could be countered by software security measures such as checking all accesses to the system, and only allowing three attempts before shutting down a terminal. The encryption of all data sent along communication channels should be considered.

case study 3

▶ Disaster avoidance

Dawson and Mason Ltd is a medium-sized manufacturing company which, over the last few years, has become more and more dependent on ICT. The company has decided to adopt the following disaster avoidance plan, which consists mainly of common sense practices – reasonable and inexpensive measures to avoid a disaster that could cost the company thousands of pounds in loss of revenue.

- Hardware and software inventory
  Each department of the company must keep a detailed inventory of all computer equipment; they must make sure the inventory is up to date. The inventory should cover all hardware, software, communications equipment, peripherals and backup media, including model and serial numbers.
- ICT facilities
  Administrative procedures are a vital part of security and disaster avoidance:
  - ✓ All perimeter doors must be kept locked if the room is unattended.
  - ✓ Windows and other access points should be kept locked if unattended.
  - ✓ Access should be restricted to authorised personnel.
  - ✓ Strangers seen entering office areas should be challenged and asked for identification.
- Local area networks
  - ✓ Backup of server files is automated on a nightly basis.
  - ✓ A rotation schedule for backup tapes should be used and several generations of backups kept.

- ✓ Two copies of the server backup tapes are generated. One backup copy is available on-site in case recovery is necessary. The other copy is stored off-site.
- ✓ Disk mirroring is used to duplicate data from one hard disk to another hard disk. Mirrored drives operate in tandem, constantly storing and updating the same files on each hard disk in case one disk fails.
- ✓ In the case of vital and sensitive data hot backup is used. Two file servers operate in tandem and data is duplicated on the hard disks of both servers. If one server fails, the other server automatically takes over.
- ✓ A UPS (Uninterruptible Power Supply) has been installed for every LAN server. The batteries should be checked regularly to ensure that they are not drained and that they are charging properly.

- Storage media
  - ✓ Magnetic media should be kept away from sources of heat, radiation, and magnetism.
  - ✓ Backup media should be stored in data safes.
  - ✓ Vaults used for storing critical documents and backup media should meet appropriate security and fire standards.
- Preventing theft
  - ✓ If a computer is used to store sensitive data, the data should be encrypted so that the data cannot be accessed even if the equipment is stolen.
  - ✓ Anchoring pads and security cables are used to prevent equipment from being stolen.
- Employee awareness

  Security and safety awareness is critical to any disaster avoidance program. A lot of problems will be avoided if employees have been trained to look out for conditions that can result in a disaster.

1. Disasters can be caused deliberately or be a natural disaster such as a fire, flood, hurricane or earthquake. Give one example of a disaster caused deliberately and one caused by accident.

2. Explain the reasons for keeping an inventory of hardware and software.

3. Dawson and Mason's plan does not mention computer viruses. Describe the actions that should be taken to prevent infection by a virus.

4. Describe the process of encryption.

5. List further measures that could be taken to prevent theft.

Planning for recovery from disaster: a contingency plan

Although it is obviously best for a business to avoid disasters, sometimes these situations cannot be avoided despite the best security measures. In such cases, if the organisation has an appropriate contingency plan in place, disastrous consequences (such as the organisation going out of business) should be prevented.

A contingency plan sets out what to do to recover from a failure. It is a planned set of actions that can be carried out if things go wrong so that disruption is minimised.

The contingency plan is likely to cover equipment, data, staff and business functions. It should take into account that the organisation will change over time, so reviews of the contingency plan must be built in. Obviously the plan should be appropriate for the size and nature of the organisation.

The contents of a contingency plan

1 **Alternative computer hardware**. The organisation will need to carry on if its hardware has broken down. Large organisations such as supermarkets and banks have more than one computer site in case of hardware problems. If a business has distributed processing facilities it may be possible to use them. Another option is the use of disaster recovery companies – specialist companies who will provide hardware until the organisation's own computers are back in action.
2 **Backup procedures**. For successful recovery from disaster, data and software must have been backed up and the backup media stored safely. Tapes and disks must be clearly labelled and dated, so that they can be restored in the correct order.
3 **Recovery procedures**. The disaster recovery plan must specify the order for restoring data.
4 **Staff responsibilities**. The plan should state who is responsible for doing what if a disaster occurs. Personnel will need to be trained to follow the contingency plan correctly and a step by step course of action for implementing the plan must be drawn up.

The contingency plan needs to be tested regularly to ensure that staff are fully aware of their responsibilities as well as to check that the plan actually works.

Activity 1

Search on the Internet for disaster recovery companies. What services do they provide?

case study 4
▶ UCAS computer crashes

In August 2002 a power failure in the Cheltenham area brought down the computers and telephone systems at the university clearing house UCAS. The A level results had just been published so it was UCAS's busiest time of year.

It was reported that workmen accidentally caused the power out by digging through a power cable – I bet you've never heard that one before.

UCAS have a business continuity plan which includes moving to an off-site facility. Fortunately this was not needed as power was restored within a few hours.

Criteria that affect the contingency plan

Different organisations have different contingency plans. The contingency plan chosen will depend on:

- the size of the organisation and its ICT systems
- the method of processing e.g. online or batch
- the length of time before the alternative system needs to be up and running
- the financial losses sustained while the computer system is down
- the costs of the various backup and recovery options
- the likelihood of disaster happening, based on risk analysis.

case study 5
▶ System failure: cashpoints fail for five hours

A power failure paralysed a bank's entire national cash machine system, leaving thousands of Christmas shoppers without cash. For more than five hours, customers were unable to obtain money from any automated teller machine.

Almost all the machines flashed up the message 'Sorry, cash point service closed'. Bank staff in shopping centres reported big queues as shoppers struggled to get money from cashiers inside branches. The timing could not have been worse; nine days before Christmas demand for cash is at its yearly peak.

The system was brought down by a power failure at the computer in Peterborough which authorises cashpoint withdrawals nationwide. Damage to a single power cable may have been to blame.

- What could have been included in the contingency plan to prevent the five hour down time and the long queues in the banks?

case study 6
▶ Fire

It was pay day at food manufacturer and retail group William Jackson, based in Hull. Anticipating her busiest time of the month, payroll administrator Diane Rush was at work by 7 a.m. preparing wages data to be transferred from the company's AS/400 computer to BACS, the system for paying wages directly into banks.

Diane noticed smoke billowing from the food factory next door and phoned Safetynet, the company's disaster recovery partner at 7.45 a.m. All staff had to be evacuated from the offices as fire swept through neighbouring buildings.

Although the tapes had been recovered, the continuing blaze meant that the payroll could not be processed on site. Under protection from the fire brigade, Safetynet successfully rescued the AS/400 from the ashes and installed the charred machine alongside their own mobile unit. Using a parallel recovery process, the payroll was successfully relayed to BACS and all 2500 staff were paid on time.

- List features from the William Jackson contingency plan.

case study 7
▶ Data recovery specialists

A company of automotive engineers archived their important drawings and documents in a locked fireproof safe in their basement.

Sadly although they were prepared for fire, a flood filled the basement with water and fine silt and over 40 tape cartridges of archives and backups were soaked through and the tapes were coated inside and out with a thin layer of sediment.

The engineers contacted data recovery experts Authentec International, who were able to extract each tape from its cartridge, remove the sediment and then place the tapes in brand new cartridges so that the data could be read. Within a few hours, the engineers had their data back.

Worked exam question

A travel company is reviewing the current disaster recovery plan for its computer-based booking system. Bookings come into the company by various means, including via post, over the telephone and via the Internet.

a) State, with a different reason for each one, three possible weak points in the booking system. (6)

b) Besides the frequency and content of the backups, and the media used, describe two other issues that should be considered when reviewing the backup strategy. (4)

ICT5 June 2003

This question also links in with Chapter 15, backup strategies.

▶ **EXAMINER'S GUIDANCE**

a) *One mark is for what is the weak point and one mark is for why it is a weak point. Answers must also relate to the need for a disaster recovery plan and not just any weak points.*

▶ SAMPLE ANSWER

- One possible weak point is the computer hardware which stores the bookings. If the computer crashed the bookings might be lost.
- Another possible weak point is physical security. If physical security is not tight, unauthorised users may break in and delete valuable data.
- A third possible weak point is if the company's website was unavailable for a period of time, the company would not be able to take bookings and valuable custom would be lost.

▶ EXAMINER'S GUIDANCE

b) *One mark here is for what should be considered, and the second mark is for why it needs to be considered.*

▶ SAMPLE ANSWER

- The company must consider where the backup media should be stored. It needs to be stored in a safe place so that it is not destroyed by whatever knocks out the computer system.
- The company must consider testing its recovery procedures so that if recovery is necessary the organisation can be sure that it can be carried out properly.

SUMMARY

ICT users must:

- **recognise the potential threats to their information systems. Dangers include:**
  - **telecommunication failure**
  - **computer crime and abuse**
  - **invalid data**
  - **system design failure.**
  - **physical failure**
  - **hardware failure**
  - **software failure**
- **plan to avoid disasters leading to loss of data. Examples of disaster avoidance measures include the use of:**
  - **virus scanning software**
  - **fault tolerant components**
  - **smoke detectors in buildings**
  - **uninterruptible power supplies or standby generators**
  - **strict password management policies**
  - **extra network links**
  - **regular maintenance.**
- **have contingency plans to be able to recover any data lost. Examples of elements of contingency plans to prevent disaster in case of failure include:**
  - **backup strategies**
  - **contract with a company specialising in disaster recovery**
  - **arrangement to use the hardware of another firm or bureau in case of failure**
  - **distributed systems maintaining duplicated data on different sites.**

Measures taken to prevent problems will depend on the perceived risk and the cost of potential loss of data. The process of risk analysis is used to determine the need for such measures.

Chapter 9 Questions

1 A medical practice, in an area prone to flooding, has carried out a risk analysis and is now preparing its disaster recovery plan. The main elements of its IT system are the patient record and prescription systems, and the network used to access and maintain them.

a) Explain what is meant by *risk analysis* (3)

b) State **two** different potential threats to this ICT system and describe a countermeasure for each one. (6)

c) Name **three** criteria that the medical practice should consider when preparing a suitable disaster recovery plan. (3)

ICT4 January 2005

2 During the fire at the Buncefield oil terminal, companies with nearby offices had to be evacuated and so were unable to access their computer systems. One company was able to set up at an alternative site because their risk analysis had suggested the fire was a possibility and they had a contract with another company to provide emergency offices and equipment.

a) What is meant by risk analysis? (2)

b) Describe **three** threats to computer systems other than fire. (6)

c) Describe possible countermeasures to the threats that you described in part (b) (6)

3 A medical practice has installed a new information system that links patient records and prescriptions to the financial systems of the practice. The financial records must be secure against fraud as they are used to claim money from the Health Authority.

a) Describe **four** factors that should be included in an ICT security policy for the practice. (8)

b) Describe **one** measure the practice could take to show that their records were accurate. (2)

c) Describe **three** criteria that could be used to select a disaster contingency plan to recover from a breakdown of this system. (6)

ICT4 June 2002

4 The company in question 2 had a disaster recovery plan that enabled them to maintain business continuity. This plan included the provision of emergency offices and equipment.

Suggest **three** other items that might have been in this plan. (3)

5 'Only 60 per cent of companies in the UK have adequate disaster recovery plans'. Discuss this statement, including in your answer:

- why such plans are necessary
- the potential threats to information systems
- the contingency plans needed to combat these threats. (12)

10 User support

Most software producers provide some form of support for users in case they have difficulty in installing or using their software. Support is sometimes provided free under the product warranty or an entitlement to help can be bought for a fixed period of time. Large organisations will have an ICT support team whose members will provide hardware and software support for users in-house.

Users may also need access to help on a regular basis. The software package may offer many features, not all of which the user makes use of on a regular basis. There needs to be a suitable way for the user to find out what he or she needs to know at the appropriate time.

Support provided by a software house

On-site help

When a software house supplies and installs a large new bespoke system for an organisation considerable support is likely to be needed for the first few weeks or months. New users will be unfamiliar with the package and may need guidance from members of the software house's development team in its use. At this stage unforeseen errors may occur in the software and modifications may need to be made. For this reason the software house is likely to supply on-site technical support during the early stages of the software's use. This is the most expensive support option for a software house.

Call-out support

This is a less wide-ranging, but cheaper, method of support than having software house personnel working on the site of the user company. A call-out support service will make a technician available to go on-site to a user organisation to provide specific support. Such support might particularly be used after the phase of on-site support has come to an end, when new features have been added to the software or when users within the organisation are extending the use they make of the package and thus need to know how to use different features. It can be expensive for a software house to provide call-out support but it is crucial that a customer does not have to wait too long for the help to arrive, otherwise the customer will lose confidence in the product. Indeed, suppliers may guarantee response times.

Telephone help desks

In addition many software suppliers offer telephone support for immediate help and advice. It provides someone with technical skills to guide the customer.

This help may be available during business hours, or for some widely used general purpose software, the help could be available 24 hours a day. The user phones the help desk (or call centre) when they have a problem. Help desk operators are technical troubleshooters who provide technical assistance, support, and advice to customers and end-users. They are experts in the software package and are likely to have a computer on the desk in front of them, which they will use to try to replicate and solve the users' problems.

When a help desk is provided for a widely used software package, it is likely that a high number of requests for help will be received. The help desk provider will need to establish procedures for logging and tracking the requests for help and the advice given. This is to ensure that all requests are dealt with in a fair and timely manner to maintain customer satisfaction.

What is logged?

When the call is taken, the user will need to give some information to the help desk operator. This should include:

- their name and telephone number
- the nature of the problem
- the name and the version number of the software
- the specification of computer it is being run on (the type and speed of processor, and the size of memory will be needed here)
- the operating system in use
- any error messages being displayed
- the licence number of the software so that the help desk can check that the software is being used legally.

The help desk operator will record this information together with the date and time.

A number of problems can arise when using a manufacturer's telephone help desk. The waiting time on the phone can be considerable at certain times of day. Many of these services are popular and it is not unusual to spend a lot of time listening to 'music' whilst a call is queued.

Some problems are common and are easy to answer but other, complex, ones will not be able to be answered on the spot, as several experts may need to confer. In these circumstances, it will be necessary for the help desk operator to phone back at a later time.

E-mail support

If the problem is not time critical, then e-mail could be used as an alternative to the telephone. This has the advantage of smoothing out the demand, so that the operator can answer queries in order throughout the day. A priority system could be used which would ensure that critical enquiries were answered first. Operators will be able to spend all their time finding solutions to problems without being interrupted by a ringing telephone.

From the user's point of view, the use of e-mail avoids wasted time on the telephone. However, instant answers to simple problems will not be possible. E-mail lacks the opportunity for human interaction offered by a telephone conversation.

Many suppliers now offer instant messaging support, as one operator can deal with several sets of instant messages at the same time.

Monitoring the help desk

A help desk is likely to use a computerised call logging system giving a unique call reference number for each user query. This allows the performance of the help desk operator to be monitored as well as providing a reference for follow-up calls. Different levels of support are provided; the level can determine the number of calls a user is entitled to make to the help desk. Logging calls enables the help desk to keep a count of all the calls made.

The help desk employees should have access to a file of registered users to enable them to check that the caller is entitled to help whenever a phone call is received. A computerised database of known errors and their solutions, together with answers to frequently asked questions should be available. This could take the form of an expert system.

The performance of the help desk should be monitored to ensure that it provides a high level of service.

Performance indicators could include:

- the number of calls logged daily or per hour
- the response time to the initial call
- the time taken to resolve the problem
- the number of repeat calls on the same problem for a particular user.

It may also be possible to record the level of the user's satisfaction of the problem resolution using a qualitative code.

The manager responsible for the provision of help desk facilities would review the performance indicators on a regular basis and make necessary changes to staffing levels and procedures. It might prove necessary to provide extra training for help desk operators.

User guides

A software house will usually provide written instructions in using a package. These are typically provided free with the software. This user guide may come in hard copy form as a book or in a soft copy that can be stored on the user's hard disk so it can be accessed whenever required. The user guide will describe how to install and use the software. For complex packages, there can be a number of different books: perhaps one aimed at a first time user, in the form of a tutorial, and another involving a complete description of all functions to serve as a reference document. Software user guides allow users to work at their own pace with the instructions beside them so they can find out how to use the software functions for themselves.

In an organisation some people, perhaps senior managers, may not be directly using a software package themselves. However, the software may produce reports that will provide them with information that they will need to make appropriate decisions. They will need to know what reports the software is capable of producing and how to interpret them. These managers would require a written manual that provides instructions for using the reports from the package, together with samples of the report so that they can determine which reports will aid them in their decision making.

On-screen help

Help facilities can be installed with a package so that immediate guidance can be given in the use of the package. Wizards can be provided to make complex procedures within the package easier for the user to utilise by breaking down a task into manageable steps, each step having a clear explanation of what data the user needs to enter. Such help is particularly appropriate when a user wants to use a feature of the software that they have not used before, or needs to be reminded of an infrequently used object. A user may wish to check how certain data that has to be entered needs to be formatted.

For infrequent or inexperienced users, detailed explanations can appear on the screen when data is being entered to ensure that data entry mistakes are avoided. For example, the format in which a date is to be entered can be shown.

Online support

A popular way of making support available to the user is to use the Internet and store help facilities on the World Wide Web. Information can be kept very up to date. Users can access patches to update software or fix errors. Such a site would offer the facility to e-mail a package expert for advice on a specific problem.

Package credibility

It is not cheap for software companies to provide and staff a customer help desk. Of course the support is not free. Someone has to pay for it and it is likely that the price of the software reflects the provision of user support. Despite its cost, user support is necessary and is a major factor in determining the credibility of the software.

The provision of user support reassures the customer when they buy the product. They are more likely to buy the product if they know that an appropriate level of support at a reasonable cost is available. If user support is not available, business users are unlikely to risk using the software.

User support shows the customer that the software company has confidence in its product. A poor quality product could result in thousands of help desk calls and would be expensive for the company.

If the user suffered a problem and no support was available, they would be unlikely to buy a product from the same company again. A help desk helps retain customers.

Support options for industry standard packages

Many industry standard packages, such as Microsoft Office or Adobe Photoshop, have a very large user base. The users will between them need to know all aspects of the software's functionality, although each individual user is likely to use only a part of the range of options a software package offers. Support is provided in a variety of ways.

Help is now usually available over the **Internet** where up-to-date advice on common problems can be stored.

Books about using popular software are produced independently by publishers and sold in most bookshops or over the Internet. For the most popular packages there are a very large number of titles available. A user needs to ensure that any book purchased is designed for a user of their skill level as books will vary from those suitable for absolute beginners to those designed for the most advanced user. Publishers of widely used software may send **newsletters** to all registered users, including **support articles** on tips, solutions to common problems and advanced functions. These newsletters provide a forum for users to share ideas and problems.

Software houses provide a considerable amount of information on packages via specialist **bulletin boards** on the Internet, often in the form of Frequently Asked Questions (FAQs). Users can search through questions that other people have asked and are likely to find a solution that resolves their own current problem. The software providers will provide websites with information about the packages that provide e-mail access to experts. It is often helpful for the user to print out a version of the advice provided for use at a later time when the same information is needed. Such facilities are particularly useful for more able users who can help themselves by reading the information provided.

For complex software, **user groups** are set up, where users can get together to share problems and ideas. Such groups can either meet physically, or more often these days, via bulletin boards on the Internet.

Many of these facilities are of most use to the experienced user who, given access to the appropriate information, can work out the solution to a problem for themselves.

Very often the help that a less experienced user needs is closer to hand. It is possible that a **colleague** or friend who is familiar with the software can help with their problem.

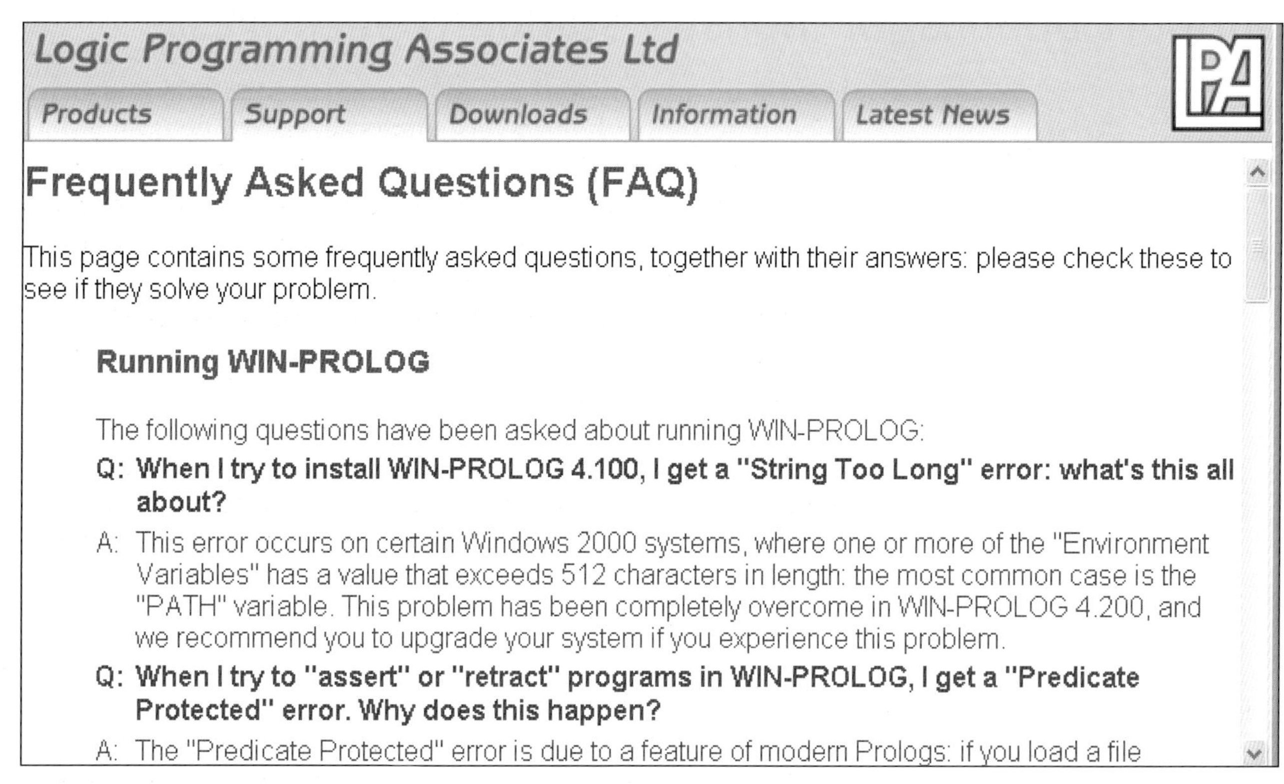

Figure 10.1 FAQs

Activity 1

- Explore the Help facilities that are available for the spreadsheet package Microsoft Excel. If you have access to the package, list the ways of obtaining help within the package.
- Describe any online help facilities that are available.
- Explore the http://office.microsoft.com/ site on the World Wide Web and list the ways of receiving help with the use of Excel.
- Explain how you would go about obtaining a newsletter with information about Microsoft Excel.
- Find the titles of three books on Excel: one introductory, one for users of some experience and one for advanced users. The following website may be of use: http://www.compman.co.uk/ Summarise the contents of each book.
- Explore the following site. List any support facilities available to users of Microsoft Excel. http://www.compinfo-center.com/pcsoft/spreadsheets.htm#top
- Can you find any further useful sites for Microsoft Excel users on the Web?

Which method of support?

The method of support a user will use depends on the nature of the problem and the skills and circumstances of the user. Many users rarely look in a manual, preferring to find out the answer for themselves although this is not always the most efficient way of operating. The first point of call is usually the on-screen help as it is always available. On-screen help can usually be easily accessed from a simple menu choice so that a user who is not clear of the format required for a particular data entry can get immediate clarification.

If the on-screen help is not sufficient to solve the user's problem he might find a colleague who knows the software well enough to solve a problem.

Checking the Internet for a bulletin board may be more convenient for an office worker than buying a book. The information given also may be more up to date. Using a telephone help desk is often the last resort for a user; it can be time consuming and require great patience.

case study 1
▶ Online class registration

A school makes use of an online registration system that allows teachers to take class registers in the classroom on a computer. Each teacher enters a unique identification code supported with a password. The attendance data is stored centrally and links to the student database. The ICT support department manages the system carrying out tasks such as: adding new teachers and pupils, entering details of classes and the pupils in those classes to the system and making modifications. Class tutors and senior managers receive regular reports on attendance. These include weekly attendance lists for each tutor group or form as well as statistical summaries. Pupils and their parents are able to access a summary of their own attendance online through the school's intranet.

Each user needs the facility to gain help when necessary so that they can make good use of the features of the software.

Teachers have access to on-screen help that relates to the stages they go through to enter the attendance for a class. Teachers quickly become familiar with the common day to day functions that they need. There are however some other functions, such as registering an absent colleague's class, that teachers only use occasionally. On-screen instructions that remind them of the data that has to be entered help them use the software in this situation. Every teacher has a printed instruction sheet highlighting the main procedures of the system for use after long school holidays!

The members of the ICT support department have technical manuals that include details of all functions in the system. They set up and maintain the appropriate data on an annual basis. From time to time they need to phone the help desk of the software house when a problem occurs that they cannot solve for themselves. An online user group has been set up where those supplying technical support to different schools and colleges share their problems through a bulletin board.

The tutors and managers are provided with a printed guide showing the reports that the system can produce and how to interpret each one. The guide includes sample reports.

The pupil or his parent accessing through the Internet is given simple online instructions explaining how to access and interpret the information relating to their own attendance. A step by step guide is provided helping the user complete all the actions required, showing exactly what data needs to be entered in every field. There are explicit instructions displayed on the screen to make data entry as simple as possible.

- Copy and complete the table below. Include further ideas of your own as well as those given in the case study.

User	Use of software	Typical help needs	Appropriate sources of help
Teacher	Entering class attendance data		
Form Tutor			
ICT support			
Pupil			

case study 2

A software house has produced a seat booking software package for sale to theatres and cinemas. The system allows front of house staff to receive seat bookings over the telephone and face to face before a performance. The tickets produced list the title of the film or play, the date and time of performance, the seat number and the price. Customers can also book online by accessing a website.

The theatre or cinema manager has to enter details of the forthcoming programme into the system. She will also be able to produce statistical reports showing such things as the sales of seats, the popularity of different shows and the cumulative takings.

- Draw up and complete a table similar to the one for online class registration.

Worked exam question

1 A software house has produced a package for sale to the insurance industry. The package has been written so that it can receive data from call centre systems, from the Internet or from salespersons' laptops.

a) Describe **three** user support options that this software house could offer its potential customers. (6)

b) The package produces information for the following types of user:

- company management
- call centre staff and the mobile salesmen
- customers who apply online.

For each of the **three** identified types of user, describe a different method of providing them with instructions and help in the use of this package, justifying your choice. (9)

ICT4 January 2004

▶ EXAMINER'S GUIDANCE

There are 15 marks in all for this question so your answer should be quite substantial. Don't forget in part (a) you need to describe three options and not just state three options.

In part (b) you will need to link the instructions method to each user.

▶ SAMPLE ANSWER

a) See page 107.

b) For the company management a **printed manual** would be suitable. It could be kept in their office and would include **directions for producing the different types of reports** available to them. The reports will help them with their **decision-making**. Now try to do the same for the other two types of user.

Documentation

Documentation consists of written material that provides information on how to use a software package. All types of software should be supported with appropriate documentation. In fact, the quality of the documentation will be one of the criteria considered when choosing software.

Different types of user will have differing documentation needs. The technical support team will need documentation that provides installation instructions including disk, peripheral devices and memory requirements. They will need to have documentation of backup routines and recovery procedures. An explanation of all technical error messages, together with the necessary action to correct them, will be required.

A data entry clerk, using the same system, will need clear instructions on how to use the functions needed for tasks. Details of appropriate error messages due to incorrect data entry should be included, together with a list of useful keyboard shortcuts.

End users who will receive reports, perhaps in printed form, will need to have documentation that explains how to interpret and make use of the reports.

case study 3

▶ Helpdesk

Computer help desk operator, salary: £14,500

I went straight from A levels to work when I joined UMIST (University of Manchester Institute of Science and Technology) at 19 as a receptionist in the computer department. Now, two years later, I work as a computer help desk operator. I work from 8:45 a.m. until 5 p.m. I don't suffer from stress, I feel valued and everyone in my department treats me as an equal.

In the morning I organise computer training courses. In the afternoon, I staff the walk-in help desk. I deal with staff and students complaining they can't log in, print or set up an account.

We get around 60 calls a day. People turn up saying, 'You're the help desk, it says on this leaflet you'll fix it.' They expect instant results and the high-ranking professors tend to get more hysterical on the phone than the students. I tend to keep calm when people lose their temper.

At the beginning I was amazed that so many students in a place specialising in technology needed help with logging in.

(From The *Guardian* newspaper)

- Describe any help desk facilities available at your school or college.
- Find out the five most frequent problems taken at this help desk.

SUMMARY

- **Software houses provide a range of support options to customers:**
  - **On-site help**
  - **Call-out support**
  - **Help desks**
  - **E-mail support**
  - **User manuals**
  - **On-screen help**
  - **Online help.**
- **Much support is expensive to provide. However, a software package needs support if it is to maintain credibility with the public.**
- **Industry standard packages have a very large number of users. Other methods of obtaining help are available to users of these packages:**
  - **Books**
  - **Newsletters**
  - **Bulletin boards on the Internet**
  - **Frequently Asked Questions (FAQs)**
  - **User groups.**
- **Documentation consists of written material that provides information on how to use a software package. Different forms are available for different categories of user.**

Chapter 10 Questions

1 Many industry standard packages have a very large number of users. For such packages help might be available from other sources than the manufacturer. For example, a range of books may be available to help users develop skills in using the software.

Describe **three** other methods of gaining support from sources other than the software's manufacturer. (6)

2 A small legal firm is about to replace stand-alone computers with a new computer network. Industry standard software will be installed. As new users of both the equipment and the software, the firm is concerned about the levels of support and training that will be needed. There are three levels of system user: the solicitors themselves, the practice management and the administrative staff.

a) Explain **two** factors that need to be taken into account when planning the training. (4)

b) Describe **two** different ways of giving technical support to these users. (4)

c) State **two** means of providing the training material, and give an advantage of each. (4)

ICT4 June 2002

3 Describe **three** ways in which support may be provided for users of ICT systems. (6)

ICT4 January 2005

4 A user purchases a copy of a widely used spreadsheet package from a computer store.

a) Describe **three** forms of documentation that are likely to be provided with the software. (6)

b) The user may require further help when making use of a feature of the software. Describe **three** sources of help that are not provided by the manufacturer at the time of purchase. (6)

5 'Now that all software has extensive online help facilities, there is no longer any need for other forms of help.'

Describe **three** other methods of user support, explaining why each is appropriate. (9)

6 A software company that maintains a *help desk* will *log* the calls that are received from users.

a) State the meaning of the term *help desk*. (1)

b) State **four** items, other than date and time, that might be entered into the log when a user call is received by the help desk. (4)

c) The manager in charge of the help desk needs to have information relating to the effectiveness of the service provided. Describe **three** measures that could be used to assess the effectiveness of the service. (6)

11 Training

Training is *'the acquisition of a body of knowledge and skills that can be applied to a particular job.'*

Today the job market is very flexible. People do not stay in one single job for the whole of their working life, but are likely to make one or more major career changes. As well as this, the nature of a particular job changes as new technological advances are made. This is particularly true for ICT users. New hardware is appearing every few months. New versions of software appear every few years. Employers need to give ICT training to their workforce on a regular basis. Training should consider both the needs of the company and the needs of the individual.

Different training needs

Different users have different training needs, depending on their previous experience, their knowledge and their job and its requirements. Some jobs involve ICT tasks that are repetitive and specific, others call for a more open-ended use. It is crucial that the level and pace of the training fits the user and the task.

Someone who has not used a computer before will need initial training. A more experienced user may need training in higher level skills. Users of special equipment (for example a bar code scanner), or special facilities (for example e-mail) will need specific training.

A database package such as Microsoft Access can be used at a number of different levels. So training needs to be available which meets these differing needs. For example, an operator of a database whose job is to enter data, may only need to be taught how to access an existing database, add and modify records.

The manager who uses the information from the database as a tool in decision making may need to be taught how to produce standard reports and carry out a range of queries. A database programmer will need to learn much more about the package. She must know how to set up a new database and amend an existing one, how to write reports and macros, and much more besides. It would be inappropriate for all the above users to attend the same course.

Skills based or task based training

Skills based training

Some training is based on learning a skill, such as typing on a keyboard, using Microsoft Windows or using a program like Microsoft Word or Microsoft Access. These skills are often used so this type of training is commonly offered in standard courses that teach participants how to use a range of facilities according to their current skills level. Such training can be fairly open-ended, leaving the trainee to decide exactly how to incorporate the skills she has learned into her current job.

Task based training

Other training is based on learning how to do a particular task. Examples of this could be: how to use a PDA to record electricity meter readings; how to process a sale with a Visa card and how to load transaction and master file tapes in a batch processing system. In such circumstances, because the training is designed specifically for the occasion, it is more likely to take place in-house. Skills acquired will be very specific and will often not be transferable into other situations.

When training to use a software application such as a sales database management system, different personnel will require different training based upon the tasks that they are required by their job to carry out on the database. A telesales person is likely to need training in data entry. They might need to know:

- what data has to be entered and what is optional
- in what order to work the data entry process
- how to deal with errors and unusual data
- how to answer enquiries.

A sales manager using the same database package might need training in how to produce a range of reports and how to 'drill down' from summarised information to find more detailed information when searching for explanations.

The database administrator will need a more technical and complex training course that provides her with an in depth knowledge of the software. She will need the skills to carry out a wide range of tasks including writing new reports, modifying the database structure to meet changing needs as well as troubleshooting when problems occur.

Skills updating and refreshing

For employees in many jobs, keeping ICT skills up to date is a nearly constant need as job requirements and facilities change. Employees will need to update their skills on a regular basis, particularly as new or updated versions of software or hardware are installed. Old skills may be superseded when new systems are installed.

Employees may also need to refresh old skills, if they have not used some piece of hardware or software for some time. Some activities are only carried out at irregular intervals and it is easy to forget how to use features of software if they are not constantly being practised.

When an employee changes job within an organisation, either because of promotion or as a result of changes in the structure of the organisation, he or she might need to be trained in new ICT skills that are needed in the new role.

case study 1

Training for use of a college electronic attendance system (See Case Study 4, Chapter 3)

A college uses an electronic attendance registration system (EARS) that allows teachers to enter the details of attendance in each class using a handheld device.

A member of the tutorial staff can access the system, on his office computer, to view the information collected in classes. He is able to produce a variety of reports relating to individual or whole class attendance over a selected time period.

The college information department manage the system. They will maintain the interface between the registration system and the college MIS. They have to write new reports when requested and they troubleshoot the system. From time to time they need to contact the developers of the registration system.

Different training is needed for each different group of staff.

1. Outline the training needs for:
   a) Teachers
   b) Tutorial staff
   c) Information department personnel.
2. State two occasions when training would be required.

Training methods

There is a wide range of training options available. It is important that the method is carefully chosen to meet the specific needs of an individual.

Face-to-face or instructor-led training

Formal training with an instructor training a group of trainees is a popular but expensive option. However this method has the advantage that the trainer can answer questions and provide immediate help and feedback. Face-to-face training may take the form of on-the-job training, or be delivered through in-house courses or external courses.

These courses will include demonstrations and practical examples to work through. Instructor-led training remains very popular as students are able to interact with each other and their tutor, sharing ideas and information.

A disadvantage of instructor-led training is that it is usually planned some time in advance which might not coincide exactly with the time the trainee actually requires instruction; in this way it lacks flexibility. If the training is not followed up by immediate practice, much of what has been learned is quite likely to be forgotten.

On-the-job training

This, as the name implies, involves learning while at work. A trainer from inside or outside the company may come and give instructions to a trainee. The trainee may spend time observing a colleague or a mentor complete a task and then have to carry out similar tasks under supervision. Staff working on a telephone, such as help desk operators, may have calls recorded to monitor that they are giving correct advice in the right manner.

Although on-the-job training has the advantage of providing training in a realistic setting, it is often difficult for the employee to learn while still dealing with the day-to-day stresses of the job.

In-house courses

In-house courses are courses specially organised for a group of employees. They are normally held on-site using an internal or an external trainer. The trainees may all have the same needs, for example, if the software used by the company has recently been replaced or upgraded. The biggest advantage of providing training in-house, run by employees of the organisation, is the cost. Outside trainers are usually very expensive. In-house trainers will have a very good understanding of the organisation itself, its procedures and structures, and will be able to tailor the training to meet the needs of the employees exactly.

When electronic registration of students, using Bromcom's EARS system, was introduced at a college, the ICT department undertook to train all teaching staff. A number of sessions were put on and teachers were invited to join a session at a time suitable to them. During the training session the teachers were each given their own EARS handheld device and were shown the different functions that the system offered. They were also handed an A4 sheet of hints to remind them what to do. The ICT staff were then available at the end of a phone to deal with problems and queries. As the only way to get a device was to attend the training session, everyone attended!

External courses

Many local colleges offer training courses in various aspects of ICT. A company may send employees to the college for a course that is offered there regularly. As the trainees could include employees of different companies, the costs will be shared and so reduced.

A college may also put on courses especially for a group of employees of a company, either in the college or at the company.

Xylos (www.xylos.com) trains more than 18 000 people each year in using ICT. Depending on needs, a team of 35 trainers use different methods, including on-the-job training, instructor led training and fully automated e-learning.

Canterbury College offers many ICT courses. There is an *Introduction to Databases* course looking at Microsoft Access including:

- creating a database
- running reports
- using queries and searching
- editing data

Start dates, times and durations can be tailored to suit the trainees.

Commercial companies also put on training courses. These are often very specialised and can be very expensive. However, many such companies offer a wide range of courses.

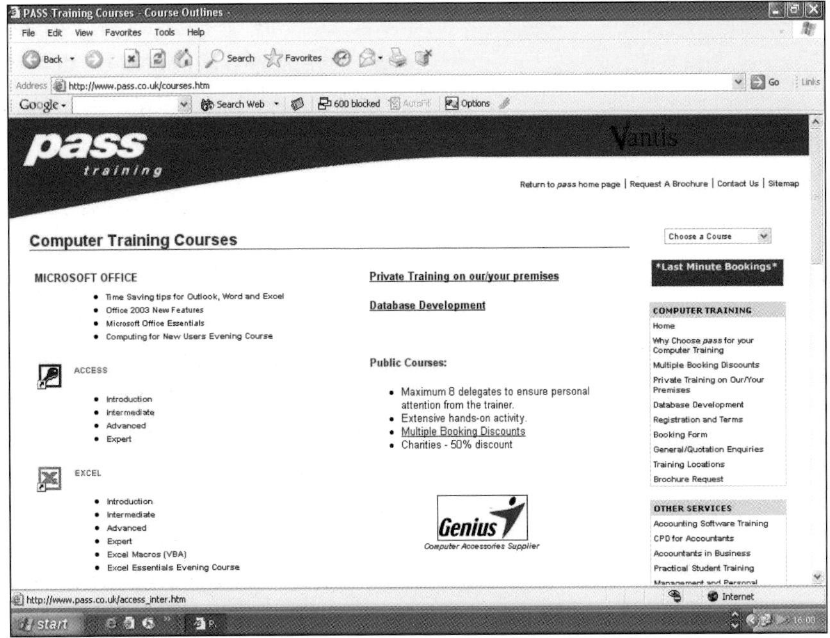

Figure 11.1 Training courses

E-learning

E-learning means using electronic methods to teach the trainee. These methods include online tutorials, interactive videos and DVDs and on-screen help. A few years ago some people felt that e-learning would quickly take over all other forms of learning, but change has not been as rapid as these people predicted. However, e-learning is growing in popularity; its big advantage is that a person can learn when and where he wants. If someone needs a particular skill for a project, then e-learning allows him to gain them straight away without having to wait for a relevant course to be run. So training can be provided at the convenience of the individual, to meet his or her specific work needs.

A factor that has held back the growth of e-learning is the lack of enthusiasm for many employees to learn in this way. E-learning, which is often very heavily graphics based, is demanding on computer and network resources (such as memory, processor time and bandwidth) so its use will only be feasible in organisations that support a good ICT infrastructure.

A company can upload e-learning materials to the Internet or the company intranet for use at work. Password protection can be used so that only their employees can benefit. They can then take their training course at home at a convenient time.

case study 2
▶ Reuters using e-learning

Reuters, the news agency, is planning a change from classroom based training to e-learning that could save them up to £1 million.

The move is an attempt to make learning integrated within normal working life. The head of training sees classroom based training as an inefficient way of transferring knowledge. He is aiming for 25 per cent of all company training to be delivered online.

- Suggest four issues Reuters will have to consider to ensure that the move to e-learning is successful.

Online tutorials

There are many tutorials available online via the Internet. Some are free, others are available cheaply. For example, there are lots of courses available at www.freeskills.com. For an annual membership fee of £99, the trainee has access to every training course. Trainees can study what they choose, when they choose, at their own pace and within a small budget.

The database courses available include: Access 2002 (XP), Access 2000, Access 97 and less commonly used programs like FoxPro, SQL Server, Oracle, Lotus Notes, Informix, Paradox and Approach.

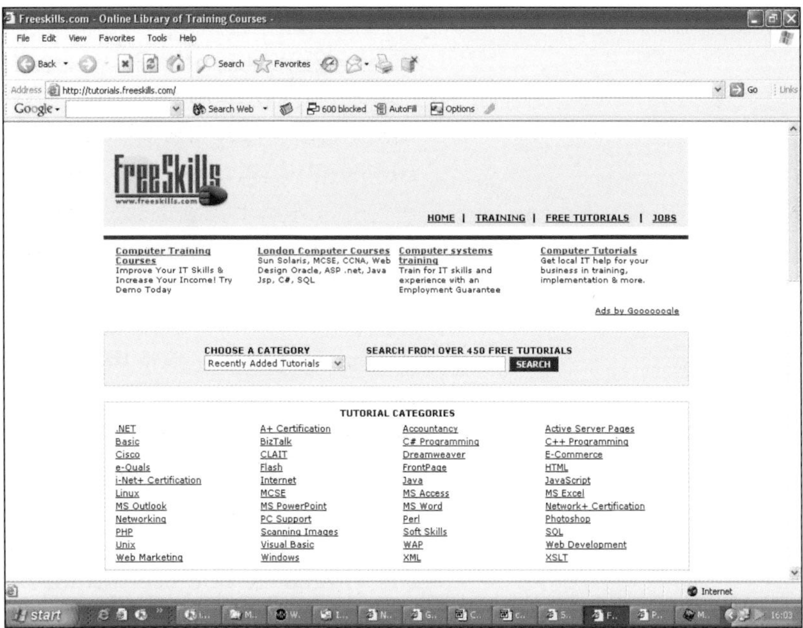

Figure 11.2 www.freeskills.com

On-screen help

Most software packages offer on-screen help simply by pressing the F1 key. On-screen help is commonly used as it is free and immediately available.

On-screen help allows you to search on keywords or to type in your question in a natural language and be given an explanation as well as examples of use. Sometimes animated demonstrations and cue cards are also available. Cue cards are small help windows that appear over the application screen to help the user.

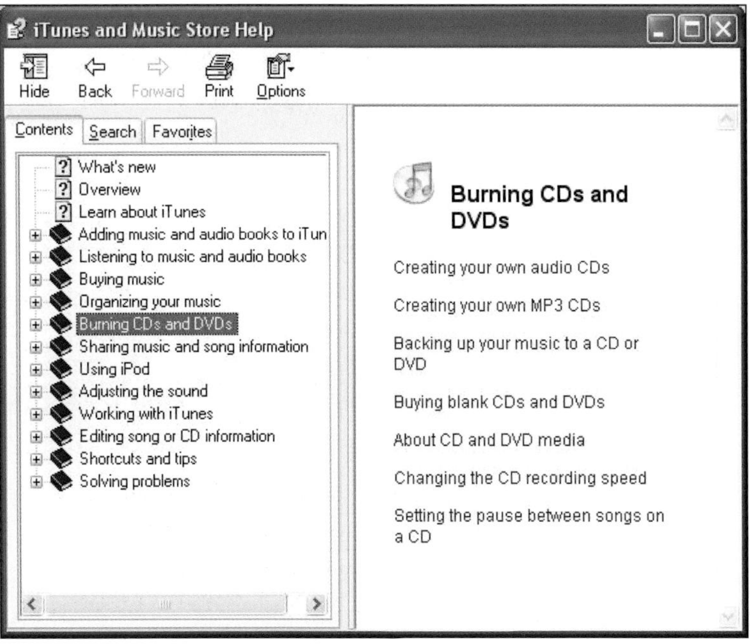

Figure 11.3 On-screen help for iTunes

Sometimes an error message will include a help button that will take you to the correct page of the help file.

On-screen help has the advantages of being always available while the software is in use, it is quick to use, is free to use and fairly user friendly.

Interactive video

Interactive video can provide professional training at your computer. Interactive video normally makes use of the facilities of a DVD system. It is interactive in that users can choose which sections to cover, miss out sections or go back over sections. The video may require the user to make responses which will reinforce their understanding and determine how quickly the trainee progresses through the course.

Interactive video is a low stress learning environment and the videos can be navigated in a logical way using an easy to use interface.

Activity 1

1. Use the Internet to find the details of courses run to teach the advanced features of Microsoft Access or another software application of your choice. A good stating point is to use a search engine such as Google to search UK pages for 'Advanced Access training course'.
2. Draw up a table comparing the location, duration and cost of courses offered by five different companies.
3. Produce a second table showing details of five e-learning courses.
4. Discuss the costs and benefits of the different types of courses you have found.

Paper based materials

Paper based materials offer a traditional method of learning. These methods include user manuals, training manuals and books.

The manual

Software manuals are widely available even though today they rarely come free with the software. They have been removed to reduce costs. Manuals claim to teach you all you need to know, but they vary in quality and are not always very easy to follow. A manual can prove to be a good reference if you have a problem. Manuals can be used when and where the user wants and progress can be made at the individual's own pace.

Books

Books are commonly available for popular software packages from bookshops. Many books are available at an introductory level. Titles include *Access for Dummies, Field Guide to Access* and *Ten Minute Guide to Access*. These books take the reader step-by-step through the basic functions of the program but don't include much depth.

Books can be dipped into from time to time when a particular problem is met or they can form part of a structured training programme. The programme will have several objectives such as learning key features of software. These features should be covered by the books in a logical order.

Training manuals

Training manuals give the user the opportunity to work at their own pace and refer quickly to the appropriate section.

Activity 2

www.mousepointers.co.uk is the URL of a company that produces computer manuals. You can buy the manuals and work through them to learn how to use various software packages.

For example in Microsoft Access there are manuals in:

- basics of Access queries
- creating tables and controlling input
- going further with queries
- understanding databases
- creating reports
- creating forms
- using macros.

Each manual costs £5.99. Figure 11.4 illustrates a page of the manual.

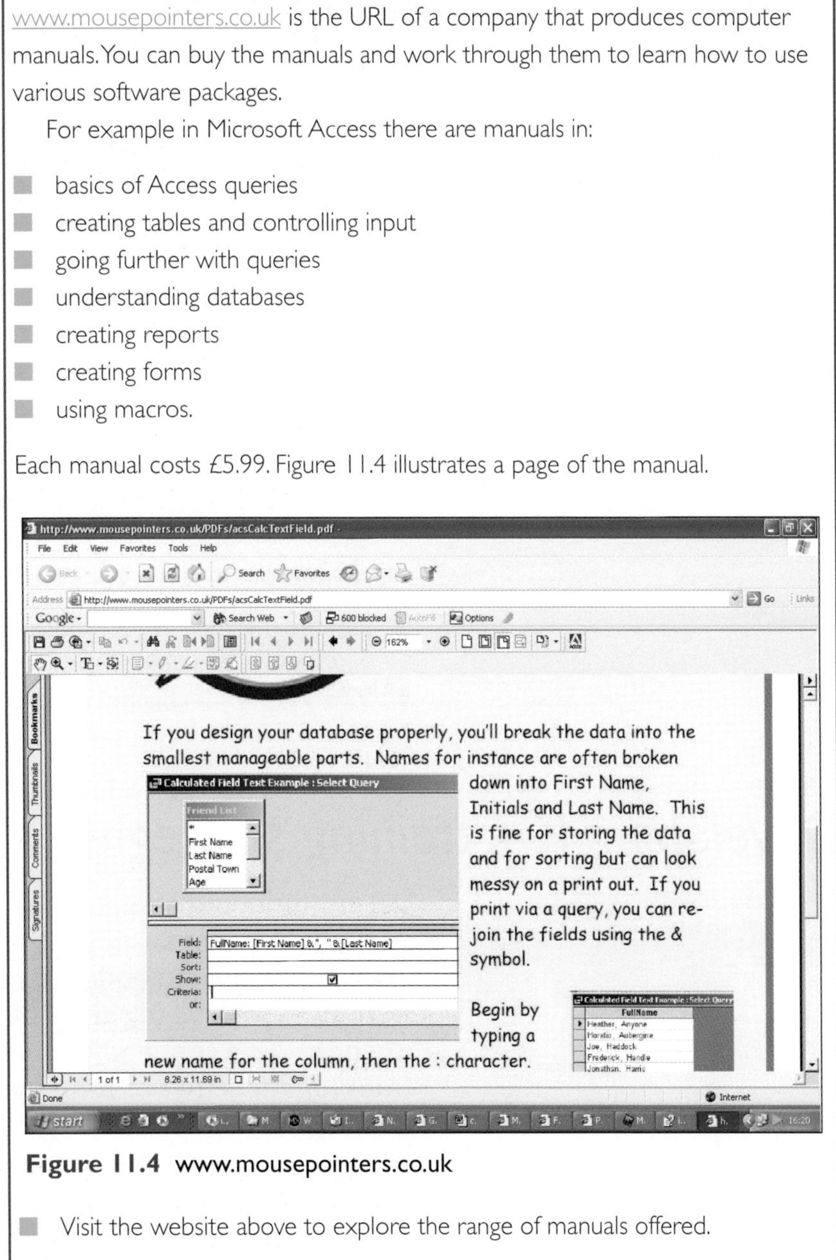

Figure 11.4 www.mousepointers.co.uk

- Visit the website above to explore the range of manuals offered.

Which way of learning?

Method	Someone there to answer questions?	Cost	Tailored to meet your needs	Where does it take place?
On the job training	✓	Can be expensive	✓	In the office
In-house courses	✓	Expensive	✓	At work but not in the office
External courses	✓	Expensive	✗	At a college or training company premises
Online tutorials	✗	Cheap	✓	In the office
Online help	✗	Cheap	✓	In the office
Manual	✗	Cheap	✗	Anywhere
Interactive video	✗	Relatively cheap	✓	Almost anywhere using a laptop

case study 3

Training in context

Middleton College is a large FE college that offers a wide range of courses. For many students ICT forms a large part of their course. There are also a number of students whose course is totally ICT based.

Middleton College has over 25 administrative staff, and the turnover of staff is quite high. The new principal has made it a priority that all his senior managers make greater use of ICT as a tool for decision making – this has caused some anxiety for several managers.

A variety of different versions of different word processing software has been used in the past by different sections of the college. Now everyone will be using Microsoft Office XP.

Different groups of staff have different word processing training needs to allow them to use Microsoft Office XP appropriately.

- Identify these different types of need, and for each suggest an appropriate training programme.

Developing ICT training strategies

ICT training in a company needs to be planned and strategies developed, based on that company's objectives. Training is often vulnerable to budget cutting as some managements see it as an expensive luxury that has to be dropped when times are hard. This can lead to a reduction in the amount of training altogether or management may look to deliver training in different ways: perhaps a move to e-learning rather than sending employees on expensive courses at distant locations that also bring travel and living costs. However, if a training strategy is to be successful, it is important that decisions involving the ways in which training should be acquired need fully to take into account the needs of both the organisation and the individual employee. It is likely that a range of different methods will be used.

Training must be planned to complement the installation of new hardware and software. In some organisations the training of personnel when new software is installed is left to the ICT department. This does not always result in the needs of the user being met in an appropriate way.

When a national museum implemented an e-mail system for the first time, the training of the new users was not carefully planned and did not take into account the real needs of these users. The ICT department decided when the training sessions should occur and the form that they should take without talking to the users to find out what would be most appropriate. As a result many people were unable to attend any of the sessions due to other commitments. The content of the training sessions was also inappropriate and did not address the protocols and procedures that need to be established if e-mail is to be successfully implemented within an organisation. It took a number of months to overcome the ill feeling and confusion caused by the mishandled training.

New legislation may bring new training needs and these need to be planned for in advance. New ventures within an organisation may also generate ICT training needs. These need to be identified early and planned for.

The ICT training needs of specific jobs must be established. These are often highlighted through the annual appraisal process, where an employee discusses his progress with his line manager and sets targets for the forthcoming year. A periodic ICT skills audit could be carried out to compare the skills required by each post with the skills of the person holding the post; this process will highlight training needs.

As employees are becoming more computer literate, so their training needs are changing over time. Many people are likely to demand more ICT training because they are interested in developing their skills further.

The ICT training needs of all new employees and current employees taking on new roles must be carefully assessed. Their current skill level should be compared with the requirements of the role and training put in place to plug the gaps.

A company's ICT training strategy will include who needs to be trained, what training they need and how this training will be delivered. Large companies may have their own training suite and in-house trainers while small companies can probably only use outside agencies.

The training strategy should fit in with other strategies within the organisation.

case study 4
ICT training at Ellis Paints

Over 800 office staff at Ellis Paints, from senior management to office juniors, had to be trained in Microsoft Office when the company switched from MS-DOS to Windows NT.

The company used a training organisation with experience in ICT training that did not exist in-house. The training organisation analysed individual needs and found a very wide range of skills. Some staff had hardly ever used a computer, while others had a very high level of ICT competence.

A programme was developed to cater for the different individual needs. The programme was based on a series of seminars and one to three days of classroom-based training designed to cater for the different levels of competence. The training included one-to-one tuition for some staff and workshops looking at specific professional requirements. According to the trainers 96 per cent of the company's staff are now trained to the initial level of Microsoft Office proficiency.

The training has not finished. Future plans include the provision of on-going support, lunchtime user clinics and the provision of online training in Microsoft Office via an intranet.

1. Ellis Paints chose to bring in outside trainers to train their staff in Microsoft Office. Describe other methods the company could have used for staff training, for each method indicate its appropriateness for Ellis Paints.

2. The senior management of Ellis Paints feel that they need to draw up an ICT training policy.
- **a)** Explain why this is necessary.
- **b)** Describe what such a policy should contain.

Worked exam question

A building society is installing a new database management system to store details of all customers' accounts. The counter clerks will need to be trained in using the new system.

a) Other than the counter clerks, suggest one category of user that will also need to be trained in using the new system. (1)

b) Explain why these users need different training from the counter clerks. (2)

c) The building society is considering whether to offer counter clerks on-the-job training or off-the-job training.
- i) Describe one benefit of on-the-job training. (2)
- ii) Describe one benefit of off-the-job training. (2)

SAMPLE ANSWER

a) One possible category of user that will also need to be trained in using the new system could be the branch managers.

b) These users need different training because their jobs are different and the tasks that they will perform on the computer are different.

c)
- i) On-the-job training takes place in the office and so is in a realistic situation with real data.
- ii) Off-the-job training takes place away from the stresses of the office and so there are no distractions.

SUMMARY

Training is vital in a highly skilled area of business like ICT. The rapid pace of change means that training is not something that happens when you start a new job but is continuous.

Training can be skills based or task based.

Different levels of training are required for different situations, for example beginner, intermediate, refresher course.

Training courses may be:

- on the job training
- in house
- external.

Other methods of training include:

- reading user manuals
- online tutorial
- on-screen help
- interactive video/DVD.

An organisation needs to have an ICT training strategy to ensure that each employee has the skills necessary to carry out his job.

Chapter 11 Questions

1 **a)** Describe **three** ways in which training may be provided for users of ICT systems. (6)

b) Describe **three** ways in which support may be provided for users of ICT systems. (6)

ICT4 January 2005

2 When introducing new or improved ICT systems, successful organisations know that, in order to achieve a successful transition, they must provide both initial training and ongoing support.

A national supermarket chain relies heavily on various information systems. It employs both full-time and part-time staff working in stores and warehouses sited around the country or at the head office.

Discuss the options available for both training and support. Make suitable recommendations for this particular company for the training and support of the different groups of staff identified below, namely:

- part-time store staff
- full-time store staff
- warehouse and home delivery staff
- head office staff
- managers at all levels. (20)

The quality of Written Communication will be assessed in your answer. ICT4 June 2005

This question also refers to Chapter 10.

3 A small legal firm is about to replace stand-alone computers with a new computer network. Industry standard software will be installed. As new users of both the equipment and the software, the firm is concerned about the levels of support and training that will be needed. There are three levels of system user: the solicitors themselves, the practice management and the administrative staff.

a) Explain **two** factors that need to be taken into account when planning the training. (4)

b) Describe **two** different ways of giving technical support to these users. (4)

c) State **two** means of providing the training material, and give an advantage of each. (4)

ICT4 June 2002

4 Internet technologies allow large companies to deliver training and assessment across their entire organisation. This can be of benefit to the companies and to their employees.

a) Describe **three** possible benefits to a company. (6)

b) Describe **three** possible benefits to an employee. (6)

c) The interaction of an employee with an online training system needs careful planning. List **four** factors that should be considered. (4)

ICT5 January 2003

5 Jane works in a call centre for a bank dealing with questions and instructions from customers. Although Jane underwent task-based training related to her job last year, she must undertake more training shortly.

a) State **two** reasons why Jane may need to undergo further training. (2)

b) Describe what is meant by task-based training. (2)

12 Project management and effective ICT teams

▶ A **project** is an activity with a specific purpose that usually takes months or years to complete. Examples of ICT projects could include expanding a school network to include a new building, installing a new booking system for a cinema chain or upgrading an internal e-mail system within an organisation. Whatever the nature of the project, it is likely to go through the same system life cycle stages (see Chapter 3) and will need planning and careful management.

It is most important that clear and realistic **objectives** are set at the start of the project and agreed by all involved. Objectives should include the timescale for completion, exactly what the development team has agreed to deliver and the size of budget available. There have been many horror stories of ICT projects that have been unsuccessful. Early attempts to computerise the Stock Exchange had to be abandoned. It is important to explore why some projects go wrong while others are successful. (See Chapter 2)

ICT projects are usually so large that they cannot be implemented by just one person. Some large projects, such as a new ticketing and passenger tracking system for the London Underground, require hundreds of thousands of man hours to complete. ICT projects are normally undertaken by a team of people working together. No one person could do all the work on their own, even if they had the time, as a wide range of skills and knowledge will be required. The project team members should be selected with care to complement each other so that together they possess the drive, skills and knowledge necessary for implementation.

Subdividing a project into subtasks

A large project is likely to be broken down into a number of more manageable **subtasks** (or subprojects). Each subtask will be allocated to a smaller, more manageable team. Such a team should consist of a number that the team leader can control easily, perhaps four to six members. Breaking up a project into tasks makes it easier to control. Some subtasks that are not dependent upon each other can be carried out concurrently (at the same time). This can bring down the overall completion time of the project and enables stricter control of the time spent on each sub area. Subtasks are more manageable as they have clearly defined and realisable objectives. Very often **milestones** are identified. A milestone is an important point in a project. Examples of milestones could be when all coding has been completed, or when the network infrastructure has been installed. Reaching a milestone represents significant progress towards the completion of the project.

Many ICT projects are made up of a number of phases. For example, when developing new software in-house for an organisation the project will be made up of the following phases:

- analysing the user requirements
- designing and prototyping a new system
- writing and testing the code
- acceptance testing
- installing the software and training the users.

Different people are likely to be involved in different phases of the project as different skills will be required. The tasks will be matched to the skills of the people in the team. For example, a team member who has good interviewing skills could be involved in the investigation stages of the project whilst a member with a flair for and good knowledge of design could be used to produce screen prototypes.

The use and organisation of ICT teams

A team is a small group of people who have been carefully selected with the aim of completing a project or subproject. They will be allocated different roles, but need to work together rather than as individuals. Tasks are usually allocated according to the strengths of the team members; getting people to do what they are good at is usually appropriate. Complementary skills are required within an ICT team (just as having a football team of 11 goalkeepers would not be successful!). Good communication within the team is essential so that progress can be monitored and potential problems avoided. They should develop to the stage where they are able to perform effectively, each member adopting the role necessary to work with others.

Every project needs a **project manager**, even if there are just one or two people working on the project. A large project with subteams will be managed by an overall project manager. Each subproject will have its own team leader who reports to the project manager. Each team will have its own plan with its own set of tasks that need to be carried out.

When implementing a project it is usually necessary to divide each phase up into smaller tasks and allocate these tasks to members of the team. Tasks will be allocated to team members on the basis of their current skills and availability as well as allowing scope for team members to develop their skills and progress. The division into tasks makes the project more manageable as each team member has a clearly defined set of tasks.

It is often possible for several teams to work in parallel to lessen the overall time taken and to bring forward the deadline. For example, if a system is being developed for a supermarket, one team might work on stock control and ordering, another team might work on the till system and a third team work on the loyalty card database.

Characteristics of successful ICT teams

A successful team is likely to have most of the following characteristics:

- good leadership
- an appropriate balance of skills and areas of expertise amongst the members of the team, with suitable allocation of tasks
- adequate planning and scheduling of tasks
- skills to monitor and control progress against the plan and to control costs
- adherence to agreed standards
- good communication skills both with end users and within the team.

Leadership

The project will be managed by a project manager who will need to direct the resources to be used in the best possible way to get the job completed successfully and on time. These resources include people, time, money and hardware. The project manager will organise the subdivision of the projects into subtasks.

A good team needs clear and consistent leadership. The team leader should have sufficient seniority to fulfil the role and should have adequate understanding of the project, the ability to see the project through to successful completion, and the skills to adequately and systematically monitor and control progress and costs. They must be able to hold the team together. A good leader will bring the best out of the individual members and encourage cooperation and exchange of ideas. Tasks should be allocated to the members appropriately, so that every member is given work of which they are capable and which, if possible, will help develop their individual skills. In this way each task will be completed in the best way possible.

Leadership is important because appropriate management and project control will encourage the members of the team to work together in an organised manner and motivate them to ensure that all deadlines are met.

Much of a project manager's time will be spent managing other people. A project manager will need to arrange meetings, ensure that team members have the resources that they need, follow up any problems that arise and ensure that all the necessary things are in place for the next phase of the project.

Activity 1

Advertisements from the ICT press:

Project manager package: £45,000–£75,000

Responsible for the day-to-day management of a client's project. Will interact directly with clients, coordinate work requirements, provide technical leadership, monitor reports on progress, control project scope, and ensure that deliverables, deadlines and budgets are maintained.

Project manager: to £45,000 + car + bonus + benefits

You will be a professional project manager with a background in systems design, able to demonstrate strong customer-facing skills. You will possess first class project management experience delivering projects to deadlines and communicating your innovative ideas at a senior level.

Project manager: to £60k

A global leader in e-commerce is seeking a dynamic project manager to lead medium to large web projects for clients. You will have a strong customer relations background with the ability to build relationships and understand new business processes coupled with a strong grasp of the technologies involved.

- Suggest ten qualities needed for a project manager of an ICT project.

Balanced team

In some situations there should be a balance of skills between team members who could have different backgrounds from areas such as systems, business operations or technical fields. This is particularly important for the overall project team and for smaller teams that are involved with planning.

In other situations it is appropriate for teams to be made up of similar personnel, each of whom performs a small part of the whole. For example a team whose task is to develop a system would consist of a number of programmers. The team often includes members with a range of skill levels, from trainees up to highly experienced specialists. This allows for the development of less experienced team members who can be set tasks within their capabilities whilst receiving help and guidance from their more experienced colleagues. These experienced team members will be assigned the most complex tasks.

Sometimes it can prove more effective to assign a team a greater range of tasks, for example the analysis and design of one functional area, rather than splitting the stages between two separate teams. There can be a greater feeling of achievement when the function is completed which can be highly motivating.

Planning and scheduling

At the start of a project objectives must be agreed between the clients and the project manager.

- **Clear timescales** must be established so that a project can be monitored using deadlines for the completion of the various stages. It is essential that the deadlines are realistic and that both parties have agreed to these so that the project is delivered on time.
- The client and the project team must establish **agreed deliverables**. Deliverables is the name given to what actually has to be produced by the project team and is likely to include fully tested and installed programs, full documentation and training material for users. These should fully meet the user's requirements and should be produced to agreed standards.
- At the start of the project, **milestones** are agreed. These are stages in the project when the client must give **approval for the project to proceed** further. This ensures that the client is satisfied with the work to date. The client would then give the go ahead for the project to continue to the next stage.

Planning is crucial to the success of any project. It is very important that enough time and thought is given to realistic planning. If they are not, then essential tasks can be overlooked which can result in a project overrunning time or going over budget. A careful analysis of risk should be carried out at the start of the project.

Scheduling involves allocating resources and facilities so that they are available when required. Resources can be human or physical. Delay in a resource being available may lead to slippage in deadlines which could incur extra expense. For example, the network cable needs to be in place before the computers can be installed. Under-floor power cables need to be installed early on before the floor is laid. There are a number of project planning techniques and associated software that are used with large projects.

An ICT project should include:

- aims and objectives
- a project leader
- a project team
- a deadline for work to be finished
- a budget for completing the work.

The budget will need to cover staffing, hardware and software costs, outlay for training, expenditure on data entry, as well as other expenses such as travel and subsistence.

Project management software can be used to draw up schedules and monitor progress and costs.

At the start, the client and the project manager will agree **acceptance criteria** for the completion of the project. These are agreed targets that must be met. Examples of such criteria are that all deadlines must be met, work should be completed within budget, the system should be working fully and all agreed security measures should be in place.

Monitoring and control

An important task for a project leader is to monitor the progress of the project as it proceeds and to report back to clients. She must ensure that it completes to schedule and that the work needed has not been underestimated. Inevitably, unexpected problems will arise and certain tasks will overrun. Sometimes extra tasks arise that were not identified at the start of the project. The project manager will have to adjust the schedule of tasks, perhaps changing around team members, authorising overtime or even contracting extra staff to ensure that deadlines are still met.

The leader must make certain that each member is working at the appropriate pace to complete their tasks on time. She must ensure that all team members are doing what they are supposed to do at the right level of effectiveness.

The project manager must control the project to make sure that it is delivering only what is required and has been agreed by the client. She must ensure that any changes to the original specification that are agreed with the client are incorporated into the current work or left for later stages as appropriate. It is the project manager's responsibility to ensure that the project is delivered to the original schedule.

The project manager will need to monitor the project costs to ensure that money has not been misused and to keep within the customer's budget. She must be able to report back to the customer with the current position.

It is important that **regular meetings** are held to review progress. There are two types of review meetings:

- more formal project/stage review meetings with the system commissioners
- internal progress meetings with just the project team/subteam to consider progress on individual tasks.

A good team will keep a careful watch on costs and should complete the project within budget. All aspects of work should be carefully costed. Progress should be monitored and alternative action taken whenever necessary, for example if progress is not being made according to plan. Regular review meetings, together with the use of charts and suitable software, can be crucial to monitoring progress and maintaining control.

Most projects will include **regular review sessions** where the team get together to compare current progress against the schedule's planned progress. Each team member will report on the progress of the tasks that he or she is currently working on. Any tasks completed since the last review will be noted. The review will enable problems to be highlighted and solutions found.

The client will expect to have a regular report on progress and this will be prepared by the project manager after a review.

Adherence to standards

Standards are agreed, formal ways of carrying out tasks. They may be nationally agreed, published standards which many system developers use, or standards that are agreed within an organisation or even a project. Standards involve the use of formal methods for the development of information systems, rather than team members drawing up their own standards.

At the start of the project, standards of working need to be set and agreed by all members. One of the benefits of using standard methods is that they allow a team member to pick up another's work easily in case of an unplanned absence.

The use of established standards also ensures that a professional or methodical way of working is used. For example, it is important that appropriate documentation is produced and kept up to date. By following set procedures the team will ensure that nothing is missed by mistake.

The adoption of the systems development life cycle model (see Chapter 3) is often used as a framework for project development.

These standards should be adhered to and monitored throughout the project.

One widely used example of such standards is SSADM (Structured Systems Analysis and Design Methodology). This is a **structured methodology** (a system of ways of doing things in regular and orderly procedures) that provides a set approach to information systems development. It specifies the stages and tasks which have to be carried out, what needs to be produced and the techniques used in production. SSADM is used in the analysis and design stages of systems development.

SSADM uses three key techniques:

- **Logical Data Modelling** – identifying, modelling and documenting the data requirements of an information system.
- **Data Flow Modelling** – identifying, modelling and documenting how data flows around an information system using a set of data flow diagrams with appropriate documentation.

- **Event Modelling** – identifying, modelling and documenting the events which affect each entity and the order in which these events occur.

Another standard technique used at the design stage of a project is **prototyping**. Prototyping, where a model of part of a system with reduced functions is developed, allows the user to be shown what the system could do before it is fully developed. Any changes to the specification could then be made before the project had progressed too far.

Standards in program writing could be the use of particular coding conventions in the choice of variable names, the layout of code and the inclusion of comments.

As well as using standard methods in the work undertaken during system development, it is necessary that the project is managed using standard project management practices. ISO 9000/ 2000 is an international standard for the management of projects that puts an emphasis on producing a suitably documented system. Increasingly, software buyers are requiring ISO 9000 certification from their suppliers.

The methods used to plan, schedule, monitor and control the project must be formalised and follow reliable and standard ways of working. Gantt charts are often used. A Gantt chart is a horizontal bar chart that is often used in project management. The user can produce a graphical visual aid of a schedule that helps in the planning, coordinating and tracking of specific tasks within a project. Gantt charts may be created using project management software such as Microsoft Project.

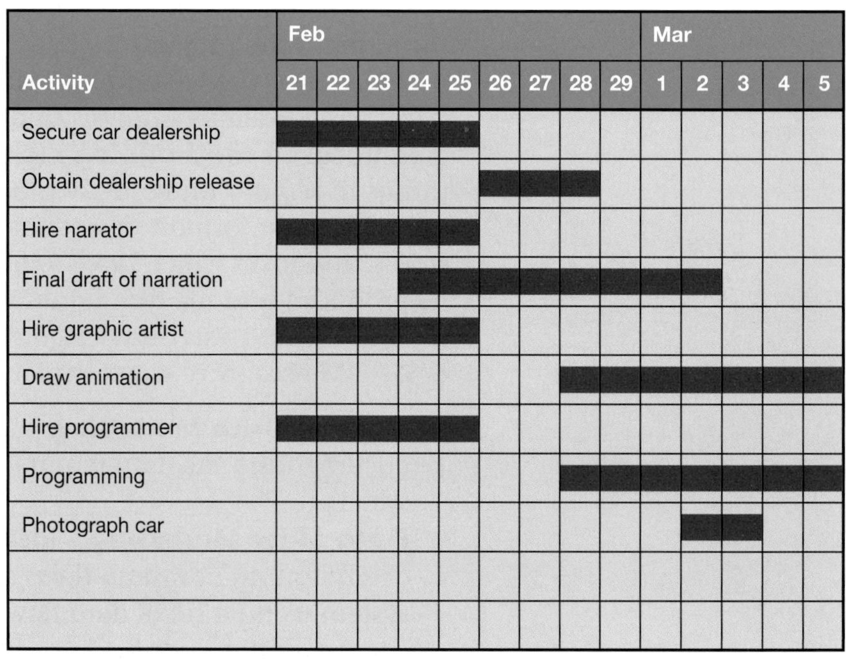

Feb
Mar
Activity
21 22 23 24 25 26 27 28 29 1 2 3 4 5
Secure car dealership
Obtain dealership release
Hire narrator
Final draft of narration
Hire graphic artist
Draw animation
Hire programmer
Programming
Photograph car

Figure 12.1 An illustration of a Gantt chart

Activity 2

Use the Internet to research the tools available for project management. Produce a report on one aspect of project management (for example, the use of Gantt charts).

The site http://www.projectkickstart.com/ provides a **guided tour**

The site http://www.smartdraw.com/exp/gan/home/ provides useful information on charting techniques – select **tutorials** and **examples**

http://www.ganttchart.com/ will also be helpful.

Communication

Within the team, there must be someone who is able to communicate well with people outside the team, for example business managers and end users, in order to gather accurate requirements effectively and to report back progress successfully. During the analysis phase of a project, team members need to be able to ask the right questions in such a way that they can establish end-user requirements. Team members should have good written as well as verbal communication skills. The writing of reports and user documentation form an important part of the development role.

case study 1 ▶ Dogged by failures

(Based on an article in the *Financial Times*)

In theory, ICT helps improve productivity, responsiveness and communication. In practice, ICT projects are often dogged by management problems that result in delays, cost overruns and failure to meet the original objectives.

ICT projects continue to have an extremely high failure rate according to a recent survey by Oasig, a group supported by the Department of Trade and Industry.

It concluded that between 80 and 90 per cent of ICT investments do not meet their performance goals, 80 per cent of systems are delivered late and over budget and about 40 per cent of developments fail or are abandoned.

1. Why do you think that so many projects fail to meet their performance goals?
2. Describe the steps that should be taken to ensure that a project does meet its performance goals.

case study 2 ▶ Camelot

The Camelot Group plc was awarded the licence to run the National Lottery. Within six months, over 10,000 retailers were selling tickets and the first draw was held, yet the first company building (the head office and main data centre) was not finished until three months later.

The National Lottery sells around 100 million tickets every week and receives over 60,000 calls per week to its National Lottery Line, mostly on Saturday nights and Sunday mornings. This requires a complex computer system with high security. With such a daunting task and a tight timescale, good project management was essential.

The project was split up into smaller tasks including:

- installing hardware in the head office and the two data centres
- training staff
- installing hardware in the retailers' shops
- training retailers
- installing the corporate network linking the head office and the two data centres, the warehouse and the eleven regional offices for both voice and data
- testing
- implementing the call centre for the National Lottery Line for customers to claim prizes
- implementing the call centre for the Retailer Hot Line for retailers with technical problems.

The Telecommunications Manager at Camelot, said, 'In normal circumstances we would have expected a project of this nature to take around eighteen months, but we did everything in only five months'.

- How could the project be completed in such a short time?
- Suggest reasons why the project was implemented so successfully.

case study 3

Sophie – a project manager

Sophie works for a large banking organisation. She manages a team of six full-time members and runs several projects at a time. A major project recently undertaken involved splitting up a current database system into two communicating halves, one dealing with front office (customer-related) operations, the other back office (internal administrative) ones. This was done so that front office services could be provided on a different hardware platform.

The project was split into three main phases:

- initial analysis when data flow and user interface needs were established
- development when the program code was written, tested and the interfaces with all other software also tested
- new system installation.

Sophie worked out that the project would require 20 man months to implement. Four members of her team were allocated to the project. Other freelance contractors with specific skills were also involved. Developers (programmers) who had specific hardware experience and knowledge of both UNIX and NT operating systems were required within the team. Analysts on the team needed both a good technical knowledge and a sound understanding of the banking business. More junior team members were employed in testing.

At the start of the project Sophie drew up a project plan that highlighted what tasks needed to be done to complete the project and who should do them. She made sure to set clear objectives for each task, defining its start and end and giving a set time for its completion. Her plan was produced using Microsoft Project. Sophie also maintained a spreadsheet of all tasks where details of problems that arose were stored.

As the project evolved, she met regularly with team members to discuss progress, giving help and direction as appropriate. If any problem became apparent she would provide extra resources to the task. She was able to monitor and control overall project progress as she could see when individual tasks were complete. She produced a project status report every three weeks which informed all the stakeholders in the project of current progress.

Whenever an unforeseen problem was thrown up by testing, the job of resolving the problem would be delegated by Sophie to a team member. She herself oversaw the progress of the project and carried out many of the tasks herself, such as managing the testing process.

Four months after starting the project it had been successfully implemented.

- Give the reasons that ensured that the project was implemented successfully.
- Describe three reasons why the project was split up into tasks.
- How did Sophie maintain control of the project?
- Why were junior team members allocated to testing?
- Describe the standards that Sophie could have been using.

Worked exam question

When an organisation develops a large information system several teams may be used.

Discuss how ICT development projects should be organised to ensure successful outcomes, paying particular attention to the following topics:

- the use and organisation of ICT teams
- the characteristics of successful ICT teams
- the use of formal methods for the development of information systems.

The quality of Written Communication will be assessed in your answer. (20)

ICT4 January 2005

▶ **EXAMINER'S GUIDANCE**

It is always tempting to launch straight in and start writing an answer to a question such as this, but it is much better to stop and think for a bit and plan your answer carefully.

The question asks you to ***discuss*** *so it is not enough just to list a series of points; indeed doing this will not gain you many marks. The bullet points in the question provide you with a structure for your answer. You should include:*

- *a brief introduction*
- *a paragraph on the use and organisation of ICT teams*
- *a paragraph on the characteristics of successful ICT teams*
- *a paragraph on the use of formal methods for the development of information systems*
- *a brief conclusion.*

The board states that 'Continuous prose is expected for this answer and four of the 20 marks are allocated to the quality of your writing'.

Activity 3

Identify as many points as you can on the use and organisation of ICT teams. Don't read any further until you have done so!

Listed below are some of the points you may have thought of:

- *several teams can work in parallel*
- *small teams of four to six people*
- *each team can have one specialism such as system testing*
- *each team has its own team leader*
- *projects may be too big for one person to carry out on their own so they are divided into subtasks.*

It is now time to put the points together into one paragraph. Study the points above and decide on a logical order to put them in. Many of these points can be extended in a way that could gain extra marks. In the paragraph below, the points have been put together and extensions to the points are shown in italics.

SAMPLE ANSWER

- Projects are divided into subtasks *which are allocated to teams.* Each team has its own team leader *reporting to a project manager.* The teams are usually small, consisting of four to six people *so that the number of people for the team leader to control does not become unmanageable.* Each team can have one specialism such as system testing *and often contains a mixture of trainees through to highly experienced specialists which allows for the development of less experienced team members.* Several teams can work in parallel *when the start of one task does not depend on the completion of another; this reduces the overall time for the project.*

EXAMINER'S GUIDANCE

A list of possible points for the third paragraph on the use of formal methods for the development of information systems is given below. Put them into a logical order and write a paragraph, extending the points whenever you can.

- *Systems development life cycle*
- *Use of structured methods*
- *Use of prototyping*
- *Clear timescales*
- *Carrying out regular project review meetings and progress meetings.*

Now write a paragraph on the characteristics of successful ICT teams. First identify the points you wish to make, put them into a logical order and then write them down, extending the points whenever you can.

All you now have to do is write a very brief introduction along the lines of:

SAMPLE ANSWER

- The development of a large information system within an organisation will involve a wide range of different tasks and require many man-hours. It is therefore very important that the project is carefully organised so that it can be completed satisfactorily and on time.

Now write a brief conclusion and put your essay together.

SUMMARY

ICT projects require careful management to ensure successful completion.

Introduction of a new ICT system into a company is usually too large a task to be performed by one person.

A large project is broken down into a number of more manageable subtasks. A subtask will be allocated to a small manageable team.

A successful ICT team is likely to have:

- **good leadership**
- **an appropriate balance of skills and areas of expertise amongst the members of the team with suitable allocation of tasks**
- **adequate planning and scheduling of tasks**
- **skills to monitor and control progress against the plan and to control costs**
- **adherence to agreed standards**
- **good communication skills both with end users and within the team.**

Chapter 12 Questions

1 Explain why projects are often subdivided into subtasks and performed by teams. (6)

2 A good leader is a major factor of a successful ICT team. State **three** further characteristics needed by a successful ICT team and for each explain why it is needed. (9)

3 Describe **three** possible causes of inefficiency in the working of a team. (6)

4 A company has three departments to handle finance, buildings and equipment maintenance. Each department currently operates a separate ICT system. The company wishes to improve the efficiency of the operations by implementing a common corporate system across all three departments. In order to achieve this improvement, the company has decided to select members of staff from each department to form a project team to plan, design and implement the new system.

a) Describe **three** corporate level factors the team should consider when planning the new system. (6)

b) At their first meeting the team decide to subdivide the project into a series of tasks. Describe **two** advantages of this approach. (4)

5 The *adherence to standards* is a factor that characterises a good ICT team.

a) Explain why the adherence to standards is necessary for an ICT team to be successful. (2)

b) Describe **one** relevant standard appropriate when working on an ICT project. (2)

c) Describe **three** other factors that characterise a successful ICT team. (6)

6 For the successful introduction of a new or updated information system, an organisation needs to have clear management objectives and effective staff teams.

a) Name **four** aspects of an organisation that may need careful management during the introduction of a new or updated information system. (4)

b) Describe **two** characteristics of an effective ICT team. (4)

ICT4 June 2004

7 At the start of a project, 'agreed deliverables' must be established.

a) Explain what is meant by the term agreed deliverables. (2)

b) Describe **two** other objectives that must be agreed between the client and the project manager at the start of a project. (6)

13 Information and the professional

Social and ethical issues

▶ The introduction and use of ICT brings social, moral and ethical issues that affect a professional working within the industry.

Some of the issues that might arise regularly include:

- Hours of work. Should staff be made to work unsocial hours?
- Unlicensed software use. A colleague asks you if he can 'borrow' a software disk. What should you do?
- Health and safety. How can we guarantee a safe working environment for ICT users?
- Deskilling of employees. Is it fair that employees find that some of their work is now done by computer, e.g. taking decisions?
- Unauthorised computer access. How can we guarantee that private data is kept secret and secure?
- Property and copyright. Is it acceptable to pass off information from the Internet as your own?
- Information overload. How can you cope when you have so much information that you cannot process it all?

Ethics

Acting ethically means making the morally correct decision. An unethical decision is not necessarily illegal. There are many situations when an ICT professional has to make decisions where ethics should play a part.

The following actions could all be considered unethical:

- Passing on information from confidential files to a friend.
- Giving outdated advice because you have not kept your skills up to date.
- Not declaring a conflict of interest, for example recommending to a client that they buy computers from a company that turns out to be owned by your brother.
- Claiming to be an expert in some area where you have little or no expertise.
- Using company information for your own ends; for example taking a file of names and addresses to use as a mailing list for a small business that you are setting up at home.

Activity 1

Read through the story of Tom's day at work and then highlight as many examples of unethical practices as you can before reading the suggestions given in the table.

Tom arrives in his office and immediately switches on his desktop workstation. He has a network user account and when he logs on he is asked for his password. He types it in: 'TOMRULES' and waits for the system to load.

First he checks his e-mails. He has 20 waiting for him. Eight of these relate to work, six are from friends and six are SPAM (unsolicited messages – the junk of e-mail). He opens the messages from his friends. One contains photo images of the friend's holiday that take a while to download.

After 20 minutes spent dealing with social e-mails, Tom opens one of the SPAM messages that has the headline 'Earn £5000 without working'. The message has an attached document. When Tom opens it he realises that the message is a hoax and immediately deletes the message.

Now Tom gets down to work. He needs to access a database for which he needs another password. He uses the one that was originally assigned to him by the database administrator and, as it is UZ682GH7J, he keeps it on a 'post-it' note stuck on his computer screen.

During the morning Tom feels ready for a break so, without logging off, he walks out to the water cooler in the corridor where he meets up with some colleagues from a different department. They stay talking for ten minutes, discussing a new computer game that one of his colleagues has recently bought. Tom borrows the game CD-ROM and returns to his desk. He is keen to try the new game so he installs it on the local hard disk of his workstation and plays the game for half an hour. He is not very good at first but quickly improves.

When it is lunchtime, Tom logs off his workstation and goes to the sandwich bar with a friend. A colleague comes in and asks Tom if he could go back to work as he has forgotten to print out a report that is urgently needed. Tom has not finished his lunch so he tells his colleague where to find the file so that she can print it out for herself. 'You'll need to log on as me: my password is TOMRULES' he says.

In the afternoon, while he is working Tom downloads ten songs from a website so that he can listen to them later on his iPod. He has another play of his new game, but he doesn't seem to be getting any better so he surfs the Internet for a while instead, visiting a couple of his favourite 'Porno' sites and downloading a couple of images that he stores on the hard drive of his workstation.

Some possible unethical practices that can be found in the account of Tom's day

Using a password that is easy to guess	A simple password presents a security risk
Reading personal e-mail	Using work time, for which he is being paid, for personal matters
Downloading photos	Putting unnecessary load on network resources
Opening SPAM e-mail from unknown source	Likely to be in breach of security policy: potential of a virus
Using database password originally assigned to him by the administrator	Not changing the password regularly could present a security risk
Sticking password on screen	Passwords should be kept secret
Failing to log off	Leaves computer vulnerable to use by others who may obtain access to data to which they are not authorised
Installing a game on the hard drive	Likely to be in breach of security policy. Unauthorised software installed without licence
Playing a computer game	Wasting work time
Telling colleague his password	Passwords should be kept secret
Downloading music	Putting unnecessary load on network resources Likely to be in breach of copyright
Downloading and storing pornographic images	Inappropriate behaviour.

case study 1
▶ Misuse of the internet in the workplace

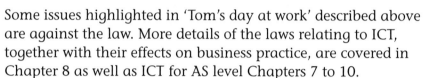

In September 2000, mobile phone company Orange sacked 40 members of staff for the 'distribution of inappropriate material.' Employees have also been sacked or disciplined at insurance company Royal and Sun Alliance, and bank Merrill Lynch, following the sending of pornographic images and e-mails.

In a recent survey, Internet and e-mail abuse were found to be the main instances of office work misconduct.

Twenty per cent of companies in the survey said that they monitored staff usage of online facilities, although only half of them had informed the staff of the monitoring.

- Describe four ways in which an employee could use e-mail or the Internet inappropriately in an office environment.

Codes of practice

Some issues highlighted in 'Tom's day at work' described above are against the law. More details of the laws relating to ICT, together with their effects on business practice, are covered in Chapter 8 as well as ICT for AS level Chapters 7 to 10.

Installing games software on your office computer probably breaks copyright law but there is nothing illegal about downloading your friend's holiday photos. However an employer would not want their employees to waste time when they should be working and slow down the computer network by downloading such images.

Professional standards of behaviour

ICT professionals are expected to act in a responsible and ethical manner. They should not pass on confidential information to a friend or waste time at work playing computer games or visiting auction sites on the Internet.

How can employers ensure that their employees work in an ethical and appropriate manner?

Employee code of practice

One way in which employers can ensure that their employees work in an ethical and appropriate manner is to have a code of practice or acceptable use policy.

Any breaches may lead to sanctions against the employee which may include: verbal warnings, written warnings, loss of pay, suspension or dismissal. The actual sanction will depend on the frequency and the severity of the breach.

An employee code of practice is simply a behaviour code for ICT users describing their responsibilities, rules for maintaining security and the penalties for misuse.

A copy of the code of practice should be given to every member of staff. It is also likely to be displayed on notice boards and possibly on a staff intranet.

Responsibilities

The code of practice will list the responsibilities of the ICT user, relating to the use of hardware, software and data. These should be listed in the code of practice. Such responsibilities might include:

- using hard disk space sensibly, i.e. deleting old files and e-mails to save space
- not using unauthorised disks
- not installing unauthorised software on the company's computers even if it complies with copyright laws
- not copying software for personal use
- not using the company's computers for personal gain
- not using e-mail for personal use
- not visiting pornographic websites or Internet chat rooms
- observing how the organisation fulfils the requirements of the Data Protection Act and the Computer Misuse Act
- not taking any action against the interests of the company.

Security

The code of practice is likely to cover all aspects of ICT security. These would include:

- only using your own userID and not letting others use it
- how often passwords should be changed
- what possible passwords are acceptable, e.g. only combinations of letters and numbers – not dictionary words or names
- that passwords should not be written down
- logging off or locking the workstation if leaving it for even a short while
- taking care to keep a laptop safe when away from the organisation's premises
- using appropriate encryption procedures when data is transmitted across public networks.

Penalties for misuse

The code of practice will describe the penalties that could result if a user broke any part of the code of practice. Such penalties could include:

- a verbal warning
- a written warning
- reduced access rights
- demotion

- suspension
- dismissal
- prosecution if a law has been broken.

However, many minor breaches of the code could occur through lack of knowledge or unintentional acts by the user. An inexperienced user might break the requirement that stipulates that a user changes his password every six weeks. Such breaches would best be dealt with by providing the user with training that demonstrated the importance of the measures in the code.

Activity 2

1. Thou shalt not use a computer to harm other people.
2. Thou shalt not interfere with other people's computer work.
3. Thou shalt not snoop around in other people's files.
4. Thou shalt not use a computer to steal.
5. Thou shalt not use a computer to bear false witness.
6. Thou shalt not use or copy software for which you have not paid.
7. Thou shalt not use other people's computer resources without authorisation.
8. Thou shalt not appropriate other people's intellectual output.
9. Thou shalt think about the social consequences of the program you write.
10. Thou shalt use a computer in ways that show consideration and respect.

from the Computer Ethics Institute, http://www.cpsr.org/issues/ethics/cei

Study the ten commandments of computer ethics produced by the Computer Ethics Institute given above.

- Which commandments are legal requirements and which ones are purely ethical suggestions?
- If you feel the commandment is a legal requirement, explain which laws are involved.

case study 2
► Jeff Wilmot

Jeff Wilmot worked in the ICT section of a district council in the Midlands. Jeff was very knowledgeable and was well respected by his colleagues.

Jeff told his colleagues that in his spare time he ran a small business setting up commercial websites for clients.

One day Jeff's line manager discovered that Jeff was setting up some of these websites while at work.

Jeff had breached the council's code of practice because he was using the council's computers for his own personal gain. He was immediately dismissed.

case study 3 ▶ University of Southampton code of practice for use of computers

The University of Southampton issues regulations for use of computer systems and networks by staff and students. The following are excerpts from these regulations:

1. Background

The use of computers is regulated by three Acts of Parliament – *The Data Protection Act 1998, The Copyright, Designs and Patents Act 1988* and *The Computer Misuse Act 1990*. Similarly the use of the public data telephone networks is regulated by *The Telecommunications Act 1984*.

These and several other Acts (including *The Obscene Publications Act 1978* as amended by *The Criminal Justice Act 1994*) identify a number of prohibited actions related to the use of computers which, if proven in a court of law may lead the perpetrator to a fine or imprisonment or both, or a suit for damages in the civil courts. The following regulations are framed to remind all members of the University of their legal obligations under these Acts of Parliament.

Any breach of these regulations will automatically be considered a breach of discipline.

2. Data Protection

Members of the University are allowed only to hold, obtain, disclose or transfer personal data (as defined by the Data Protection Act 1984) as permitted by the University's current registration with the Data Protection Registry and in accordance with Data Protection Principles as set out in that Act. If in doubt the University's Data Protection Officer should be consulted before any personal data is stored in a computer system.

3. Copyright

Members of the University will comply with the provisions of the Copyright Designs and Patents Act 1988 (as amended) in relation to any computer program or data set and shall not act in any way contrary to the terms of any licence agreement applying there to.

4. Computer Misuse

i) Members of the University are allowed only to use those computing resources, data or voice communications facilities, which have been allocated to them by the responsible computing management.
ii) Computing resources, including data and voice communications networks may only be used for properly authorised purposes.
iii) Members of the University may not lend or give resources to any other person.
iv) Members of the University may not access, alter, erase or add to computer material which has not been generated by them.
v) Authorised users of computer systems must take reasonable care to prevent unauthorised use of the computing resources allocated to them.

vi) Members of the University may not use computer systems or networks in such a way as to compromise the integrity or performance of the systems or networks.

5. Data and Voice Networks

i) Members of the University must abide by any 'Conditions of Use' of data or voice networks which are published by the responsible computing management for the protection of the integrity and efficiency of the network.

ii) Members of the University must not cause obscene, pornographic, discriminatory, defamatory or other offensive material, or material that otherwise infringes a right or inherent right of another person to be transmitted over the University, national or public networks, or cause such to be stored in University computer systems.

6. Withdrawal of Service

i) The responsible computing management may withdraw access to facilities from any user for the purposes of investigating a breach of these regulations.

ii) The responsible computing management may withdraw access to facilities from any user found to be guilty of a breach of these regulations.

- Categorise the statements above as relating to: the responsibilities, authorisation, security or penalties for misuse.
- List those statements that relate to ICT legislation.

Activity 3

1. Draw up an ICT code of practice for students at your school or college. You will need to include statements that relate to:
   - behaviour
   - use of ICT equipment
   - use of school network
   - access to, and use of, the Internet
   - legal requirements
   - plagiarism (copying the work of others and passing it off as your own).
2. Include any further statements that you feel should be included.
3. Draw up a further code of practice for teachers at your school or college.
4. For each statement, describe the appropriate sanction if the requirement is not met.

Worked exam question

Discuss the social, moral and ethical issues for a professional working within the industry, that might arise when introducing and using information and communication systems. (6)

ICT4 January 2003

EXAMINER'S GUIDANCE

This question says 'Discuss' so the answer should be in continuous prose. As there are six marks available, the question is looking for three examples with a detailed explanation to get full marks. As the question refers to introducing and using information and communication systems, almost any issue involving the introduction or use of computer systems would be relevant.

SAMPLE ANSWER

One issue to be considered when using ICT systems is unethical conduct such as visiting unsuitable websites in work time. Staff should sign an employee code of practice which states what they can and cannot do.

Another issue to be considered when using ICT systems is the use of unlicensed software; that is not using software according to the terms of the licence agreement. Companies should carry out spot checks to prevent this.

A third issue to be considered when using ICT systems is providing a safe working environment for ICT users. There are safety hazards in using a computer for long periods of time such as backache, RSI and eyestrain. A safe environment will include suitable equipment such as adjustable chairs and wrist rests.

SUMMARY

The introduction and use of ICT brings social, moral and ethical issues that affect a professional working within the industry. Employers need to establish a code of practice for their employees.

- **An employee code of practice will lay down the responsibilities of ICT users**
- **The code of practice is separate from any legal requirements.**

For example it may suggest that you:

- **cannot use e-mail for personal use**
- **cannot play computer games or visit Internet chat rooms in work time**
- **must not use the work's computers for personal gain.**

It will also cover security standards such as:

- **password policy**
- **not using another user's ID**
- **logging off when leaving your workstation.**

The code will also describe the penalties that could result if a user breaks any part of the code of practice. For example:

- **a verbal or written warning**
- **reduced access rights**
- **demotion**
- **dismissal**
- **prosecution, if a law has been broken.**

Chapter 13 Questions

1 A hospital computer network manager ensures that all new users read and sign a code of practice before they are issued with the log-in user identity.

a) Why is it necessary for employees to sign this code of practice? (2)

b) Describe **three** topics to include in a code of practice. (6)

2 Suggest **three** items related to passwords that should be in a company's code of practice. (3)

3 A military base has a computer network where security is paramount. Military personnel all sign a code of practice. Suggest **three** topics to include in a code of practice to ensure that security is not compromised. (3)

4 A company's code of practice forbids the use of memory sticks in the company's computers.

a) Give **two** reasons why the company should include this in the code of practice. (2)

b) Describe another topic related to hardware that might be in the code of practice. (2)

5 New employees joining a company are each asked to sign an agreement to adhere to a code of practice for using the organisation's computer system.

Explain **four** issues that such a code of practice should address. (8)

6 Bill Gregson is an IT consultant advising people on computerising their work. Bill recommends to clients that they should buy their computers from the computer manufacturers Cheapo, run by Bill's friend Clive Baxter. These computers are usually out-of-date models. 'These are the bee's knees. They'll never let you down. I swear by them. You don't want that modern stuff – too unreliable,' says Bill. State which laws or ethical standards have been breached (if any) and why. (4)

7 A company network manager is concerned that some users are installing unauthorised games software in their network user areas. Other users are believed to be downloading videos from the Internet and storing them in their user areas.

a) Suggest **two** reasons why installing unauthorised games software will be a concern to the network manager. (2)

b) Suggest **two** different reasons why downloading videos will be a concern to the network manager. (2)

c) What should the company do to prevent this sort of abuse? (2)

8 In 2005 a council in Scotland dismissed nine workers for inappropriate use of the Internet in work's time. The workers had contravened their ICT code of practice.

a) What is meant by a code of practice? (2)

b) Other than dismissal, what procedures could be used to discipline members of staff who break the code of practice? (2)

14 Policy and strategy issues

Information technology policy

Organisations spend a lot of money on ICT: for the hardware, the software and for the people who support it. Any large organisation should have an ICT management policy to ensure that best use is made of their investment in ICT and that any systems introduced are of benefit to the organisation. The senior management of an organisation need to take a long-term view of ICT management.

Without a centralised policy, as an organisation grows, different sections can develop their own systems that meet their specific needs; they may choose different hardware platforms and different software. This can lead to difficulties, making it hard to transfer data and information throughout the organisation because of hardware or software incompatibility. Without careful planning, systems can grow in an unstructured way, leading to inefficiency, redundancy and incompatibility. Although each department might work effectively and produce the information needed for their particular function, integration of the systems would be hard or impossible to achieve. Thus the overall information that the organisation would need for its management information system could not be brought together.

An ICT management policy should address the following:

- Ensuring that any systems that are introduced are of benefit to the whole organisation.
- Identifying the type and content of data that is stored and what information should be passed to whom.
- Ensuring that there is consistency of hardware and software across the organisation.
- Ensuring that adequate procedures are in place for compliance with all the related legislation (see Chapter 8).
- Ensuring that appropriate training provision is in place (see Chapter 2 and Chapter 11).
- Identifying required backup procedures to ensure that, in all systems within the organisation, data can be recovered in an efficient and structured way (see Chapter 15).
- Ensuring that maintenance and support can be provided to all ICT systems within the organisation, at a realistic cost.

Within any organisation, some ICT functions will be specific to a particular department.

Having a clearly defined ICT management policy that ensures that there is a consistency of hardware and software across the organisation should make it possible to provide appropriate maintenance and support at a realistic cost. ICT technicians within the organisation will only need to be familiar with a limited range of hardware and software.

An established ICT management policy should establish order within an organisation in terms so that different systems within the organisation complement each other. It should identify the content of the data that is stored within systems and what information should be passed to whom.

A timescale needs to be laid down for the replacement of hardware. For example, desktop PCs may be given a life of three years. Other equipment may be given a longer or shorter life, as appropriate. This allows the managers involved with purchasing equipment to plan ahead as the replacement costs of hardware can be anticipated. With centralised control, new technology can be implemented over a reasonable period without having to change every piece of equipment at the same time.

Establishing an ICT management policy

An organisation may decide that it needs an ICT management policy when it grows in size and the management realises that ICT systems have been established in a rather haphazard way with no central planning, or when many problems are arising within the organisation. Sometimes a new overall policy has to be established when two organisations merge.

It is crucial that consultation takes place before policy decisions are made, particularly relating to the purchasing strategies for hardware and software. In order to make sure that departmental requirements are met, discussions must take place with the departmental manager as he will know what is needed within his own department. Including user departments in the decision making should result in the departments supporting and implementing the decision because they feel that they have ownership of it.

Strategic implications of software, hardware and configuration choices

The choices that are made concerning the purchase of hardware and software, and also the kind of network infrastructure and operating system that are installed are likely to have major implications within the company. Such purchases are very costly and represent a major investment. New systems are unlikely to be totally replaced very frequently, so major purchase choices will dictate the ICT structure and direction of the organisation for some time.

It is advisable that all ICT purchases are made through a central point so that standardisation can be controlled.

The skills required, both from current employees and future recruits, will be established. A major training programme may be required. For many employees this training may just show them how to do their current jobs in a different way.

An organisation may become reliant upon the support given by the supplier or manufacturer. If a change in supplier or manufacturer is made then new relationships will need to be made with personnel in that organisation.

When making a configuration choice of the network infrastructure and operating system, it is important to choose a set up that is both flexible to use and able to be expanded as requirements change and grow. Organisations do not stay the same. They can diversify into new areas that will make new, extra demands on the ICT systems.

Software

Aspects of software choice are considered in Chapter 16. Decisions have to be made as to whether appropriate software already exists which can be bought and modified if necessary or whether it must be developed from scratch.

The use of an Office-type suite and other commonly used software should be standardised throughout a company. This will allow easy maintenance and support from the ICT technical team within the organisation. Documents and other data can be shared easily between users. Training can be standardised across all departments for the relevant applications.

The use of a standard operating system across a whole organisation will provide a standard look and feel. Software can support certain file formats; if the same standard software is used, all departments can share documents and guarantee that they can be understood.

Hardware

Ideally, an organisation's ICT technical department would have identical workstations for all users. This would simplify maintenance and would allow the best discount deal to be worked out with the manufacturer. However, in reality, such a situation is unlikely to occur, except in very small organisations. To replace all workstations in one go is likely to prove too costly. Most organisations carry out a rolling programme of replacement to spread replacement costs more evenly.

Even when the hardware purchases are standardised within an organisation, maintenance problems can arise if computers are configured in different ways.

Future expansion needs must always be considered, although these are unlikely to be exactly known.

Range of user needs

When drawing up an Information Technology management policy, the needs of all users must be considered. These needs are likely to be very diverse. The jobs carried out by different personnel will have very different ICT skill requirements. The skills required by users will vary from basic data entry or occasional word processing to a wide and varied technical knowledge of hardware and software. Some users will use a workstation or other ICT equipment for nearly all their work whilst others will be occasional users. The skills that users already have, together with their confidence in the use of ICT, will also be a factor.

Different departments within an organisation will have differing requirements that may result in them preferring to have different hardware or software.

There can often be a conflict between the user and the organisational needs. In some cases, a 'one solution for all' policy is just not appropriate. There will be specialist software requirements that are required just for one department due to the nature of the work done. For example, the accounts department within an organisation will require specialist accounting software that no one else in the organisation will need. It is very important that discussions take place with the head of department so that an agreement can be reached on the software to be used. If possible, software should be chosen that is able to export data files in a format that can be imported into the other software used within the organisation.

When choosing generic software that is likely to be used by all sections of an organisation, standardisation is usually chosen.

case study 1
▶ Software change

A new head of department, Sean, was recruited to run the sales department of a business, StrongRope that manufactures and sells rope. The spreadsheet software that was used at StrongRope was different from the one that was used in Sean's previous job. As he felt more comfortable with the old software, he persuaded his team to change to the package that he was more familiar with and purchased the required licences from his own budget.

All seemed to go well for a while, but soon some of his team became frustrated as they could not use the new software as well as they wished and there was no help available within StrongRope, as everyone else used a different package. The in-house support team did not have the expertise with the new spreadsheet software, the cost of providing specific support was beyond Sean's budget and the company was not prepared to pay either.

The issue blew up when the Managing Director found out that his PA had been unable to produce a report, that should have ▶

included linked data from the sales department spreadsheets, as there was no common data format for transfer. He told Raj, the head of ICT who was unaware that Sean had installed a different software package.

Raj realised that there were likely to be problems with the spreadsheet software as the company had a special agreement with the original spreadsheet provider that gave them the required licences at a lower rate so long as the company did not use any other spreadsheet.

The Managing Director immediately told Sean to get rid of the new software and to revert to using the original.

1. List the reasons why Sean should not have used the old software.
2. How could the problem described above have been prevented?

Worked exam question

A soft drinks manufacturer uses one particular hardware, operating system and applications package combination throughout its organisation. One department finds that this particular set-up does not suit its needs. The manager of this department decides to purchase different hardware and operating system, and the specialist applications that he requires.

a) Describe two reasons why the manager's action may not be advisable. (4)
A large organisation should have an Information Technology management policy.
b) Give two reasons why such a policy is necessary. (2)

ICT5 June 2003

▶ **EXAMINER'S GUIDANCE**

In part (a) one mark is awarded for what the problem is, and one mark is awarded for why it is a problem. You have to think of two problems. One part could be:

'Maintenance contracts may be compromised (1) separately purchased hardware may cause problems not covered under contract (1)'.

Some possible areas to consider are: the portability of data, training, licensing, cost and organisational support. For each of these write a sentence in the form given above.

In part (b) it is important that you discuss an Information Technology management policy not a code of practice (issues relating to staff usage). It is important to learn the definitions for these terms.

Activity 1

- Write a report for your head teacher/principal stating what you feel should be included in an ICT policy for your school or college.

Methods of enhancing existing capabilities

Future proofing

Future proofing concerns finding ways of making sure that a system has a reasonable life and does not need to be totally replaced too soon.

Computers have developed so rapidly that machines that are four or five years old seem slow and cannot cope with recent software. When buying a new computer system, it is important to buy one that won't be out of date too soon.

Old data must be able to be transferred to a new system. Programs must have **backwards compatibility** (the ability to read files from previous versions). DVD drives must also be able to read CD-ROMs. New computers no longer have a built-in floppy disk drive as the technology has become outdated. However, external floppy disk drives that work from the USB port can be used so that any files that have been stored on a floppy disk can still be read.

Hardware performance is constantly being improved by manufacturers in terms of both processing speed and memory capacity. New versions of software include extra features and usually require extra main and backing storage memory. It is important that any computer purchased has sufficient main memory and hard disk capacity to cope with likely future requirements, both from software and expanding files.

The possibility to expand memory at a later date should be built in as well as the capacity to add extra cards and peripherals if needs change. Computers often have **expansion slots**, a connector inside the computer into which an **expansion card** can be plugged. The expansion card would contain a new feature such as additional RAM or a graphics accelerator.

Considering future needs is even more important when setting up a **network**. When establishing the cabling in and between buildings, care must be taken that future growth in network traffic is catered for. The development of wireless networking is growing very fast so it is important that any new network is set up to allow wireless access. The network infrastructure of cables, switches, servers and so on, is costly to purchase and install. Frequent changes to these basic, underlying services can be disruptive to work and need to be avoided through careful forward planning. There must be flexibility in the number and positioning of workstations so that changing future requirements can be catered for.

Upgrading hardware and software

Hardware and software development

After some years of use, a company may wish to **upgrade** their computers. Changes in available devices, such as the development of flat screens, may make upgrading desirable. An increased volume of data or a desire to decrease processing time could make it necessary to replace a computer with one that has a faster clock speed and more RAM. Required changes in software might make the hardware upgrade necessary as new versions of software often have greater resource requirements.

If computers are kept for a long time, they can become obsolete and spare parts become unavailable so that they cannot be repaired when they break down.

As technology advances, tasks can be carried out in a way that could not once have been achieved. This could result from such developments as increased processor speed, increased memory capacity or enhanced transfer speed over a network. For example, improved technology may have resulted in the production of printers that produce a better quality of print than was available previously.

Alongside the increase in hardware performance, software development has also made rapid progress. There has been a move towards software that has a greater range of functionality as well as graphical user interfaces which provide an interface that is easier and less frustrating to use.

Organisation ethos

The organisation may have a policy to upgrade hardware after a certain time in order to provide an up-to-date image for the company or to maintain good staff morale.

Having up-to-date ICT resources can inspire confidence in customers and other business contacts. It should also provide the best service to customers.

This is a particularly important reason for regular upgrading in a company whose business is in ICT, for example, in hardware manufacture, software development or support. Such an organisation needs to portray an image that it is 'ahead of the game' and at the forefront of ICT development.

Task-driven change

Changes in the way that tasks within the organisation are carried out might force an upgrade of hardware or software.

For example, a decision that salespersons should collect all information regarding clients directly would require them to be issued with laptop computers. The currently-used software would have to be upgraded to allow for the transfer of necessary data to and from the laptops on a daily or weekly basis.

A decision by senior management to provide the facility of Internet sales for customers would have networking and software upgrade implications.

case study 2
▶ Howse, Hulme and Byer (HHB), estate agent

HHB is the name of a small estate agent that has eight offices within a 50-mile radius.

Information on customers and the details of houses for sale are stored locally at the nearest office. Customer details and data regarding the houses, such as the number of rooms and their dimensions, locality etc., are stored in a spreadsheet in a four-year-old computer. Photographs of properties are stored in filing cabinets.

HHB wishes to upgrade its methods to enable the photos to be stored on the computer together with short video clips. Details of all houses that they are currently trying to sell should be available online in all their offices.

- What hardware are HHB likely to need if they upgrade their system?
- Discuss the extra functionality that would be needed in the software.
- What benefits would there be for HHB if they upgrade their current system?

Software change

Many commercial software packages are regularly updated and new versions brought on to the market. An organisation will have to decide if and when it is appropriate to move to the new version.

Consideration will have to be given to whether the extra features offered by the new version will be of real benefit to the organisation's users. It is advisable to wait until the new version is tried and tested so that it will prove to be robust in use.

Occasionally, it is appropriate to change to new software which provides the same functionality as that currently used, but more cost effectively as the licences for the new software are cheaper.

If the new version has a different look and feel from the old version, as well as having extra features, it might be necessary to undertake a programme of staff retraining to ensure that everyone is able to make efficient use of the software.

A new version of a software application frequently has a greater systems resource requirement than an older version. It is likely to take up more hard disk space than the old version, require more RAM and may need a faster processor to run it. Problems can arise when not all the workstations in an organisation are able to run the new version and have to keep using an older version. This can lead to some file incompatibility as it is likely that files produced by the new version cannot be read by the old.

Users may require training in the use of the new version of the software if it includes new features. Although new features could be ignored until the user feels ready to find out about them, upgrades can also include changes to existing features which could cause confusion and irritation. Unless training is provided, users will initially take longer to perform familiar tasks. Extra support will be needed for users when software upgrades have been made.

In a large organisation, an upgrade can be trialled in one department before use throughout the whole organisation. In this way expertise can be built up and problems highlighted on a small scale. However, if this is done there are likely to be complications in file transfer between departments.

Very often, it is not necessary to purchase a full copy of a new version of software, just an 'upgrade' copy that will convert the current version to the new one. This is usually a cheaper option, but does have some disadvantages.

A graphic designer who runs his own business uses the Quark software package on Apple Macs. Over a number of years he has bought upgrades to the original version that he purchased. Although the original version provided all the features he required, he needed to install the upgrades as his clients and publishers used the more advanced versions and would send files to him which could not be read by the older software.

Recently the system was struck by a virus that resulted in all the software having to be reinstalled. This took a considerable time as every upgrade had to be installed separately, in the correct order.

When an organisation undertakes a major system upgrading a decision has to be made on the new hardware platform. Ideally it should be compatible with the old platform.

Compatibility of hardware and software

When different hardware manufacturers produce machines that all support the same software and data files the machines are said to be compatible. The processors of compatible systems will have a similar architecture with the same instruction set.

Some applications are dependent upon a particular hardware configuration (e.g., processor type or clock speed, memory configuration, VDU configuration). For example, Microsoft Office 2003 will only run on a PC with a minimum clock speed of 233MHz. The term compatible hardware is often used to refer to those hardware systems that conform to a particular minimum hardware specification, having similar architecture and supporting the same peripheral devices.

Software packages are said to be compatible if they are able to share data files with each other.

case study 3

▶ Pump up the program

(Based on an article by Brian Clegg in *PC Week*)

Software upgrades are a mixed blessing. Upgrading is plagued with hidden costs and difficulties such as incompatibilities with previous versions or other installed software and insufficient system resources. Even the users who beg for the latest version will need extra training and support.

An important consideration of upgrading is the cost of new software licences. The amount paid can be subject to negotiation: vendors have a variety of approaches. Oracle's support agreement for server products includes free upgrading. This removes any concern about the cost of new licences, but limits the ICT manager's choice. IBM effectively insures against upgrades, offering a protection scheme to provide low cost upgrades provided you pay 15 per cent extra on the original licence.

The biggest upgrade expense can be training users. If benefits are to be gained, there is a training need, and companies that aren't prepared to provide that training will have hidden costs in the time taken to perform once familiar tasks.

However, training is the most disputed area. At one large company, a manager comments, 'we do not put much resource into user training. It does not work for most people and they can't afford the time out from fee-earning work. We find most people who want to use software pick it up and use it to a level they are happy with themselves. If they get really desperate they can call my department for help'.

Sometimes an upgrade will generate hidden training requirements. A senior network analyst with the same company recalls problems with a new version of Microsoft Project. 'There were differences in the way Project handled changes, for example, tasks that had slipped. We treated the upgrade as if it was a matter of pure extra benefits, but ignored the differences in the way the product worked, resulting in problems.'

The message from the ICT managers is that you should take charge of upgrading – don't leave it to the vendors to tell you when to do it.

- List the costs of upgrading software identified in this article.
- Describe the training needs that can arise from upgrading software.
- Explain the reasons why software vendors make such frequent changes to their software.

case study 4
Upgrading systems

Camelot upgrade

In 2003 the National Lottery operator Camelot upgraded its ICT infrastructure. This upgrade meant that Camelot could offer new games and could sell lottery tickets via digital television, the Internet and mobile phones.

Camelot started thinking about the upgrade in 2000 and started work on the upgrade in 2001 with a team of 50 staff working on the project.

Direct Line

The insurance company Direct Line has upgraded its call centre technology to improve the service to its customers, currently over 5 million. They replaced computer workstations and installed new software. The call centres can deal with 170,000 calls a day (about 35 million a year). The computers process 9.5 million transactions daily, so reliability is essential. The old system had reached the limits of its capacity.

The new system provides more customer information so that the operators can answer calls more effectively.

The company had been waiting to upgrade for some time, but did not want to do so until reliable technology that would last was available.

1. What do we mean by the term 'network infrastructure'?
2. What is a 'call centre'?
3. Why do you think it took so long for Camelot to upgrade their system?
4. Compare the reasons of the two companies for upgrading their systems.
5. List other reasons that can cause an organisation to upgrade its hardware and/or software.

Worked exam question

A school ICT coordinator wants to upgrade the school computer network, which consists of a large number of workstations and two servers, all of which are at least three years old. The operating system (OS) is over five years old.

- State five reasons she could give to her senior management that would reinforce her case for upgrading. (5)

ICT 5 June 2001

SAMPLE ANSWER

Possible reasons include:

- Additional functionality
- Take less time for users to log on
- New system may be accessed by students from home
- Students will have similar software on their home computer
- Unreliability of old equipment
- To improve the image of the school

Emulation

When a decision is made to upgrade hardware it is likely that much of the software used will be upgraded too. Indeed the need for new software could well have been the driving force for hardware change. However, it is possible that some of the old software would still need to be run on the new hardware. If a change to incompatible hardware is made, it may be possible to run old software using an emulator.

A **software emulator** is a program which, when it runs, makes a physical computer run as if it were a computer with a different hardware specification. When a program is being developed to run on a number of different hardware platforms, the developer might use an emulator instead of buying many different machines.

An emulator is a type of **systems software** that acts as an interface between the hardware of a system and any application program running on the system. This allows for application software to be run on a hardware platform other than the one for which it was designed. It enables a computer to give the appearance of it being a different platform. Microchips are available to provide **hardware emulation**.

Emulation provides a way of ensuring that old software, incompatible with new hardware, can still be used. It is a solution which is an attractive choice when a few, small systems need to be continued using old software. Emulation can also prove useful when a minority of computer users need to work on different hardware platforms from the majority of the organisation's users. For example, the design department in a large organisation might need to use Apple computers rather than PCs for their design work. The use of emulation software will allow them to use certain PC software that is used by the rest of the organisation.

Using emulation software also allows for existing hardware to be used when some new application software is purchased so that further investment in new hardware, that may be of limited use, will not have to be made.

Using software emulation allows access to a greater range of application software than that which is available on the user's hardware platform and allows data to be transferred between platforms. The user may have access to more file types which might be specific to particular software that is not available on the current system.

It may also be possible to access hardware which may only be developed for the other platform.

Using emulation software can provide a cheap short-term solution to a problem without the need to invest in costly hardware until the user is sure that the more expensive change is justified.

For some users the possible easy access to two sets of operating systems is an advantage.

Because an extra layer of program is required, the original software will run more slowly and may be too slow to be of practical use; it will not exploit the features of the new hardware.

The emulator can make heavy demands on system resources such as memory, hard disk space and processor time.

Software emulation may not provide full functionality of the application software so that the user can only access some of its features. The available functions may limit productivity.

Software support will be more complex as it will be difficult to ascertain whether a problem lies with the application software or the emulation software.

It is possible that the organisation will have to buy extra software licences for the application software to run under the emulator.

Advantages of emulation

- Emulation allows old software that is incompatible with new hardware to still be used.
- Existing hardware can be used with newer software.
- Access to two different platforms provides a user with the advantages of both sets of operating systems available at once.
- Cheap short-term solution to a problem before deciding whether to invest in new hardware at a later date.

Limitations of emulation

- There may be functions missing that are needed in order to be productive.
- The emulator may run too slowly to be of practical use.
- The software takes up space on the hard disk of the existing system.
- There may be a need to buy software licences for applications to run under the emulator.
- Support may be more complex.

Activity 2

Did you know it is possible to turn your PC into a primitive 1980s games computer like the Atari or the Spectrum using an emulator? You may wonder why in these days of sophisticated games graphics anyone would want to play a retro game like Space Invaders but dozens of such emulators exist.

- Investigate them. Use a search engine to search for PC Emulator Atari. List 10 features of the emulator.

The original IBM Personal Computer, the **IBM PC/XT** was first released in 1981. It had 64Kb of RAM, 40Kb of ROM which included a BASIC interpreter. Website www.xt-ce.com/ provides details of an emulator that allows software produced for the XT to be run on a Handheld Personal Computer (H/PC), a mobile device that can be used in the palm of the hand and uses a new operating system, Windows CE.

- Explore the website. List the reasons why an emulator is required.

SUMMARY

- **Organisations should have policies for ICT management.**
- **Software, hardware and configuration choices have strategic implications for an organisation.**
- **Hardware and software purchased within a company should be standardised to ensure:**
  - **compatibility with existing data**
  - **compatibility with existing hardware**
  - **that colleagues can share data where necessary**
  - **that colleagues can communicate where necessary (e.g. by e-mail)**
  - **that technical support is available**
  - **that legal software licensing requirements are met**
  - **that training is available**
  - **that the hardware can cope with possible future demands.**
- **ICT users within an organisation have a wide range of needs that have to be considered.**
- **Organisations decide to upgrade their hardware and/or software provision for a number of reasons including:**
  - **hardware/software development**
  - **organisational ethos**
  - **task-driven change**
  - **software change.**
- **When upgrading, compatibility with existing systems needs to be considered.**
- **Emulation software and hardware provide ways of running software on a different hardware platform.**

Chapter 14 Questions

1 **a)** Define the term *software emulation*. (1)
b) State an example of an appropriate use of software emulation, describing why it is used. (3)
c) Describe **one** advantage and **one** disadvantage of using software emulation. (4)

2 A graphic designer makes use of a particular hardware platform and particular software packages. Her clients often send her files produced on computer systems that are incompatible with hers. One solution for the designer is to use emulation software.

Describe **one** advantage and **one** limitation the designer will have if she pursues this solution. (4)

ICT5 June 2002

3 A mail order company has been using a particular stock control package for a few years. They now wish to upgrade the software.
a) Explain **three** reasons why the company may wish to upgrade the software. (6)
b When upgrading the software, *compatibility* with existing systems needs to be considered.
i. Define the term *compatibility*. (1)
ii. Name an existing system within a mail order company that should be considered. (1)
iii. Describe **two** ways in which the systems could be incompatible. (4)

4 A successful telecommunications company is rapidly growing in size. The senior management has decided that the company needs to establish a policy for ICT management.
a) Explain why an ICT Management Policy is required. (2)
b) Describe **four** issues that should be addressed by the ICT Management Policy. (8)

5 A publishing company wishes to standardise its ICT systems. Managers from all departments of this company are consulted before any standardisation takes place.
a) Describe, using an example, **one** reason why this consultation is necessary. (2)
b) As part of this standardisation strategy, it is decided that:

- no computer hardware will be used for more than a fixed number of years
- all departments will have a standard set of applications software
- the software must support a certain set of file formats.

Explain **two** reasons why the company has decided to adopt this strategy. (4)

ICT5 January 2004

6 An estate agency company has a chain of 15 offices all situated in the North West of England. It has recently merged with a smaller agency in the area that has five offices. Both agencies have computer systems that have been in use for several years. The management have decided to upgrade the hardware and software for all the offices.

Discuss the implications of the upgrading, paying attention to the following:
a) The hardware requirements and the factors that will affect the choice
b) The software requirements and the factors that will affect the choice
c) Any particular problems that will arise as a result of merging two different computer systems used by the merging organisations. (20)

The quality of Written Communication will be assessed in your answer.

7 Within a large organisation it is advisable that all purchases of hardware and software are *standardised*.
a) State what is meant by the term *standardise*. (1)
b) Describe **four** reasons why standardisation is desirable. (8)

15 Backup strategies 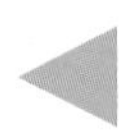

The need for a backup strategy

▶ The aim of producing file backups is to make sure that if data from a computer system is lost or corrupted for any reason, the files can be recovered and the computer system restored to its original state. The loss might occur due to:

- a hardware fault such as a hard disk crash
- an incident where a file might, for example, be accidentally deleted or data is lost as the result of a natural disaster, such as a flood or an earthquake
- deliberate actions such as sabotage or terrorism.

An organisation's information management strategy must include a strategy for backing up files to cover all eventualities, including accidental damage, deliberate damage and damage due to equipment failure. The strategy will depend on the data involved and its use. The strategy will cover:

- when is the best time to backup
- how often to do it
- what type of backup will be used
- whose responsibility it is
- what media will be used
- where the backup media will be kept
- keeping a log of backups taken
- testing the recovery of backed up data.

Drawing up the strategy

After carrying out a **risk analysis**, a formal strategy should be established that ensures that regular backups of critical data are taken in a consistent and appropriate manner.

They need to be done in such a way that, if necessary, the system could be restored in a reasonable amount of time. What is considered reasonable will depend on the nature of the data being backed up.

It is important that the backup procedures should not affect the provision of service; ideally they should be invisible to the user.

Organisations should have a strategy for the **archiving** of old data that is no longer needed online. Archiving removes old, no longer used data and stores it on removable media, for example on magnetic tape. The data is unlikely to be needed so it is stored offline but can be accessed if required.

Backing up is keeping a second copy of current data.

Archiving is a good idea as it frees up hard disk space and not so much data has to be backed up.

When is the best time to backup?

It is important to establish when backup should take place. This is often at night as many systems only run during working hours. The software will do this automatically without human intervention. However the backup tapes will need to be changed every day.

A **backup log** should be kept. In this should be recorded the details of all backups taken with details of time, date, the medium used (identified by a volume number) together with the name of the person who carried out the backup.

With an online sales system, suitable backup facilities must be in place to ensure that all lost transactions can be restored. Consideration of the volume of data involved in the system and the importance of the speed in which restoring from backed up files is necessary must be taken into account. Arranging backup for systems which are online for 24 hours a day can be complicated.

When a network is used, the process of backing up can be centralised and all servers can be backed up from one place. In most cases the user is responsible for the backup of any data that is stored on the hard drive of their own workstation.

How often should an organisation backup?

The strategy will need to specify which files need to be backed up at what frequency. A good management plan will ensure the backups are performed at the appropriate intervals. Most organisations backup at least daily but some backups may need to be performed more or less frequently.

The frequency of backup must be determined. Obviously, the more frequent the backup, the less out of date will be the data when it is restored. However, whenever a backup is undertaken, processor time is tied up and files (or just records if record locking is used) can be unavailable for other use. An appropriate balance needs to be found and factors such as the acceptable length of delay in restoring files in the case of failure as well as the importance and nature of the data need to be considered. Sales data for a supermarket, which affects orders and deliveries, will be backed up hourly, if not more frequently. User data, such as passwords and user names, need only be backed up every week.

To use removable storage media it must be possible to allocate time when backup can take place without interfering with the normal running of the system. In many organisations, systems are not in use at night and so full backups can be taken then.

What type of backup will be used?

Does the organisation need to backup every file or just those that changed today? See full backup, differential backup and incremental backup below.

Whose responsibility is it?

The responsibility of backing up a system should be allocated to a specific person within the organisation. It is his responsibility to ensure that backup and recovery procedures are practised from time to time and that careful checks are made to ensure that whatever backup measures are being taken actually work, so that backed up data can be read at any time. It is important that all recording and playback equipment is compatible.

What media will be used?

A number of factors will influence the decision of backup method and storage medium. These include:

- the seriousness of the consequences of lost data
- the volume of the data
- the speed at which the data is changing
- how quickly recovery needs to take place if a situation occurs when data has to be restored from backed up version(s)
- the cost of the various methods.

Large businesses with a lot of essential data are likely to use high capacity storage media such as magnetic tape. They may also use an autoloader – a magnetic tape drive that can fetch tapes from a library automatically and load them. This makes unattended large-scale backups possible. They are frequently used when backing up data stored over a network. The volume of data that can be backed up without the need for human intervention is increased hugely and runs into thousands of gigabytes. It is limited only by the number of tapes that the library can hold.

Backing up small quantities of data

It is not always necessary to have a device that is dedicated to backup.

Smaller businesses and home users may use storage devices for backup that were designed for archiving or transferring data. Examples of these are:

Floppy disk	Very low capacity (1.44 Mb); suitable for storing a few small files. Floppy disks are being used less and less as more convenient storage media with greater capacity are now available.
CD-R and CD-RW (Compact Disk Recordable and Re-writable)	Normally can store up to 700 Mb on each disk.
Memory stick	Easy to use, connecting to any USB port and highly portable. Can store more than a CD-R and increasing in capacity.
DVD-RAM (Writeable Digital Versatile Disk)	The same size but greater capacity than a CD-R – up to 4.7 Gb.
External hard drive	Avalable in hundreds of Gb. They connect to a USB port and can be used to increase disk capacity or as a backup.

Where will the backup media be kept?

There is no point in backing up if the backup media is destroyed by the same flood or fire that has destroyed the computer system. The place where backup copies are to be stored must be specified in the backup strategy, as well as the length of time and number of back copies that are kept.

Activity 1

Many organisations have excellent strategies in place to backup their networked systems and databases but neglect to consider the backup needs of the growing number of laptop computers that are used by employees. Laptops are particularly at risk as they are more vulnerable to theft and potential damage.

An employee's laptop could contain a range of data and programs whose loss could range from annoying to critical, such as software applications, highly configured Windows systems, communication setups to connect to the Internet and the organisation's network, documents and other data, and Internet bookmarks.

An insurance salesman uses his laptop to keep records of sales, clients and payments using special purpose software and to keep in touch with work colleagues through e-mail. He seeks your advice on a backup strategy and asks you to help. Can you suggest answers to these questions?

1. How often should he backup?
2. When is the best time to do it?
3. Should he backup every file every time?
4. What backup medium should he use?
5. Where should the backup medium be kept?
6. How should he log his backups?

case study 1
▶ A college backup strategy

A sixth form college runs a network used by teachers and students as well as all administrative services such as MIS and examinations. The network supports over 20 file servers. Backup is an important part of the work of the IT department.

To carry out its backup the department uses a software utility program called BackupExec developed by Veritas, a company specialising in backup solutions.

As little use is made of the college system outside working hours, the department carries out a full backup every night. The backup is initiated by the software and DLT7000 tapes are used to store the backed up files. The tapes are slotted into a 16-slot autoloader.

The rotation system described on page 176 is used. The last and previous weeks' tapes are held off site while those for this week are held in the autoloader. The monthly backup is kept for a year.

The backup process starts at 1630 in the afternoon and is completed around 0630 the following morning. Jeremy, senior IT technician at the college, is in charge of checking that the backup has successfully completed when he arrives at work in the morning. The backup software produces a log file which will inform him whether the backup:

- completed with no errors
- completed with errors
- aborted.

Most mornings the backup will have completed with no errors; a complete failure causing the backup to abort is a rare occurrence. If the backup completes with some files failing to be backed up, Jeremy has to follow up each error. If the backup does fail completely he will have to decide whether or not to risk running without a backup for a day or to slow the network down while the backing up is repeated.

If a user of the network deletes or overwrites a file by mistake, Jeremy can restore a previous version for them. The backup software keeps a catalogue of the path of all the files it backs up. It will then read through the tape until it finds the required file.

Files on the servers are not the only things that need backing up. For example, configuration settings for the firewall are stored as a text file. Over time the settings will have received many modifications and if the file were lost it would take many man-hours to recreate.

1. What is the advantage of using an autoloader?
2. Comment on the effectiveness of the college's backup strategy.
3. Why is it important for one person to have the responsibility for backup?
4. Explore the Veritas web site (www.veritas.com) to find out the functions offered by BackupExec software.

How long to keep data

The longer an organisation keeps its data, media that are more portable, such as magnetic tapes, are needed. Older backups will be needed in case later backups fail. Consideration of any legal obligations for the business, as well as other business needs, should be made when determining how long backed up data should be retained. If the data needs to be stored for a long time, the media should be periodically inspected for signs of damage.

Recording of transactions in a log

Unless a file is backed up after every transaction, which is most unlikely to be feasible, a record will need to be kept of all the transactions that have taken place since the last backup occurred. In the case of file failure, the latest backup copy would be used to restore the file. It could then be brought up to date by rerunning all the transactions, stored on the log, that had occurred since the backup was made. Of course, the transaction log itself must be backed up otherwise failure could cause a loss of transaction. One important transaction you wouldn't want lost might be the booking of a flight.

In some systems it is necessary to perform transaction log backups every 15 minutes during the day to keep the data entry loss to less than 15 minutes.

Systems that are live for 24 hours a day may need to look at alternative methods of ensuring that data is adequately backed up.

Program files do not change very frequently except during development; backups only need to be created when new versions are installed. However, many software applications need to be configured to meet the requirements of the hardware that is installed. They can also be customised to meet the user's specific needs using macros and templates for example. It is advisable to keep backups of all such modifications. A user can easily delete the files that store the configuration details and without a backup file the configuration and customisation would have to be undertaken again. All backup copies should be regularly checked.

Data files are regularly changing and will therefore need regular backing up.

Scheduling backups and tape rotation methods

Tape backup systems have been in use for years on computer systems. It would be very unwise to use the same tape for every backup session. The backup process might fail part way through execution without producing a complete tape; the old version would have been overwritten. So a number of tapes will need to be kept and, if the tapes are not going to get muddled up they need to be carefully labelled and stored. This will allow the correct tape to be accessed when needed to restore the system.

A **tape rotation system** is used to ensure that the correct versions are kept.

Full backup

Perhaps the easiest way to backup is where a full image of the system is copied to tape every single day. A different tape is used each day. This ensures that the system can be restored from only one tape. It may take many tapes, and, if the volume of data is large, a considerable time to carry out each day. This type of backup is common for small servers that are not in operational use 24 hours a day. The limitation of taking a full backup is that it can take a considerable time to carry out; if a system is running at the same time it is likely to slow down processing.

Differential backup

A differential backup only backs up the files which are different from or were updated after the full backup. This allows the full system to be restored with a maximum of just two tapes. The limitation of using differential backup is that when some time has elapsed since the last full backup, the backup of all changed files will be time consuming.

Incremental backup

An incremental backup backs up only the files that have changed since the last backup to the tape. The advantage of an incremental backup is that it takes less time to backup but if a failure did occur it would take more time to restore files to the current position as several tapes may have been used.

For example a business might use an incremental backup strategy as follows:

Monday night:	Full backup on tape A
Tuesday night:	Incremental backup (Tuesday's changes) on tape B
Wednesday night:	Incremental backup (Wednesday's changes) on tape C
Thursday night:	Incremental backup (Thursday's changes) on tape D
Friday night:	Incremental backup (Friday's changes) on tape E

If the business needed to restore on Saturday, all five tapes would be needed.

Choosing a physical tape to use for backup

A **rotation method** determines how tapes are fed through the system.

Grandfather, father, son

The grandfather, father, son method is a simple process that has been used for many years. Tapes are labelled by the day of the week with a different tape for each Friday in the month and a different tape for each month of the year. (Using a tape for Saturday and Sunday is optional depending on whether files are updated over the weekend). The rotation would be made as follows:

MONDAY TUESDAY WEDNESDAY THURSDAY FRIDAY1
MONDAY TUESDAY WEDNESDAY THURSDAY FRIDAY2
MONDAY TUESDAY WEDNESDAY THURSDAY FRIDAY3
MONDAY TUESDAY WEDNESDAY THURSDAY MONTH1

MONDAY TUESDAY WEDNESDAY THURSDAY FRIDAYI
MONDAY TUESDAY WEDNESDAY THURSDAY FRIDAY2
MONDAY TUESDAY WEDNESDAY THURSDAY FRIDAY3
MONDAY TUESDAY WEDNESDAY THURSDAY MONTH2

MONDAY TUESDAY WEDNESDAY THURSDAY FRIDAY1
MONDAY TUESDAY WEDNESDAY THURSDAY FRIDAY2
MONDAY TUESDAY WEDNESDAY THURSDAY FRIDAY3
MONDAY TUESDAY WEDNESDAY THURSDAY FRIDAY4
MONDAY TUESDAY WEDNESDAY THURSDAY MONTH3

etc.

Since some months have more than four weeks, it will take over 20 tapes for regular backups over one year.

Physical security of backup medium

As data can be lost due to disasters such as fire, it is necessary that backup files should be kept in a separate place from the original storage medium.

In some large cities there exist firms that run a backup service. They come to client organisations at a fixed time, usually daily, collect the day's backup tapes which they take away to store safely in their own premises. At the same time they provide the client with the tapes, correctly labelled that need to be used for the next day's backups. If the backups are needed to restore the system, the firm will rush the appropriate tapes to the client organisation.

Often a fireproof safe is used. A locality should be chosen that is climate-controlled, secure and easily accessible.

Data files can also be backed up by transmitting them across a network to save a copy of the data in a remote location. (See Case Study 2: Using a remote backup service).

Recovery method

It is important that when files have been backed up the backup copy is verified, in other words checked against the original to ensure that it has been copied exactly. If this is not done, the backup files could prove to be useless and the original file could not be recreated.

If the original data files are lost or corrupted, the data can be recovered by using programs that restore the data from the backup files. It is necessary to restore the files in the correct order by following agreed recovery procedures. The file will first be recreated using the most recent full backup and then each subsequent incremental backup file should be accessed, in time order, to update the file. Any transaction log should then be used to restore the most recent transactions.

If the files are used in the wrong order, the restored data will not be correct. Care must be taken in the careful labelling and organisation of backup tapes and disks to ensure that no mistakes are made.

Other backup strategies

Remote backup

An organisation can use a remote backup service, similar to the one described in Case Study 2, by transferring files to a remote site using a wide area network. The limitations of using remote backup are that data is vulnerable as it is being transmitted over a network and will need to be encrypted.

case study 2
▶ Using a remote backup service

There are now several companies such as DataHaven (http://www.datahavenltd.co.uk) who offer a remote backup service.

How it Works

12.30 am – Your computer 'wakes up' and prepares a compressed backup of the chosen files which it then encrypts for security.

1.00 am – Your computer logs onto the Internet and connects to a DataHaven *Remote Backup* host computer. Computers exchange accounting information. Your computer then sends its daily compressed and encrypted backup to DataHaven's host computer.

1.15 am – Backup is finished. An encrypted copy of all your critical data files is now safely off-site in our secure storage facility.

From http://www.datahavenltd.co.uk

The fact that so many companies offer this service suggests that it is very attractive. Prices start at around £10 a month depending on the amount of data to be backed up and the frequency of backup. ▶

Companies choose to use a service like this for the peace of mind. Installation is simple and they no longer have to worry about changing backup tapes, storing backup tapes in a safe place, damaged or lost tapes, maintaining backup hardware, testing backups and training their staff.

1. Why is the data compressed?
2. Why is the data encrypted?
3. List the benefits to an organisation of using the services of DataHaven.

Online backup

The methods described above are used by many organisations and are appropriate for small and medium sized systems. However, organisations with very large systems that hold vast data warehouses of information, need to look at alternative methods for providing backup. As well as having very high volumes of data, the organisations running such systems can neither afford to lose even a small amount of data, nor lose operational time while data is being restored from a backup. An alternative way has to be found to provide against the hazards of data loss.

One way is to use **disk mirroring**: storing identical data on two different disks. Whenever data is stored to disk, it is stored on both disks. If the main disk fails, the exact data is available on the second disk.

The mirror disk does not have to be located in the same place as the first disk. If it is in a different building then the data is still protected from disaster such as from fire or terrorist attack.

RAID (Redundant Array of Inexpensive Disks) is a fault tolerant system which uses a set of two or more disk drives instead of one disk to store data. By using two disks to store the same data, a fault in a disk is less likely to affect the system.

case study 3
▶ Porsche cars move to online backup

Porsche store vehicle and warranty information as well as customer information. They have recently moved from traditional tape storage to online backup. Tapes used to be stored off-site, so that in the event of a problem, most historic information was safe. But more recent data, that had not yet been transferred, was vulnerable. If a fire, or similar disaster were to have happened on a Friday, then Monday, Tuesday, Wednesday and Thursday's tapes would still be on-site.

The new storage technology will reduce manual error as previously staff have had to swap tapes over.

1. How could the manual swapping of tapes have led to error?
2. What is meant by online backup?

Batch processing systems

Batch mode is a common method of computer processing used when there are large numbers of similar transactions. It is used when processing such systems as a payroll or utility billing which are run at regular intervals, perhaps once a day, once a week, once a month or once a quarter. All the data to be input is collected together before being processed in a single operation.

In a typical batch processing system all the transactions are batched together and entered offline into a transaction file which is then sorted into the same order as the records in the master file. The records from the transaction file are merged with the corresponding records of the master file and the updated records are stored in a new master file.

The old master file is called the **father file** and the new version the **son**. This method of processing produces automatic backup since, if the son file were to become corrupted, it could be recreated by running the update program once again using the same transaction file with the father file to restore the son file.

When the son is in turn used to create a new version it becomes the father and the old father becomes the **grandfather**. The number of generations that are kept should be decided upon. Obviously it will be necessary to keep the transaction files as well as they will be needed in the process to restore the up-to-date master file.

Activity 2

Produce a leaflet on appropriate methods of backup for a new student of ICT A level who has just bought a home PC. Explain in your leaflet:

- the need for a backup strategy
- appropriate methods of backing up
- the hardware choices available for backup and the merits and costs of each (research on the Internet).

SUMMARY

- **A full backup occurs when all the data stored on a medium, such as hard disk is copied to another medium such as magnetic tape.**
- **A periodic backup occurs at set time periods.**
- **A differential backup is a variation of full backup where one tape is created that contains a full image of the system and subsequent tapes receive copies of the files which are different or were updated after the image backup.**

- An **incremental (or modified) backup** only stores changes that have been made since the last backup.
- The following factors need to be considered when establishing a backup strategy:
  - the value of the data
  - the appropriate medium for backup storage
  - the rotation of the backup media
  - the frequency of backup
  - the use of a log to record transactions – a transaction log is a record of all the transactions that have taken place since the last backup occurred
  - the use of full and/or incremental backups
  - the number of generations of backup that should be kept
  - the method of recovery
  - how the physical security of backup medium is to be assured within the organisation
  - whether to use a remote backup service
  - who will be responsible for the backing up of the system and restoring any lost data.
- Different strategies are needed for backing up program and data files.

  Using a remote backup service replaces the need to:
  - keep backup tapes securely
  - label backup tapes carefully
  - train staff
  - practise recovery procedures
  - test backup regularly.
- Recovering lost data
  - Files must be restored in the correct order.
  - Alternative hardware must be available if required. An organisation may have a contract with specialist companies that provide emergency hardware. In the short term it may be necessary to work from another location.
  - Backups of data and software must be readily available.
  - Staff must be trained in what to do.

Chapter 15 Questions

1 A computer repair service uses different information systems to keep records of clients, current jobs and parts held in stock. These are accessible from a number of workstations, on a Local Area Network, which are used by several employees.

Describe **four** factors that need to be addressed in forming a suitable backup strategy that the company can use. (8)

ICT5 June 2004

2 A local college with over 5,000 students has classes from 9 a.m. until 9 p.m. Monday to Friday. Software installation and management of network users on the college's computer network are generally carried out during the holidays. Student files however are changing every day.

Suggest a suitable backup strategy for this system, explaining:

- what should be backed up
- when the back-up should take place
- how frequent the back-up should be
- what media should be used, and
- where the back-up media should be stored. (10)

3 A local council has a local area network at the town hall that is connected to the Internet so that residents can pay their council tax online. Files are created, deleted and amended every day.

The council has a back-up strategy. Every evening from Monday to Friday at 6.00 p.m. the network is shut down and a global backup is made of every file stored on the file server.

The council has five backup tapes named Monday, Tuesday, Wednesday, Thursday and Friday. The Monday tape is used on Mondays and so on. The town hall is closed on Saturdays and Sundays.

State, with a reason for each, **four** improvements that could be made to the backup strategy. (8)

4 A bank uses batch processing to update bank accounts following transactions. A new transaction file is created every day and used to update the files every evening. The transaction file tapes are clearly labelled and kept for a week before being reused.

a) Why is it important to label the tapes? (1)

b) Explain why the tapes are not used until the following week. (2)

16 Software

► Choosing a software package to use on a home computer is usually relatively simple. There are many magazines and websites that review different software packages, describe features, comment on ease of use and make recommendations.

They will often provide further details such as minimum processor speed, hard disk and memory requirements and the results of benchmark tests.

Choosing the appropriate software to use within an organisation is a much more complex task. There might be hundreds of workstations throughout the organisation being used for a wide range of tasks by hundreds of different users.

External consultants may be employed to carry out formal evaluation of possible software packages so that the one that most closely fits the client's needs can be identified.

Establishing clients' needs

The first step that needs to be taken is to establish the end-user requirements by finding out what is essential and what, though not essential, is desirable so that suitable software can be investigated. The capabilities of the software will need to be evaluated and then the needs matched with the capabilities. This process is similar to the investigation stage of your coursework for ICT3 and ICT6.

An **initial meeting** between the client and the supplier is essential for the supplier to understand the constraints placed upon the purchase of the new software. The supplier needs to demonstrate that they have a clear understanding of the client's needs. At this stage, at the start of the process, both parties must establish clear criteria for software choice. These criteria need to be agreed between the two parties.

Once the criteria have been established a process of **observation** of the current system is undertaken so that the tasks that are carried out can be evaluated and it can be seen where the current system works and where it doesn't work.

The exact type of data that is currently used can be identified by studying the **documentation** of the system.

To establish the end-user requirements, a detailed investigation will be needed; it should involve **interviewing** the different end-users at different points in the system to get their perspective on the current system. A large system is likely to have a number of end-users, each of whom carries out a different task. For example, a stock system for a mail order retailer will be used by clerks making orders in response to telephone requests; others will enter data as deliveries of products are made; in the warehouse employees will record the dispatch of products; the sales manager will receive reports about the sale of different products.

The process of investigation should highlight whether or not the organisation has realistic aims that can be met, as well as find out what is important to the user. The investigation should establish the nature of the systems that are already in place. This will allow the current starting position that is to be developed to be clearly seen.

The budget restrictions should be made clear at the start of the process. If this is not done, much time can be wasted exploring solutions that are not financially viable. In such situations, wrong software choices could be very costly. It is important firstly to determine the needs of the user and which aspects of the software type are most important to them. This could be a time-consuming and costly process that, as described above, involves a number of people. It is a process that should not be skimped.

Evaluating software

If a number of commercial packages already exist that might fit the needs of the user there will be a number of sources of information on which to base a decision.

For many packages there will be reports available, either in the ICT press or in trade magazines. Very often such publications will carry out extensive evaluations of new software, carrying out benchmark testing and even comparing a range of similar packages. These should prove a useful starting point in making a software choice.

Many software producers will provide a CD-ROM with a version of the software that a prospective user can use for a limited time period for evaluation purposes. An alternative method used for distributing software for evaluation purposes is via the Internet.

The capabilities of the available software packages should be looked into and compared with the user's agreed needs so that the best match can be found. It may be appropriate to talk to some existing users of the software application being considered. Seeing the software in action can help to highlight problems that might occur and give insight into its suitability for the prospective organisation.

Of course, no suitable software may exist, in which case alternative solutions need to be sought (see Chapter 21).

Manufacturers will usually provide demonstrations of the system in use. These may be provided at an organisation which is already using the software.

Many colleges are currently considering purchasing VLEs (virtual learning environments) to allow teachers to manage students' learning through ICT in an organised way. One of the first things that an ICT manager in such an institution would do would be to visit colleges that had installed one of the VLEs that are already on the market. By questioning the users and observing the software in use, the ICT manager would gain useful information on which to base a purchase decision.

When major applications are being considered, personnel from the software producers may provide a prototype implementation that is configured to the specific needs of the prospective user. This would provide the opportunity to see the system in action in the user's environment.

A range of alternative software solutions should be investigated and objectively compared.

The evaluation process should match the software capabilities to the client need. It must establish which software packages are available that will be able to complete the client's task. It is necessary to draw up software evaluation criteria that will be used to help decide which product to use. The criteria used in any particular situation will be wide ranging and will enable an objective choice to be made. The criteria that have been decided upon with the client are applied to each software package in turn and the performance of each recorded. Obviously some criteria will be more important than others, so **weightings** are applied to the criteria accordingly.

Software evaluation criteria

The requirement specification will be agreed by the user and the developer. The evaluation criteria will need to be based on this specification. The following evaluation criteria are likely to be used.

Functionality

The term functionality of software means what it actually does. The more features it offers the greater its functionality. Functions of a word processor might include mail merge, thesaurus and grammar check. However, it is important that the functions the software supports are the ones that the organisation needs. The software must provide all the functions present in the system that is being replaced. There is no advantage in using software that has a number of irrelevant functions because their presence could confuse the user.

Performance

The performance of a particular software application is determined by how well it carries out the required features. **Benchmark tests** are often used to measure performance. Examples of such tests could include the speed of locating a record or the file storage requirements. The new system should be more efficient than the one it is replacing; for example the time taken to produce a particular report using the new software should not be longer than with the current system. It is important to establish whether or not the software can cope with the demands of the user.

A benchmark is a standard set of computer tasks designed to allow measurements to be made of computer performance. These tasks can be used to compare the performance of different software or hardware. Examples of tasks are: how long it takes to copy a 1 Mb file across a network, how many pages can be printed in one minute and how long it takes to save 1000 database records to disk. (Taken from the BCS Glossary)

Usability and human–machine interface

It is important that the software interface is suitable for the intended user and use. In most cases, an interface should be intuitive to use, consistent with clear and appropriate help facilities. An application might have all the functionality required but might prove to be very difficult to use and learn. If a system is not easy to use then users may not continue to use it. For a beginner it would need to be very user-friendly with clear screens and instructions. If it is to be used by more experienced ICT users shortcuts would need to be available.

Compatibility

Ideally new software should be compatible with the software currently in use; that is, the new software should be able to read data files from the old software. If it is not, ways will need to be found to transfer data. Many everyday packages, such as spreadsheet, graphics or DTP, are produced as compatible units. Very often the operating system that is used will influence the choice of software as some packages are only produced to run under particular operating systems. If it is similar to the existing software little training will be needed, otherwise extensive retraining might be needed.

Transferability of data

The ease with which data from current files could be transferred into those for the new system is an important factor. This could be achieved easily or there might be a need for major data conversion which could prove unwieldy or expensive. In the worst case, all the data could have to be re-entered.

Robustness

Robustness refers to the extent to which the software will run using realistic volumes of data, supporting the required number of users day after day without crashing or causing errors. It is important to establish how well the software has been tested. If it has a wide user base it is likely that errors will already have been highlighted and corrected. If it has been used in circumstances similar to those required by the new system its robustness can be easily assessed. It is crucial that the software can be shown to function effectively using the volume of data that is likely to be used.

User support

The kind of support that is provided will need to meet the likely requirements from users. Initial training may be needed when the new software is first used. Once the system is established for the client, the software suppliers are likely to provide occasional troubleshooting support when needed. Many software publishers provide a telephone helpline for registered users. If adequate support is not automatically provided, the cost of acquiring it must be considered. This might involve extra training for the ICT technicians within the organisation.

The quality of documentation may vary considerably between different software packages. The full range of users' needs to be considered: from the beginner to the personnel providing technical backup within the organisation.

There are likely to be books, videos or training courses available for widely used software.

Resource requirements

It is important to consider whether the software will run on the existing hardware platform or whether new equipment will be required. The processor speed, main memory and disk space requirements will need careful consideration. Whether or not it will run under the current operating system is a crucial factor to be considered.

Another resource to be considered is the personnel needed to run the new system within the client's organisation.

The choice of particular software might result in the need for changes to other currently used software as well as any software that is intended to be replaced. Some choices might result in further staff being required to run the new software. The costs of retraining current staff to use new packages must be considered.

Upgradability

Whether or not upgraded versions of the software are likely to become available in the future could be an important factor. The credibility of the company that produces the software will be crucial.

Portability

It is important to ensure that adequate filters are provided to allow data to be transferred to other systems in the way that the system demands. It may be necessary for data to be able to be exported to other software. A company may use other software to create reports, so the package must have export functions.

Cost/benefit

Cost will always be a very important factor when deciding upon software purchase. The wider implications of a particular choice need to be explored. For instance, whether additional hardware and other associated software will need to be bought.

It is important to establish how long it would take to recoup the financial costs of installing the new system. The client needs to see a good return on their investment that is measurable, for example, through greater efficiency or added functionality that reduces costs.

Considerations such as training needs and file conversion costs must also be included. The development cost of installing the new software will also need to be considered. Different licensing arrangements will need to be explored as well as the software manufacturer's attitude to upgrades. Some companies provide these free while the cost of others can be a major expenditure.

Other considerations

The supplier of the software must be chosen with care. A well-established company with a good range of products on the market that are well used and well supported has greater credibility than a new, untried company. If a company does not appear to have a stable future any software currently produced may cease to be supported or developed if the company were to cease to trade. Even if it were bought out by a larger company, a particular software application may not be supported under the new management.

Activity 1

A large market research company is considering several different software packages in order to assist with the analysis of data collected on behalf of clients.

A table has been drawn up to list the different categories of evaluation criteria together with reasons for the choice. The criteria have been left for you to fill in.

Criterion	Reason
	The software will have to provide statistical functions so that the research company can produce the relevant analysis
	The company will be dealing with vast quantities of data and the software will have to cope without crashing
	The company will require results to be produced in a reasonable time so the software package must be more efficient than current methods.
User support	The company will require access to initial training, as well as help with troubleshooting.
	The company may use other software to present the results of their analysis and so this package must have an export function
	Any existing data the company holds that is useful for analysis should be available to the new software package without the need for re-entering data
	The company cannot guarantee ICT literacy level of end user; they want old and new employees to be able to use the package quickly
	The software will have to be of use for a significant length of time so the company will not need to have further investment in the same area in the future
	The company has hardware systems in place and the new package will have to function effectively with these
	The company may be prepared to pay extra in order to gain extra functionality

(based on an AQA ICT question 2002)

Activity 2

a) Josh has details of his family tree stored in a paper file. He is now thinking of storing all the information on computer and has found three possible software packages that he thinks might be suitable. He has never used any software like this before. State three evaluation criteria that he might use saying why they are appropriate.

b) A local branch of a political party wishes to design an illustrated newsletter, which will include contributions from two local councillors and their MP. There are a number of packages that they could purchase and they have to decide which one is best. Describe three evaluation criteria they might use saying why they are appropriate. (The criteria chosen in part (b) must not have been used in part (a).)

Evaluation report

When an evaluation has been completed, a report is written to present the overall findings of the evaluation for the senior management who commissioned the evaluation. The management would then make a decision based on the information provided. The function of the report is to document how the different software packages available performed against the criteria set and how they would measure up to the expectations of the organisation. The findings of the report should enable a decision to be made.

After explaining the purpose of the particular report by defining the user requirements, the report should include:

- A summary of the **methodology** used to produce the report detailing how the information was gathered and how the evaluation had been carried out, so that the clients understand what has been done. This would include a description of all benchmark tests undertaken.
- The report should show which packages were being considered as possible solutions. It should also detail the required functionality that was being checked for in the evaluation.
- The **actual evaluation**, where the appropriate evaluation criteria are discussed. The results of the evaluation for each of the packages should be described with the advantages and disadvantages of each solution clearly laid out. This would show how well each system compared to the agreed criteria; a scoring system could be used.
- **Recommendations** for purchase of the software that best fits the client's needs would then be made based on the evaluation.
- The recommendations would be backed up with **justifications**, explaining how the recommendations were arrived at, based on the evidence given in the report.

case study 1 ▶ College timetabling

A large college wishes to replace its timetabling software that allocates staff and students to classes. The current software is proving inadequate as the college has been growing in size and the number of subjects taught has increased substantially since the current software was installed.

As there is no one on the college staff who has sufficient expertise, the senior management have employed consultants to help them in their choice. The management team meet with the consultants to agree the requirements of the system. The management team are keen that the consultants understand exactly what they require. The consultants ask many questions so that they can get a clear picture of exactly what the new software will be required to do. They then carry out further investigations to help them understand exactly what is needed.

A few weeks later the consultants provide the management team with a summary of the requirements. This contains a list of the most important features that the new software should have, which include:

- Data must be quick and easy to enter with the minimum likelihood for errors to be made.
- The software must allocate students to classes at a speed twice as fast as the current software achieves.
- Clear, easy to understand timetables and other reports must be produced within an accepted time.
- The software must be able to cope with the allocation of 2,000 students to up to 6 different classes from 45 subjects without crashing.
- During the time of year when timetabling takes place, there must be call-in help available within 12 hours if the software fails in any way.
- No extra staffing should be required to run the system.

The management team, with some minor changes, agree the requirements with the consultants and together they decide upon the weightings of the listed evaluation criteria; i.e. putting them in order of importance.

The consultants then establish what software is available that carries out timetabling tasks. They carry out all the tests that have been agreed on each of the software packages, and carefully record the results. They also record their findings in respect to all the other evaluation criteria.

Once they have recorded all their findings they decide which software package to recommend. No package exactly meets all the agreed criteria, so they choose the one providing the best match, taking into account the evaluation criteria weightings that they agreed initially. They then produce an evaluation report which they take back to the college's management team.

The team agree to their recommendation and purchase and install the new software. They are very happy with the chosen software.

1. What is the purpose of the initial meeting between the management team and the consultants?
2. What form could the 'further investigations' carried out by the consultants have taken?
3. For each of the criteria described in the case study, state which category (functionality, performance, usability etc.) it falls into.
4. Give three more evaluation criteria that would be appropriate for this application.
5. Describe what the consultants would include in their final report.

Worked exam question

A large college requires a new Management Information System to be created, which will replace several separate departmental systems. This new system will be used to provide information to external agencies, as well as statistical information to college staff. A small software company has won the contract to supply this software, although it has no previous experience of working with educational establishments.

a) The college and the software company feel that it is important to discuss the requirements of the system.
Explain why this meeting is important for both parties. (3)

b) Evaluation criteria have been established by the two parties to compare the possible solutions that the software company could produce. These criteria include 'cost-benefit' and 'compatibility'.

i) Explain why 'cost-benefit' is a useful criterion in this situation. (2)

ii) Explain why 'compatibility' is a useful criterion in this situation. (2)

iii) Name and describe **two** other criteria that would be useful in this situation, stating why each one is useful. (6)

c) A report is produced for the college that compares various possible solutions. Name **four** sections that are likely to form part of the report, stating the purpose of each section. (8)

ICT5 January 2005

▶ **EXAMINER'S GUIDANCE**

The answer to part (a) can be found earlier in the chapter in the section ***Establishing clients' needs.***
Possible answers to (b) (i) and (ii) could be:

'The college needs to see a good return on investment that is measurable (1) e.g. through more efficiency or through added functionality that reduces costs (1)' and 'The college will have systems in place (hardware and/or software) (1) and the new package will have to function effectively with these (1)'.

In part (iii) you will be given one mark for naming a relevant criterion and two for a reasonable description. You need two criteria.

One criterion could be **performance**. You could give the reason as: 'the college will require results to be produced in a reasonable time (1) so the software package must be more efficient than current methods' (1).

Other possible criteria could be functionality, robustness, support or transferability. Write a sentence for each – remember you need to gain two marks in your justification.

Part c) has eight marks. The first four marks come from remembering the four sections (methodology, results, recommendation and justification). Then you must give the purpose of each.

For example 'The methodology (1) – how the report has been derived (1)'.

Complete the answer for the remaining three sections.

Activity 3

- Establish evaluation criteria for choosing a **search engine**.
- Put your criteria in order of importance.
- Carry out an evaluation using three different search engines.
- Produce a report giving your recommendations. Make sure that your report includes the sections outlined on pages 186–189.

SUMMARY

- **First the clients' needs must be clearly established.**
- **Software evaluation should address the following criteria:**
  - **functionality**
  - **performance**
  - **usability and the human-computer interface**
  - **compatibility**
  - **data transferability**
  - **robustness**
  - **user support**
  - **resource requirements**
  - **upgradability**
  - **portability**
  - **cost-benefit**
  - **supplier.**
- **In choosing which software to buy, companies must establish their needs and find software that satisfies these needs.**
- **An evaluation report should include:**
  - **a summary of the methodology used**
  - **the actual evaluation**
  - **recommendations for purchase.**
- **The recommendations must be backed up with justifications.**

Chapter 16 Questions

1 A large market research company is considering several different software packages in order to assist with the analysis of data collected on behalf of clients. Give **three** criteria that should be considered when evaluating these software packages. For each criterion explain why it may be important to this company. (9)

ICT5 June 2002

2 A car importing company has decided to purchase a new ICT product tracking system. The company has employed a consultant to help them to make their choice. The consultant will produce an evaluation report for the company.

Describe **three** sections that should be included in the evaluation report. (9)

3 An employment agency currently holds information about job seekers and job vacancies on an information system that is several years old. As a consultant, you have been asked to help this company look at alternative software solutions.

Discuss what you would do in order to produce a report for this company. Your discussion should include:

- how you will establish your client's needs
- the criteria you will use to evaluate possible solutions
- how you will match software capabilities to your client's needs
- the content of the evaluation report you will write for your client.

The quality of Written Communication will be assessed in your answer. *(20)*

ICT5 January 2004

17 Database management concepts

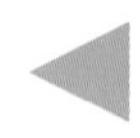

The British Computer Society gives the following definition for a database: *A database is a collection of data items and links between them, structured in a way that allows it to be accessed by a number of different applications programs.*

BCS Glossary of Terms 11th edition.

In other words, a database is simply the data.

The software package that allows the user to access the data is the database management system (DBMS).

The database management system

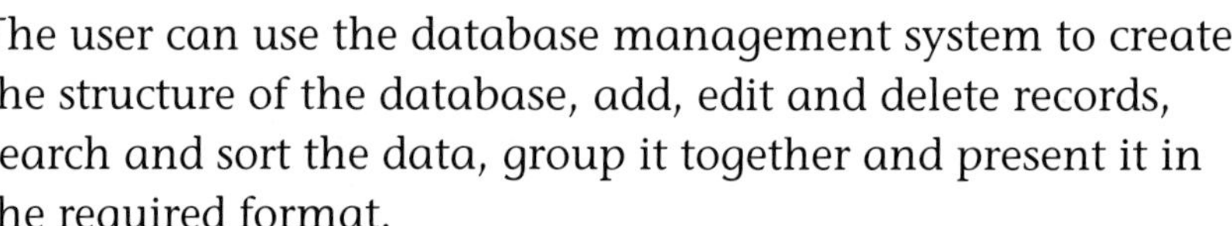

The user can use the database management system to create the structure of the database, add, edit and delete records, search and sort the data, group it together and present it in the required format.

The DBMS usually provides a user-friendly interface and works automatically without the users needing to know how it works. It can search for required data, perform calculations using the data, update the data and carry out other tasks such as maintaining indexes.

The DBMS will support a number of different user applications. The DBMS allows user queries to be made, usually using either SQL (structured query language) or QBE (query by example) to communicate with the DBMS.

A DBMS stores the data separately from the programs that use the data; thus the programs and the data are independent of one another.

There has been a huge growth in the use of database management systems over recent years. A number of DBMS packages can be bought for use on a stand-alone PC such as Microsoft Access, Lotus Approach, Paradox or Oracle. Multi-user systems, where a number of users, linked to a network, can access the same data are widely used in business. In such a system the data can all be stored on a central file server or the data can be spread over several databases held on different computers. (This is a *distributed database* – see page 224.)

The functions of a DBMS

The functions of a DBMS are summarised as follows:

- **Database definition**. As most commercial databases are relational, the structure of the database will be made up of tables and the relationships between the tables. A specific language, data definition language (DDL) is used to specify the database structure.
- **Data storage, retrieval and update**. The DBMS allows users to store, retrieve and update information as easily as possible. These users are not necessarily computer experts and do not need to be aware of the internal structure of the database or how to set it up. Data from the database can be retrieved by using queries.
- **Creation and maintenance of the data dictionary**. This is a file containing the details of the structure of the database including details of tables, fields, field types, field lengths and any other characteristics.
- **Managing the facilities for sharing the database**. Many databases need a multi-access facility. Two or more people must be able to access the database simultaneously and to update records without causing a problem.
- **Backup and recovery**. Information in the database must not be lost in the event of system failure.
- **Security**. The DBMS must check user passwords and allow appropriate privileges.

The role of the Database Administrator (DBA)

The database administrator is the person in an organisation who is responsible for the structure and control of the data in the organisation's database.

The DBA will:

- be involved in the design of the database.
- maintain a data dictionary.
- publish naming conventions for elements of the database, such as field and table names. It is important that all users of the database follow the same convention to avoid confusion.
- carry out any changes to the database requested by users, such as adding additional fields.
- inform database users of any changes affecting them.
- monitor the performance of the database. If there are a large number of users, the response time might become unacceptably low.
- make appropriate changes to the database structure if such problems arise.
- provide appropriate help and training.

- allocate passwords to users and protect confidential information by implementing and maintaining appropriate access privileges that restrict what data an individual user can access and/or change. These are necessary to prevent inexperienced users from mistakenly changing or deleting data as well as for purposes of data security.
- set up reports for users; the administrator will have a detailed knowledge of the DBMS package and so will be able to create reports that provide the user with the information required in a clear format.
- manage backup procedures including testing that the backup is working.
- manage restoring data if corruption does occur.
- archive data and carry out any year end and other special housekeeping tasks.

Table name	Column name	Column type	Column note
auto_inc	column0	int(8)	Primary key
clients	blob1	longblob	
	blob2	mediumblob	
	blob3	longblob	
	blob4	longblob	
	profit	decimal(8,2)	
	customer_type	enum('douteux','normal','grand_compte')	
	last_modif	timestamp(14)	
	id_client	varchar(10) binary	
	id_employe	varchar(10)	
	nom_client	varchar(20)	
	nf_contact	varchar(15)	
	pr_contact	varchar(15)	
	tel	varchar(12)	
	adresse	varchar(22)	
	ville	varchar(12)	
	dept	char(2)	
	toto	double(8,2)	
	stamp	timestamp(14)	
	tata	date	
	tutu	enum('customer','prospect','beta-tester')	
	NumCol	bigint(8)	
clients2	photo	longblob	
	id_client	varchar(10)	Primary key
	id_employe	varchar(10)	
	nom_client	varchar(20)	
	nf_contact	varchar(15)	
	pr_contact	varchar(15)	
	tel	varchar(12)	

Figure 17.1 Data dictionary

case study 1
▶ Interview with Kim, database administrator

Kim is the DBA for a college administrative database. The database includes data on admissions, exam entries and attendance and is used by teachers, tutors, senior management and a range of administrative personnel. Data is used to produce exam entry information, statistical returns for the local skills council for funding purposes as well as for many internal purposes.

An interview was carried out with Kim to find out what her job involves. This is a summary.

How much time do you spend working on the database?

90–95 per cent of my week is spent working on a database, either our main database, unit_e, or one of our in-house databases. The other part of my week is spent liaising with staff and taking part in meetings.

Can you list tasks in a typical week?

I don't really have a typical week except in very general terms, for example, writing reports, analysing or amending procedures, maintaining existing databases. I have a weekly tasking meeting with the vice-principals and the bursar.

How many users of the system are there?

There are over 80 users who have some access to unit_e at the moment.

What different access rights do different categories of users have?

We can assign 'select', 'insert', 'update' and 'delete' rights to individual objects or tables. We assign rights to groups: users have the rights of the group we put them in. We have a read-only group that most college staff are a member of; other groups have additional rights on particular objects.

Do you have a training role?

Each new user needs some training as unit_e is not a very user-friendly application. Users need to know how course and class codes are structured and require a basic knowledge of how to search a database before they can really benefit from the system.

Others, who use the system as a main part of their job, will need more detailed training that ensures that data is recorded in a consistent manner. Specific processes that users may have to carry out frequently are documented in training documents so that individuals can refer to them as necessary.

Do you write ad hoc reports for users?

Yes, usually for management. For example, I have just produced a report on the destinations of students on leaving college, broken down by the school they came to us from. A requirement will be discussed and its potential assessed for making it available to everyone. If it will serve as a useful tool for the majority of users it will be made generally available via the unit_e reporting application.

1. What other tasks are often carried out by a database administrator?
2. List ten reports that are likely to be produced by the application.
3. What is meant by the term *ad hoc* report?
4. Why is it necessary for Kim to meet with the college bursar and vice-principals every week?
5. The college also employs a data entry clerk, Mary, whose task is to enter details of new students and other changes to the database.
   a) What access rights to student data would you expect Mary to have?
   b) What training would Mary have required when she joined the college?

Advantages of storing data in a well structured database

Organising data in a well structured relational database brings a number of advantages over older, traditional individual file-based systems.

- **Data independence**
  The data and the programs using the data are stored separately. Any changes to the structure of a database, for example adding a field or a table, will not affect any of the programs that access the data. In a file-based system, a minor change in a file structure may require a considerable amount of reprogramming to all the programs that access that file.
- **Data consistency**
  When the database is well structured, each data item is stored only once, however many applications it is used for. There is no danger of an item, such as an employee's address, being updated in one place and not in another. If this happened the data would not be consistent.
- **No data redundancy**
  Redundancy occurs when data is duplicated unnecessarily. In a flat file-based system, the same information may be held on several different files, wasting space and making updating more difficult.
- **More information available to users**
  In a database system, all information is stored together centrally. Authorised users have access to all this information. In a file-based system data is held in separate files in different departments, sometimes on incompatible systems.
- **Ease of use**
  The DBMS provides easy-to-use queries that enable users to obtain instant answers. In a file-based system a query would have to be specially written by a programmer.
- **Greater data integrity of data**
  It is important that the data stored in a database is maintained so that it is as correct as possible. A range of measures can be taken to ensure the integrity of the data stored in a database. Validation checks can be built-in to check that only sensible data can be entered into the database. For example, a range check could be set up for the date of birth of a new student in a school to make sure

that the student's age is within appropriate limits. Checks, such as parity and checksums, should be used to make sure that stored data has not become corrupted. All these checks were studied in the AS modules.

- **Greater data security**
  The DBMS will ensure that only authorised users are allowed access to the data. Different users can have different access privileges, depending on their needs. In a file-based system using a number of files it is difficult to control access. Relational databases provide different methods of database security.

  The simplest method is to set a password for opening the database. Once set, a password must be entered whenever the database is opened. Only users who type the correct password will be allowed to open the database. The password will be encrypted so that it can't be accessed simply by reading the database file. Once a database is open, all the features are available to the user. For a database on a stand-alone computer, setting a password is normally sufficient protection.

  A more flexible method of database security is called user-level security, which is similar to the sort of security found on networks. Users must type a username and password when they load the DBMS. The database administrator will allocate users to a group. For example, in Microsoft Access there are two default groups: Admin (administrators) and Users. Additional groups can be defined. Which group a user is in will determine what level of access they have. For example, some users may be able to see some fields such as name and address but not others such as financial details.

  User-level security is essential where users can legitimately access some parts of a database but not those parts which contain sensitive data.

Data consistency: a data item will have the same value whatever application program is being used. In a well structured relational database, this is achieved by storing every data item only once.

Data integrity: the data that is stored in the database is reasonable as it has not been accidentally or maliciously altered.

Data redundancy: data that is duplicated unnecessarily.

Data independence: data and programs are stored separately. Changes to the structure of the data (for example, by the addition of an extra field in a table) do not result in all programs having to be rewritten.

case study 2

A company sells many of its goods through door-to-door salesmen. Each salesman has details of his customers stored in a file. Some of the fields stored in the file are shown in figure 17.2.

Forename	Surname	Address 1	Address 2	Post Code	Phone	Last visit	Value last sale
Stephen	Hopkins	22 The Copse	Hightown	PL3 4FR	879654	22/05/03	223.45
Susan	Carville	15 High Street	Kenton	PL4 2FF	445565	25/03/03	176.34
Philip	Higgins	253 London Rd	Hightown	PL3 4FT	809745	12/05/03	87.50
Paul	Fryett	1 Maple Lane	Hightown	PL3 6TG	864351	12/05/03	104.00
Mohammed	Hadawi	57 Greenhill Lane	Kenton	PL4 5RT	476765	09/06/03	338.79
Hamish	MacGregor	12 Wickham Way	Kenton	PL4 6TY	879804	17/04/02	2.50

Figure 17.2 Details of customers (held by salesman)

The central accounts department deals with the billing of customers. They make use of another file, some of the fields of which are shown in figure 17.3.

Invoice Number	Forename	Surname	Address 1	Address 2	County	Post Code	Value	Amount Outstanding
2003/34	Phillip	Higgins	253 London Rd	Hightown	Berks	PL3 4FT	87.50	87.50
2003/35	Mohammed	Hadawi	57 Greenhill Lane	Kenton	Berks	PL4 5RT	67.00	0.0
2003/189	Mohammed	Hadawi	57 Greenhill Lane	Kenton	Berks	PL4 5RT	338.79	338.79

Figure 17.3 Customer accounts (held by accounts department)

Storing data in this way, in two separate files involves data redundancy as the customer name and address are stored in two different places, leading to wasted space. Storing the data in this way can also lead to data inconsistency. For example, if the salesman is informed of a change of address for Philip Higgins, he can make a change to the address field. It is quite possible that he forgets to inform the accounts department, so that Philip Higgins' address is not updated on the accounts department. When such an event occurs, and the same data item is stored differently in two different places, data inconsistency occurs.

- The accounts department of an organisation maintains a file that is used every month to produce payments for all employees. The human resources department maintains a personnel file that stores details of all employees. It is updated when new staff join the organisation or when current employees are regraded. What possible data inconsistencies could arise because these two files are maintained?
- Consider inconsistencies that could arise when separate files of patients are used by different departments within a hospital.

Entity relationships

Entities

An entity is an object, person or thing represented in a database. Examples of entities include CUSTOMER, EMPLOYEE, PRODUCT and ORDER.

Note:

1. Each entity will normally be represented by a table in the relational database.
2. Entity names are normally in the singular and are written in upper case, e.g. CUSTOMER and not CUSTOMERS or Customer.

Attributes

The information that is held about an entity is called its attributes. For example, for the entity, CUSTOMER, attributes might be surname, forename, address, phone number, etc. Attributes are normally stored in fields.

Entity relationships

The link between two entities is called a relationship. Diagrams showing these relationships are called **entity relationship diagrams** or ER diagrams. The diagram is

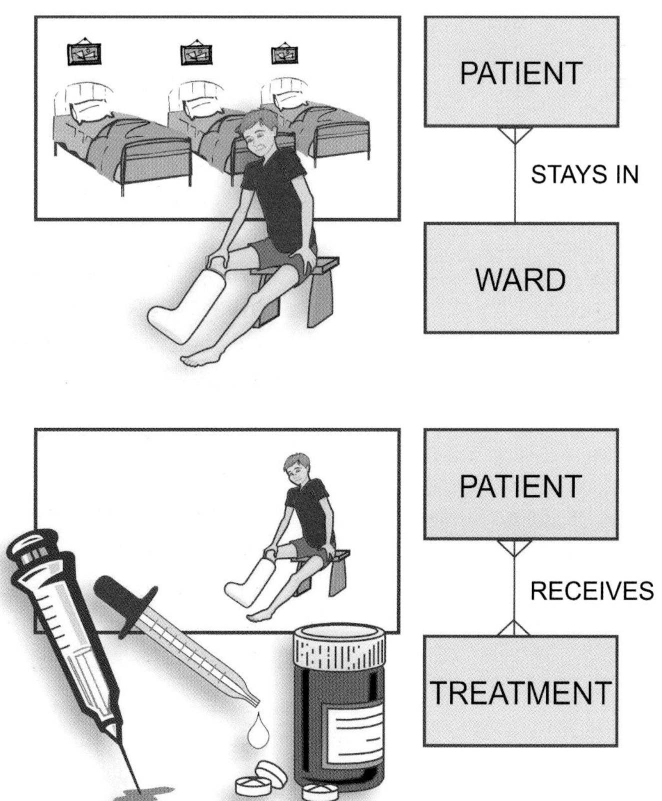

Figure 17.4 Examples of relationships

made up of entities drawn in rectangles and lines joining the entities that represent their relationships.

One-to-one, one-to-many or many-to-many

There are three types of relationship between two entities.

1:1
MAN
IS MARRIED TO
WOMAN

One-to-one (1:1)

One occurrence of the first entity is only ever associated with one occurrence of the second, e.g. one man can only be married to one woman.

1:m
MOTHER
CHILD

One-to-many (1:m, 1:*)

One occurrence of the first entity can be associated with more than one occurrence of the second entity. For example, one mother can have many children.

m:m
PATIENT
TREATMENT
m:m
STUDENT
CLASS
m:m
ORDER
PRODUCT

Many-to-many (m:m; *:*)

More than one occurrence of the first entity can be associated with many occurrences of the second entity. For example, many orders can contain many products.

Dealing with many-to-many relationships

As part of your study of relational databases at ICT AS level, you saw how the relationship between tables was made through the use of foreign keys. A foreign key is a field in one table that is the primary key of another table. Thus data can be linked between the two tables.

Figure 17.5 shows how the PET and OWNER tables from a database at a veterinary practice can be linked by the use of a foreign key.

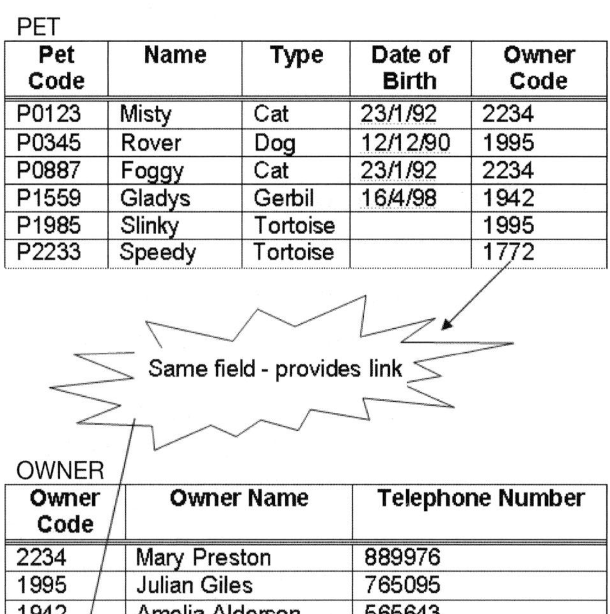

PET

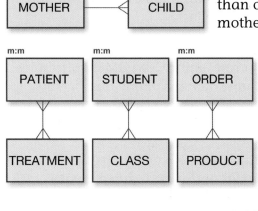

Pet Code	Name	Type	Date of Birth	Owner Code
P0123	Misty	Cat	23/1/92	2234
P0345	Rover	Dog	12/12/90	1995
P0887	Foggy	Cat	23/1/92	2234
P1559	Gladys	Gerbil	16/4/98	1942
P1985	Slinky	Tortoise		1995
P2233	Speedy	Tortoise		1772

OWNER

Owner Code	Owner Name	Telephone Number
2234	Mary Preston	889976
1995	Julian Giles	765095
1942	Amelia Alderson	565643
1772	Sally Ann Taylor	876875

Figure 17.5 Linking two tables using a foreign key

Unfortunately, foreign keys cannot be used directly to make a many-to-many link. In a relational database it is necessary to break up many-to-many relationships by creating an extra entity that will have two one-to-many links.

For example, a company maintains a database of stationery orders made for its employees. Two entities, ORDER and PRODUCT have a many-to-many relationship as an order may contain a variety of products and a product may be in a variety of orders. To implement in a relational database, an extra entity must be created, in this case named ORDER/PRODUCT that links the other two entities. The ORDER/PRODUCT table would contain the primary key fields of both the PRODUCT and the ORDER tables, thus enabling an order to have more than one product.

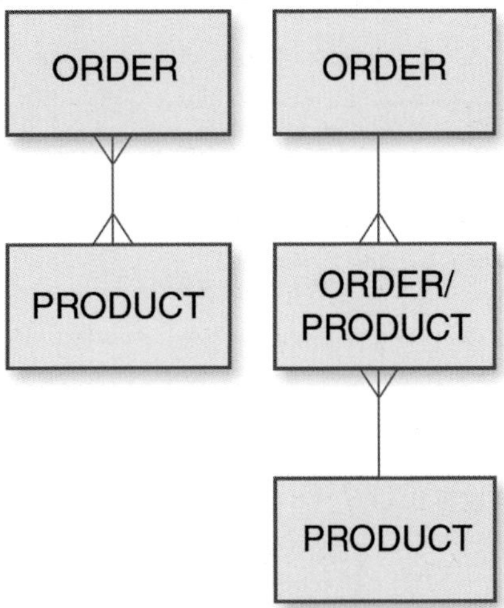

Figure 17.6 Implementing many-to-many relationships using a relational database

Database normalisation

Database normalisation is the process of breaking down complex data structures into simpler forms. It is the process of designing appropriate tables and relationships to minimise data duplication, avoid many-to-many relationships and allow efficient access and storage of data in a relational database.

The process is made up of a number of defined stages.

1. Write down all the attributes required by the system. Referring to the order form shown in figure 17.7, and listing all the attributes:

   Order Number
   Date

Customer Number
Customer Surname
Customer Forename
Customer Title
Phone Number
Item Code
Description
Quantity
Unit Cost
Total Cost

There can be any number (minimum 1) of these fields in any orders. They are called repeated fields. E.g. for one order number 12376 there will be many of these values.

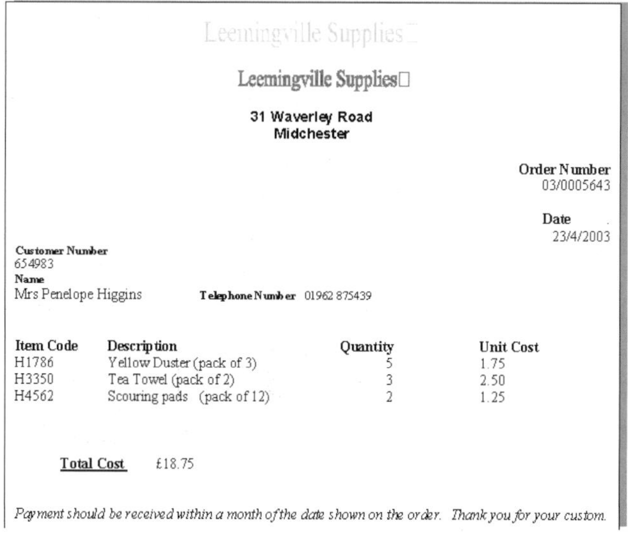

Leemingville Supplies

Leemingville Supplies

31 Waverley Road
Midchester

Order Number
03/0005643

Date
23/4/2003

Customer Number
654983
Name
Mrs Penelope Higgins **Telephone Number** 01962 875439

Item Code	Description	Quantity	Unit Cost
H1786	Yellow Duster (pack of 3)	5	1.75
H3350	Tea Towel (pack of 2)	3	2.50
H4562	Scouring pads (pack of 12)	2	1.25

Total Cost £18.75

Payment should be received within a month of the date shown on the order. Thank you for your custom.

Figure 17.7 Order form showing attributes required to be stored in database

This data structure is complex, as it contains a number of repeated fields – one order can contain a number of these fields (Item code, Description, Quantity and Unit Cost).

The process of normalisation will transform this data structure into a number of simple tables, linked through the use of foreign keys.

This unnormalised data is sometimes referred to as **Zero Normal Form (0NF)**.

2. At this stage there is only one table, the ORDER table. Fields are written in brackets after the table name, the primary key field(s) is underlined and repeated fields have a line over them.

   ORDER (Order Number, Date, Customer Number, Surname, Forename, Title, Phone Number, Item Code, Description, Quantity, Unit Cost, Total Cost)

   Order Number has been chosen as the primary key as it is a unique number for each order. A line is drawn over the four fields to indicate repeated fields. There can be many entries for these fields in one order.

3. The next stage is to remove the four repeated fields (Item Code, Description, Quantity and Unit Cost) from the ORDER table.

A new table is created called ITEMORDER as it consists of the details of the order for one item. The two tables are now:

ORDER (<u>Order Number</u>, Date, Customer Number, Surname, Forename, Title, Phone Number, Total Cost)

ITEMORDER (<u>Order Number</u>, <u>Item Code</u>, Description, Quantity, Unit Cost)

Note that the key field Order Number has been copied to ITEMORDER. If this were not done, there would be no link between the items ordered and the main order. However, Order Number by itself is not correct as a primary key for ITEMORDER as there may well be many entries in ITEMORDER for the same order.

This is now in **First Normal Form (1NF)**.

4. The **compound key** of the two fields Order Number and Item Code together form the primary key for this table. The next stage is necessary only if the first normal form produces a table with a compound key. All attributes in this table should be examined to see if they are dependent upon just one part of the compound or composite key.

   Examining the table ITEMORDER we find

   - *Order Number* is part of the key
   - *Item Code* is part of the key
   - *Description* is always the same for a given Item Code, regardless of Order Number so it is dependent on Item Code
   - *Unit Cost* is always the same for a given Item Code, regardless of Order Number so it is dependent on Item Code
   - *Quantity* relates to the Item Code but will vary for different orders – thus it is dependent on <u>both</u> Order Number and Item Code.

   We can create another table, ITEM that holds all data about a particular item. The attribute Item Code is also left in the ITEMORDER table to provide a link. The three tables are now:

   ORDER (<u>Order Number</u>, Date, Customer Number, Surname, Forename, Title, Phone Number, Total Cost)

   ITEMORDER (<u>Order Number</u>, <u>Item Code</u>, Quantity)

   ITEM (<u>Item Code</u>, Description, Unit Cost)

   This is now in **Second Normal Form (2NF)**.

5. The next stage is a 'tidying up' stage where all tables are examined for dependencies (links between attributes). It is exactly the same process as that carried out for second normal form except that it is carried out for tables without a compound key.

   Such links can be found in the ORDER table where Customer Number, Surname, Forename, Title and Phone Number are all linked, Surname, Forename, Title and

Phone Number can be said to be dependent on Customer Number. These attributes can be taken out to form a new table – CUSTOMER. Once again, Customer Number is also left in order to provide a link.

The final design of tables is as follows:

ORDER (Order Number, Date, Customer Number, Total Cost)

CUSTOMER (Customer Number, Surname, Forename, Title, Phone Number)

ITEMORDER (Order Number, Item Code, Quantity)

ITEM (Item Code, Description, Unit Cost)

This is now in **Third Normal Form (3NF)**.

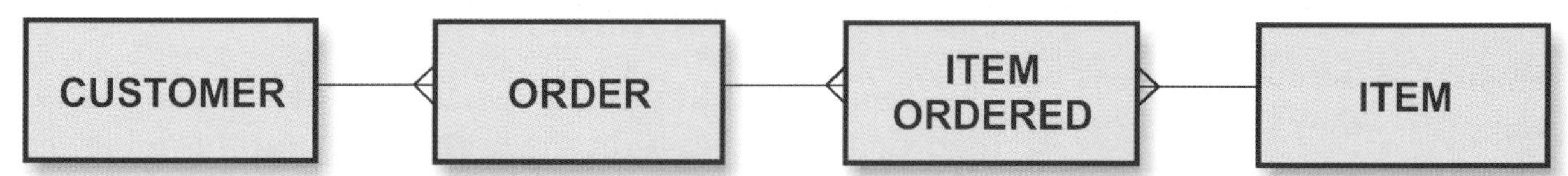

Figure 17.8 Entity relationship diagram for Order database

The database can now be created. The four tables described above should be created; the fields underlined should be set as key fields. The relationships shown in the ER diagram should be made between the tables. Note that some data duplication remains, but this is necessary redundancy as the fields are used to create links.

Activity 1

For each of the following, write out the attributes in standard notation. Normalise, showing first, second and third normal form. Then draw an entity relationship diagram.

1. A college library system: each record contains data about a student and the books they have borrowed

Student Num	Name	Address	Tutor Group	Tutor	Book#	Title	ISBN	Return Date
3124	Mary Smith	32 Hill Street Bluedale	D22	H Jones	2234	'PCs for Fun'	1 877556122	13-6-06
3124	Mary Smith	32 Hill Street Bluedale	D22	H Jones	3356	'Geography is good for You	1 655536327	21-6-06
5464	John Bloggs	27 Mill Road Grenham	D23	J Pell	5883	'Biology for Brilliance'	1 223334554	18-6-06
3369	Peter Kelly	119 Leigh Hill Grenham	D22	H Jones	4343	'French for Frivolity'	2 346798443	16-7-06
3369	Peter Kelly	119 Leigh Hill Grenham	D22	H Jones	2112	'History is Hilarious'	3 444576661	27-6-06
7765	Gary Tolan	The Heights, Blogdale	D44	M Kelly	3412	'Sociology for Slackers'	4 558787432	14-6-06

2. Scouting goods suppliers: each record contains data about different scouting goods and the available suppliers, together with the price charged.

Product No	Description level	Stock Price	Supplier no	Supplier name	Phone	Selling
80098	Small woggle	19	3345	Woggles R Us	020 3133 8675	£1.25
80099	Medium woggle	31	3345	Woggles R Us	020 3133 8675	£1.39
78780	Large woggle	67	1123	Superwoggle	020 7777 8654	£1.99
90933	Cub scarf: green	33	0093	Communiform	01962 874532	£4.99
90934	Cub scarf: red	12	0093	Communiform	01962 874532	£4.99
22123	2 man tent	4	4659	Tent City	01287 765 234	£213.75
22124	4 man tent	1	4659	Tent City	01287 765 234	£359.99

3. Employee training records: each record contains employee details and the courses they have attended.

Employee No	Name Code	Dept Code	Department	Course	Description	Venue	Venue	Date
321-93	Hilary Barr	HR	Human Resources	G1	Getting on with people	IH	In house	23-05-04
566-92	Penny Blyth	F	Finance	EX-A	Advanced Excel	PT	Pembly Tech	15-06-05
566-92	Penny Blyth	F	Finance	M2	Financial Modelling	HH	Highham House	02-01-06
566-92	Penny Blyth	F	Finance	AP2	Appraisal level 2	IH	In house	01-02-99
321-92	Neil Flynn	HR	Human Resources	G1	Getting on with people	IH	In house	23-05-04
321-92	Neil Flynn	HR	Human Resources	AP2	Appraisal level 2	IH	In house	11-12-03

4. Fine arts sales: each record contains details of a work of art being sold in auction.

Catalogue No	Title	Painter	Seller Code	Name	Phone	Reserve	Medium Code	Medium
M0134	Hill Sheep	Conrad Dale	AT1	Andy Tomkins	0151 878 6787	£250	O	Oil
P9009	Abstract	Sally Salter	CD4	Colin Drake	0121 844 8444	£1200	I	Bronze
M9843	Abstract	Conrad Dale	PT1	Primrose Tilly	01281 877666	£700	O	Oil
G6677	Tempest	Anonymous	CD4	Colin Drake	0121 844 8444	£12000	W	Water colour

Activity 2

For the document shown in figure 17.9 carry out the following tasks:

- List out the data fields in 0NF using standard notation.
- Underline the key field and draw a line over all repeating fields.
- Work through the process of normalisation, showing the data in 1st, 2nd and 3rd normal forms.

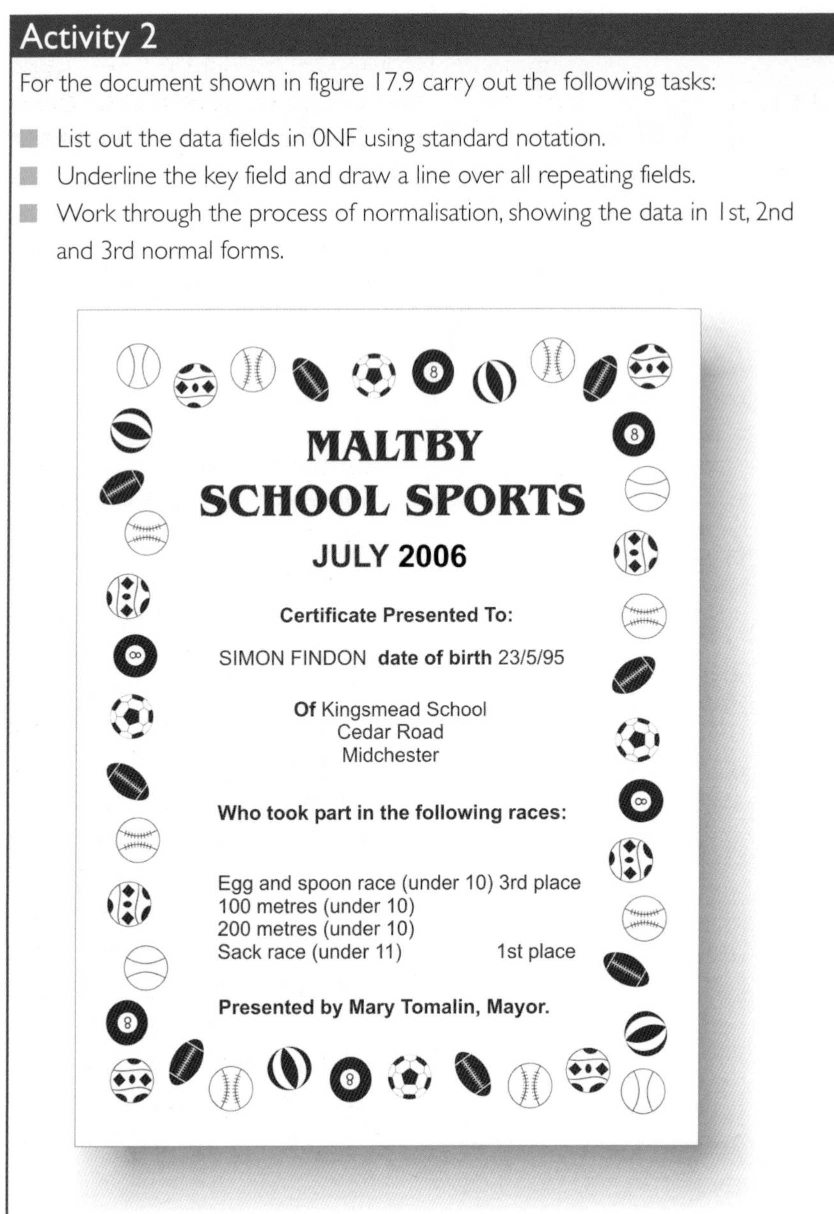

Figure 17.9 Maltby School Sports Participant Certificate

Client/server database

A client/server database is a multi-user database used over a network that has a file server. All the data for the database is stored on the file server.

The server. The server is a central computer where users of the network can store data. As the server stores a lot of data and can be accessed by several users at once, it has to have a fast processor, a large amount of RAM and a high capacity storage device, usually one or more hard drives.

The client. The client is a computer on the network that can access the data stored on the server. This computer does not need to be as powerful as the server. If a user wishes to search the database using a client computer, the request for data is sent to the server. The search of the database is carried out by the server and the records selected, i.e. those that match the search criteria sent from the client, are then sent back to the client for any local processing.

Advantages of a client/server database over non-client/server database

- A large database is an expensive resource; by making it available to a wider user base it will be used more cost effectively.
- As all the main processing is done by the server, the client workstations do not need to be so powerful and are therefore, being of a lesser specification, cheaper to buy.
- Having the data stored only in one place, on the server, rather than keeping copies on different user workstations means that consistency of data is maintained.
- Communication between client and server is minimal as only requests for data and the results of searches are communicated rather than the entire database. Department specific report formats can be held on the appropriate client workstation so that users can produce the required information in the most appropriate format.
- The centralisation of the database allows for a greater control over the data which is less likely to be accessed by the wrong people.
- Backup can be carried out centrally.

case study 3 ▶ Client/server database

Quester is an independent venture capital company, specialising in providing funds for technology-based growth companies. Founded in 1984, Quester manages over £260 million in funds, specialising in a variety of markets including software, the Internet, telecommunications, new media and healthcare.

Before launching a new venture capital trust called VCT4, Quester realised its current database would not be able to cope with the increased complexity of the business. A new, reliable and robust, database was needed to store the company's contact and investment data.

Quester opted for a client/server database so that all their staff can access the database from their network workstations; the new system is faster and more dependable and managing the data is easier and more efficient. Quester are already considering adding additional functionality to the database and the option of connectivity to palmtop computers.

SUMMARY

A **Database Management System (DBMS)** is software that accesses data in a database.

The functions of a DBMS are:

- database definition
- data storage, retrieval and update
- creation and maintenance of the data dictionary
- managing the facilities for sharing the database
- back-up and recovery
- security.

A **database administrator (DBA)** is the person in an organisation who is responsible for the structure and control of the data in the organisation's database.

A DBA's tasks include:

- designing the database
- maintaining a data dictionary
- making any changes requested by users
- monitoring the performance of the database
- dealing with queries for the user
- providing help and training for users
- allocating passwords and access privileges
- managing backup procedures for the database.

Data independence means that data and programs are stored separately. Changes to the structure of the data will not affect the programs that access the data.

Data consistency means that a data item will have the same value whatever application program is being used. In a well structured relational database, this is achieved by storing every data item only once.

Data integrity means the data that is stored in the database is reasonable as it has not been accidentally or maliciously altered.

Data redundancy means data that is duplicated unnecessarily.

An **entity** is an object, person or thing represented in a database.

The information that is held about an entity is called its **attributes**.

An **entity relationship (ER) diagram** is used to show how entities are related to each other. Relationships can be one-to-one (1:1), one-to-many (1:m, 1:*) or many-to-many (m:m; * :*)

Normalisation is a process of breaking down complex data structures into simpler forms. It consists of three stages: 1st, 2nd and 3rd normal form, each of which produces a form that is simpler than the previous one. 3rd normal form will consist of a number of simple tables, linked through the use of foreign keys.

A **client/server database** is a multi-user database. The data is stored on the network file server and can be accessed by network workstations (clients). A centrally stored database:

- is cost effective as it is a good use of resources
- maintains consistency of data
- reduces traffic between client and server
- provides better security
- can be backed up centrally.

Chapter 17 Questions

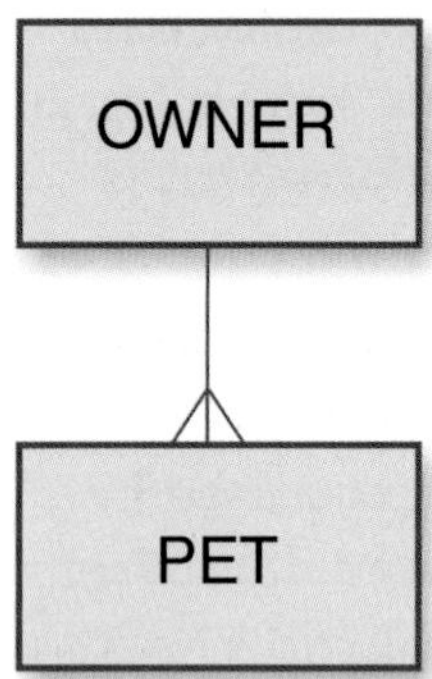

Figure 1

1 a) Name the type of relationship in the diagram above. (1)

b) Briefly describe what this relationship means. (2)

2 Computer networks are an integral part of life in the 21st century. The infrastructure must be efficient if these networks are to be of use.

a) Define the term client, as it applies to computer networks. (2)

b) Define the term server, as it applies to computer networks. (2)

c) Describe **two** advantages of a client/server database over a non-client/server database. (4)

ICT5 June 2005

3 a) Explain what is meant by a *relational database management system.* (3)

b) A successful relational database will have undergone normalisation. Describe what is meant by *normalisation.* (2)

ICT5 January 2003

4 A charitable organisation needs to coordinate all the data that it holds at several locations across the world. They have discovered that there is often conflicting data held in different sites, and time is wasted in reconciling them. A consultant has recommended that they use a relational database management system. The organisation has accepted this advice and is now advertising for the post of database administrator. In the advertisement it states that each applicant should write a supporting letter. You have decided to apply for this post.

Write a letter in support of your application, paying particular attention to:

- the role of a database administrator
- how a relational database management system can help with this problem
- the advantages of a client/server solution to this problem.

Quality of Written Communication will be assessed in your answer. (20)

ICT5 June 2003

5 As an ICT manager in a medium sized company, you have been asked to create a job specification for a database administrator.

a) Describe **three** responsibilities you would include in this specification. (6)

b) The database that this person will be in charge of is a client/server database. Describe **two** advantages of using this type of database over a non-client/server database. (4)

ICT5 June 2002

6 The secretary of a local tennis club is constructing a database to store data on members' personal details and records of attendance. He has been told that a relational database management system can assist him. Having found an article on relational database construction, he does not understand some of the terminology it contains. He asks you for advice.

a) Explain the following terms:

i) normalisation
ii) data independence
iii) data consistency
iv) data integrity. (8)

b) The secretary constructs his database structure and asks you to examine his work before he enters any data. You notice that he has not included any validation. With the aid of an example, explain why data validation is important. (3)

c) Give **three** reasons why he should consult with other members of the tennis club committee before finalising the design of the database system. (3)

ICT5 June 2002

18 Communication and information systems

Computer networks play an ever-increasing role in modern communications. It is common to find networks used in schools and colleges, doctors' and dentists' surgeries, and shops and offices of all kinds.

There are two types of network: wide area networks (WAN) and local area networks (LAN), although a network may be a mixture of both.

Public WANs such as the Internet can be accessed legally by anyone, either free or on payment of a fee. Private networks have restricted access, for example only to employees of a company.

Local Area Networks (LAN)

A LAN is a collection of computers and peripherals that is normally located in one building or site. Traditionally, the devices in a LAN have been connected together by cables, but technological developments mean that wireless LANs are now very common. At its simplest, a LAN consists of a few computers sharing some resources. The computers connected to the network in this way are called workstations or terminals. Wireless workstations connected to the network by radio waves are becoming increasingly more common.

A LAN will usually have one or more file servers – powerful, high performance computers with large disk capacity. Data is stored on the server and can be accessed from any terminal. If a printer is to be shared by all workstations, then a printer server is required; a high performance computer that manages the allocation of the printer to different jobs and maintains a queue of waiting jobs. A LAN may have several different printers for different purposes, for example a high speed A4 laser printer for business documents, a slower, lower quality printer for producing draft documents and an A3 colour laser for diagrams.

On larger sites it is common to have more than one LAN linked together with bridges.

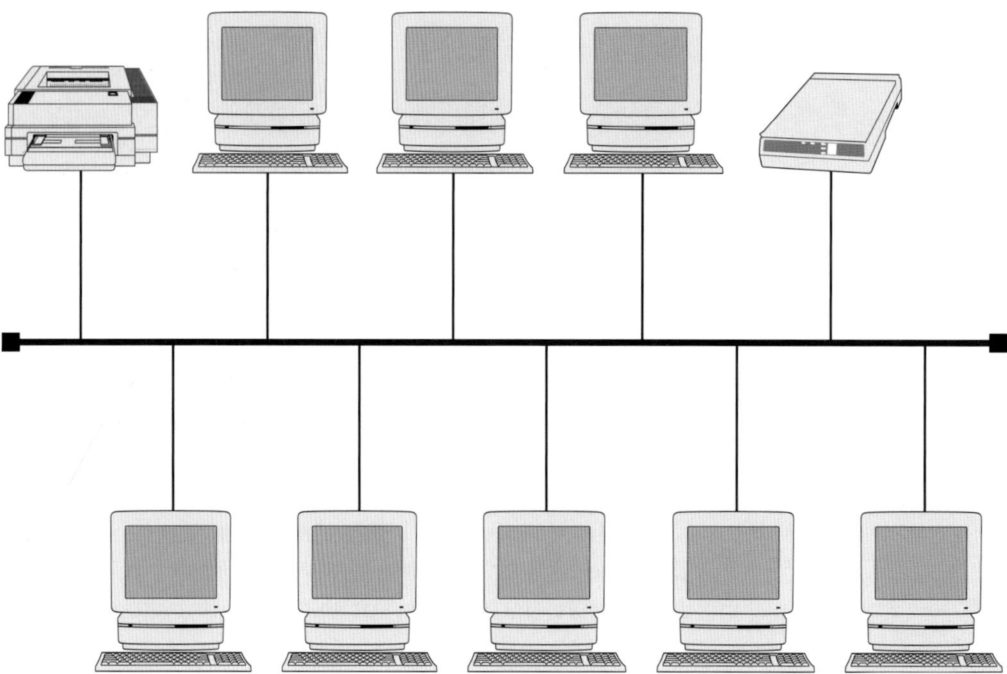

Figure 18.1 A LAN

Wide Area Networks (WAN)

A WAN is a collection of computers spread over a large geographical area, which can be as small as a few miles or as large as the whole world. Communication between computers is made in a variety of ways including microwave link, satellite link, dedicated cables or the telephone network. The telephone link can either be made through the public dial-up lines where the message is routed alongside others, or through a leased line which provides a permanent connection. Leased lines are practical when the volume of data being sent is large and communication is frequent.

Data sent between two computers on a global network might travel through a number of different communications media. The route is created via switching computers that create the necessary path from source to destination computers.

The Internet

The Internet, a shortening of 'international networks', is more than a WAN. It is a network of networks. The Internet backbone is a high-speed network provided by telecommunications companies. The Internet uses a wide range of different

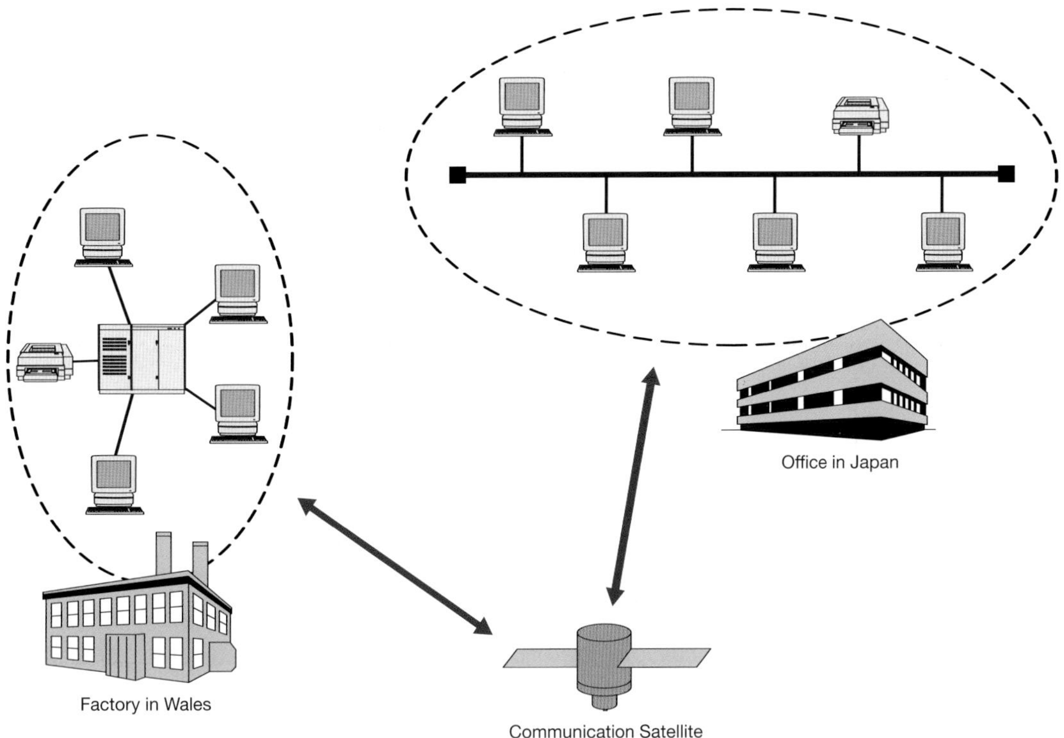

Figure 18.2 A WAN

telecommunication media and provides the facility to exchange information on a global scale. Each network that is connected into the Internet can be located anywhere in the world, can be of any size and can be based on any hardware platform. All of this is hidden from a user of the Internet.

The World Wide Web (WWW)

The Internet is the network structure that supports the transfer of information in the World Wide Web (WWW or Web). The World Wide Web is a collection of information held on the Internet in multimedia form. This information is stored in the form of web pages on computer locations called websites. These pages can contain text, graphics, sound or video clips. Organisations and individuals can create websites each of which can contain many pages. These need to be organised into a structure that makes them easy to access by a visitor to the site. Web clients and web servers communicate with each other using Hypertext Transfer Protocol (HTTP). Web pages are usually prepared using Hypertext Markup Language (HTML). There are a range of software tools available, such as DreamWeaver, that enable the relatively easy creation of web pages and sites.

Browser software and search engines, studied in the ICT AS level course, allow a user to locate websites and pages.

Ways in which a network can improve communication and productivity within an organisation

- **E-mail** can increase the speed of communication by replacing paper messages whilst avoiding the constant interruption that can result from the use of the telephone. Information can easily be sent to all staff within a company.
- **Videoconferencing** can reduce the time and cost of travel for meetings, bringing together participants from different locations without the need to travel.
- A **centralised database** allows all areas of the organisation to have access to the same data at the same time. Data can be added from across the organisation.
- An **intranet** allows information to be shared throughout an organisation without the need for circulating, filing and retrieving physical documents. Information can be delivered to the employee's desktop; every employee receives information at the same time.
- **Collaborative software** allows employees in different areas of the organisation to work on the same document or project. Diaries and other computer files can also be shared.
- **Telecommuting** allows personnel to work at home thus reducing office overheads and absence due to family circumstances.
- Access to the **Internet** provides all the facilities of the World Wide Web so that sources external to the company can be accessed. It opens up the opportunities of e-commerce.
- **Electronic data interchange (EDI)** allows one organisation to transfer electronic data from their computer system to that of another organisation thus removing the need for paper transactions.
- A retail organisation can use **point of sale (POS)** terminals with **electronic funds transfer (EFT)**.
- A **network** allows stock control to be managed in real time. When goods are sold via a POS terminal, the level of stock can automatically be decreased. Other computers on the network can be provided with up-to-date stock levels.

Internet infrastructure

If an individual user is part of a network, for instance, at school or in the workplace, access to the Internet is likely to be made through a permanent connection between the network and the Internet.

If a user is accessing the Internet from a stand-alone computer, a link will be made through an **Internet Service Provider (ISP)** such as Wanadoo or AOL, which in turn is connected to the Internet. The user links to their ISP's computer using a standard telephone line and a modem, an ISDN line or broadband fibre optic cable.

For a network to connect successfully to the Internet it must be able to communicate with it. All computers accessing the Internet must use a **set of protocols**. These protocols include standards for technical details, identification of computers and naming of data files. (See Chapter 23 for details of standards and protocols used to support the World Wide Web).

When data is to be sent over the Internet it is broken down into small packets of data. Each **packet** or message is sent individually and can take a different route from source computer to destination computer. When all the packets have reached their destination they need to be reassembled into their original order, as some packets might have 'overtaken' others and so arrived out of order at the destination.

The job of ensuring that data is sent from source to its correct destination via the Internet is carried out by **routers**, dedicated devices that are located around the world. When a router receives a message it checks the destination address and sends it either to the appropriate computer if it is directly linked or to another router on route to the destination. The same process is carried out by every router until the message reaches the destination computer. The best route at any point will be chosen, so if certain links are down or congested, the message can be sent via a different route. Before sending a data packet on, the router will check that the packet it has received has been transmitted correctly from the previous point. **Integrity checks** such as parity checks, studied at AS, may have detected that data has been corrupted. If this is so, the router will need to request that the packet is sent again.

Each computer connected to the Internet has an address, a number known as an **Internet Protocol (IP)** address which provides a consistent way of referring to a specific computer. The IP address is made up of 4 numbers, for example:

192.165.0.228

The IP address must be unique so that only the specific computer is identified. If more than one computer had the same address then data could not be routed towards a computer.

The IP address can be converted into a domain name which is easier to remember and use than an IP address. www.hodder.co.uk is an example of a domain name. Domain names have to be applied for and once allocated they are stored using the **Domain Name System (DNS)**. The DNS is the way that Internet domain names are located and translated. Maintaining a central list of domain names and the corresponding IP addresses would not be practical. The domain name system is a global network of servers that translate host names, such as www.hodder.co.uk, into the IP addresses. The DNS server that is located close to a user's access provider will map the domain name to an IP address for forwarding them to other servers in the Internet.

The uniform resource locator (URL) is a unique website identifier that points to a specific web site. A typical URL: http://www.microsoft.com/index/index.com consists of 3 parts:

- The **protocol** (set of rules) used for connection to the server (http in the example above)
- The **domain address** of the host computer (www.microsoft.com/) This is, as described above, equivalent to the numerical IP address.
- The **path and filename** of the object being requested (index/index.com)

Parts of a domain name

Domain names make it easy for people to find and visit websites. For example, the UCAS website has the domain name **www.ucas.as.uk**.

This domain name consists of four parts:

- www means it is a website
- ucas is the organisation's name
- ac reveals that it is an academic institution
- uk is the country where the site is registered

A domain name must be unique; no two organisations on the World Wide Web can have the same domain name.

Activity 1

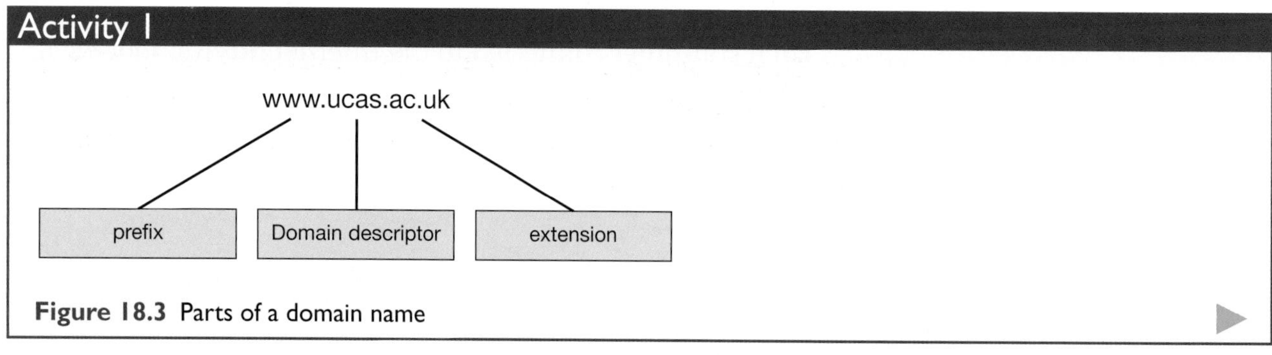

Figure 18.3 Parts of a domain name

1. Use the Internet to research the following extensions; copy and complete the table:

Extension	Identifies	Extension	Identifies
.ac	An academic institution	.com	
.co		.edu	
.net		.gov	
.sch		.org	

2. The protocol **http** (Hypertext Transfer Protocol) is used to access a website. Other protocols include **https** and **ftp**. Use the Internet to find out the function of each of these protocols.
3. Use the Internet to find out how you can obtain a domain name to use for yourself and how much it might cost.

Applications of communication and information systems

Hundreds of thousands of organisations throughout the world use networks as part of their everyday business. The use of the network for most has become an essential tool and they are almost totally dependent on the network and the information it provides.

Computers in all branches of Sainsbury's supermarket chain are linked to computers in the company's distribution warehouses and its head office. Sales information is used in the warehouse to establish order levels for each store. The performance of each store can be monitored centrally. Each store has its own LAN, linking POS terminals to central servers. Each LAN is linked to a nationwide WAN.

Trafficmaster is an organisation that provides traffic information to road users and motoring organisations. They have a WAN linking 7500 sensors located in sites on motorways and trunk roads in Britain. The sensors detect traffic speeds and so the information service can warn motorists of problems ahead. Information can be sent to motorists via radio, telephone or an in-car receiver.

The London Stock Exchange is over 200 years old but started screen-based trading in 1986 replacing face-to-face trading between dealers on the stock market floor. In 1997 a fully electronic, automated trading system was introduced. Today, a fast, secure, reliable network is essential for trading stocks and shares.

case study 1

▶ Acquiring the European Computer Driving Licence

An FE college has a range of employees working in administrative jobs who need to improve their ICT skills so that they can best meet the demands of their job. The college is spread over several sites and the employees needing to build their ICT skills work in a range of departments in the college such as the library, the examinations office, human resources or the finance department. All are very busy. In the past, such staff were sent away on courses or, occasionally, a trainer was brought in for a day so that a number of staff could be trained at the same time. Unfortunately this was not always satisfactory for a number of reasons. The service provided to the college could be severely affected if several members of the department were being trained at the same time. There was also little consistency of training provision across the different sites. The training courses were very expensive for the college. Although the college kept records of who had attended courses, they had no idea of what each individual had actually learnt and whether they were able to use their newly acquired skills in their work.

The members of staff themselves were not satisfied with the provision. They felt that they were not necessarily being taught what they personally needed to know in the class and some felt left behind and failed to grasp what they had been taught.

A management decision was made to provide access to an online course, called the European Computer Driving Licence (ECDL), available to all college personnel. This meant that staff did not have to be released from their work for an extensive period of time but could access the training during quiet spells in their daily routine. This approach saved the college money as there was no longer a need to employ an instructor to deliver the courses or to send staff on courses. The online course provided a method of recording assessments so that an individual member of staff's progress could be checked to see that they had acquired the skills that they needed. All the staff in the college were now receiving consistent training irrespective of the site they worked on.

Each member of staff was now able to work at his own pace so that sections they found difficult could be repeated again and again until they had grasped them. They received instant feedback on their progress from the regular assessment that allowed them to address weak areas immediately. Members of staff were able to work at any location, including home, and at a time convenient to them rather than when the trainer or a course was available.

1. What advantages to the college were there from moving to an online delivery of ICT skills?
2. Can you think of any disadvantages to the college of moving to an online delivery of ICT skills?
3. What advantages to the members of staff were there from moving to an online delivery of ICT skills?
4. Can you think of any disadvantages to the members of staff of moving to an online delivery of ICT skills?

Worked exam question

Internet technologies allow large companies to deliver training and assessment across their entire organisation. This can be of benefit to the company and their employees.

a) Describe **three** possible benefits to the company (6)

b) Describe **three** possible benefits to an employee (6)

c) The interaction of an employee with an online training system needs careful planning. List **four** factors that should be considered. (4)

(relates to Chapter 20)

ICT5 January 2003

▶ **SAMPLE ANSWER** Possible benefits include:

a)
- Time – employees can train during quiet periods
- Training is consistent across the company wherever people work
- Content can be edited and kept up-to-date at all times

b)
- Can work at their own pace and go back if required
- Computer system gives feedback on performance – can concentrate on weaknesses
- Can undertake training at home or at work whatever is convenient.

c) See Chapter 20.

Distributed systems

In the early days of computing, data processing took place in a central mainframe computer. User workstations were purely dumb terminals with no processing power linked to the mainframe. As computers have increased in power but decreased in price, it has become more common for the processing to be performed over a network of computers rather than by the central mainframe.

Two main approaches to processing are used: **distributed systems** and **client/server systems**.

A distributed system is a system where processing is carried out by sharing tasks between physically separated computers on a network. A distributed system will consist of a network of connected computers which can share resources. One computer may store customer data while another stores product data. Alternatively, data could be distributed between different geographical regions within an organisation. The system allows the data on one computer to be accessed from any other computer and combined in appropriate ways. Distribution should not be obvious to the user and the system should appear to be operating at the local machine.

Distributed processing means most data can be processed locally, faster and without continually sending data to and from the central computer. Furthermore processing capacity is spread around the organisation, which allows the work of one branch to be covered by another in case of breakdown.

Most large international organisations will use distributed systems. A company based in the USA selling products online might store the product data in the USA while keeping all client-based data in the local country. It would not be possible to store client data from the European Union in the USA as this would contravene data protection legislation.

A large chain of public houses would use a distributed system. Details of all transactions would be held locally and links made with the head office via a WAN at the end of the day or week to transfer sales details and download any new pricing or product information.

Distributed control

When all data was processed on a central mainframe computer, control was firmly in the hands of the data processing department. They could decide in which order work was done and set their own priorities.

With distributed systems, local branches or departments are able to access the data that they need for themselves as long as they have the appropriate access rights. A distributed system can allow the management of a local division of an organisation to set their own priorities and have greater autonomy. The computer at the head office of an organisation would not need to have access to day-to-day information as all operational, and much tactical, decision making would be made locally.

Distributed databases

A distributed database is a collection of different interrelated databases spread over a network. Some computers on the network each hold part of the data and cooperate in making it available to the user. If the data required is not available on a particular computer, it is able to communicate with other computers in the network so that the data can be obtained. Each computer will usually keep a separate copy of frequently used data to reduce unnecessary network traffic. Distributed database management software manages the distributed database and makes it appear to the user to be a single database.

An example of a distributed database is the Internet Domain Name System (DNS). Details of hostnames and their Internet address are stored in several databases on several computers.

A hotel chain might use distributed databases to store details of reservations. Each hotel stores its own reservations on a local computer. However, because all the hotel computers are networked and a distributed database is used, it is possible for hotel staff to see reservations at other hotels and for company managers to monitor reservations throughout the company.

Because the database is distributed, different users can access it without interfering with one another. However, the DBMS must periodically synchronise the scattered databases to make sure that they all have consistent data.

A distributed database can either be online at the host computer in a central location but also available to remote locations, have part of the database at the host computer duplicated and placed in a remote computer, or have copies of the entire database and DBMS at each remote location.

Advantages of distributed databases

The use of a distributed database brings many advantages to an organisation.

- The use of a distributed database can allow **local control** of processing local data. For example, in a chain of supermarkets, different pricing structures can be used in different shops to reflect local demand.
- As data that is most frequently used locally can be stored locally, **network traffic is kept to a minimum**. This provides faster response times. Queries can be localised, so that if a certain search is only performed locally, it can be stored there.
- The **effect of a breakdown is reduced** as distributed processing provides the opportunity of replicating data in more than one location. If failure causes data to be lost at one site an up-to-date copy will immediately be available at another site.
- The use of a distributed database allows **data to be shared** by different users or branches of the same organisation or even different organisations. The data from one location can be available at another even though the hardware platform or operating system may be different.
- There is **no need to have a powerful, central server** so there does not have to be reliance on a single computer.
- **New locations can be added** to the database without requiring a complete rewriting of the entire database.

Limitations of distributed databases

Of course, there are a number of issues that need to be considered before a decision is made to install a distributed database.

- A distributed system, which hides its distributed nature from the end-user, is **more complex** than a centralised system. This means that such a system is much more expensive to install and maintain.
- As there is no centralised control there will be an **increased management overhead** as someone at each site must be responsible for the management of the data on that site.

- The need to transfer data from one location to another increases the **security risks** to the data; having more access points will increase the likelihood of unauthorised access. Techniques such as data encryption will need to be used to ensure that data is kept secure.
- As all the data is not stored in one location, if one station were to fail with inadequate backup, other locations might suffer a loss of data.
- If some data is stored and updated in more than one place, there is an increased chance of **data inconsistency** (see Chapter 17). Procedures will need to be put in place to ensure that the chances of data inconsistency are minimised.
- There is a reliance on the communication links being maintained; if there were to be a link problem then data could not be shared.

SUMMARY

- **Local and wide area networks play an expanding role in today's businesses with many companies dependent on their networks for communication.**
- **The Internet is the network structure that supports the transfer of information in the World Wide Web.**
- **The World Wide Web is a collection of information held on the Internet in multimedia form.**
- **The Internet requires an extensive infrastructure of high specification computers and links to support its use.**
  Routers ensure that data is sent from source to correct destination.
  Data is transferred in packets of predetermined size. Each packet can be sent via a different route.
  Each computer connected to the Internet has a unique address, its Internet Protocol (IP) address. This can be converted into a domain name such as www.hodder.co.uk.
- **A distributed system is a system where processing is carried out by the sharing of tasks between physically separated computers on a network.**
- **Distributed systems allow processing to be done on local stations rather than centrally.**

  Distributed databases are essentially different databases stored at different locations but linked together to appear to be one database.

Chapter 18 Questions

1 **a)** Define the term *client/server database.* (1)
b) Describe **three** advantages of a client/server database over a non-client/server database. (6)
c) Describe **two** disadvantages of a client/server database over a non-client/server database. (4)

2 Explain the term *uniform resource locator* (URL). (3)

3 A large company has many retail outlets around the United Kingdom selling consumer electronic devices such as televisions, audio equipment and personal digital assistants. The current stock control system is now inadequate for the company's business needs.

An important decision for the company to make is how to implement its new stock control system. It is essential that each outlet will have access to the stock control data of all the other outlets. Each outlet must also have control over its own stock.

Discuss how this company might implement a stock control database system with the above features. Include in your discussion consideration of the following issues:

- resource requirements
- management of the data
- management of the system.

The quality of Written Communication will be assessed in your answer. (20)

ICT5 June 2004

4 When 'http://www.abc.co.uk/userguide.htm' is entered into web browser software a web page is displayed.
a) Explain the meaning of the 'http' part of the address. (2)
b) State what the 'www.abc.co.uk' part of the address is called. (1)
c) Explain what each of the following stands for:
i. www
ii. abc
iii. co
iv. uk (4)
d) www.abc.co.uk can also be given in numerical form such as 192.165.0.232. State what this number is called. (1)
e) Explain what 'userguide.htm' represents. (2)

5 **a)** Define the term 'distributed database'. (2)
b) Describe **one** situation when it would be appropriate to use a distributed database. (2)
c) Describe **one** limitation of using a distributed database. (2)

6 A large international organisation makes use of wide area networking in a number of ways. Access to the Internet and the use of e-mail are two examples. For a number of employees the use of the network allows them to 'telecommute'. Telecommuting allows an employee to work at home using ICT to link to the work place.
a) i. Describe **one** advantage to the employee and **one** advantage to the organisation of telecommuting. (4)
ii. Describe **one** disadvantage to the employee and **one** disadvantage to the organisation of telecommuting. (4)
b) Describe **three** further ways in which the use of a wide area network can be used by the organisation. (6)

7 Explain the role of the following in a wide area network:
a) routers (2)
b) packets. (2)

19 Networks

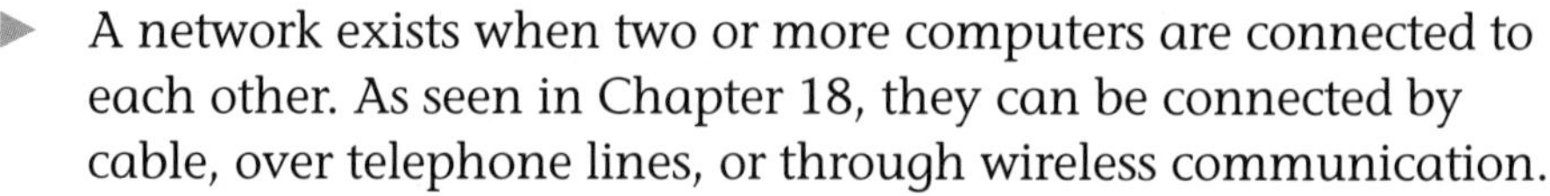

A network exists when two or more computers are connected to each other. As seen in Chapter 18, they can be connected by cable, over telephone lines, or through wireless communication.

Networks are used because users can share resources available to their computer, such as data files, software, printers and modems. However, networks present a greater security risk than stand-alone machines because it may be possible to access your files from another workstation.

Network security

When an individual uses a stand-alone computer system, ensuring data is secure is a relatively simple matter. Use of a keyboard lock can prevent other people from using the computer and accessing files. The use of a screen saver with a password can prevent casual prying when the user is away from their desk.

When a computer is part of a network, then security is more complex. The larger the number of stations and the larger the number of users, the greater the risk of abuse, particularly if the network can be accessed remotely, i.e. from a computer off-site.

As a network is likely to be used by most if not all the employees of a company, it is likely that all the company's data will be stored on the network. As a result any breach in security could be catastrophic for a company. Important data could be altered, deleted or simply read by competitors.

Preserving network security

To promote security, network users are normally allocated a unique username protected by a password. This allows a directory to be allocated to each user so that users cannot access each other's files.

Users can be allocated a maximum directory space and logging in restricted to certain times of the day.

Network operating system software can be used to allocate different **access rights** to different users; some users could be allowed no access, some to read, others to read and modify, whilst others to read/write/delete and modify. It is also possible to restrict access to specific resources in a system, for example, only members of the accounts department could be given access rights to print using the printer in their office.

Network weak points

The use of passwords on their own are not enough to guarantee security. Security on a network is only as good as the weakest link, which is normally the staff. Staff should follow simple procedures to help maintain security as outlined below.

These procedures should be part of the user's code of practice. Anyone not following these procedures should face disciplinary measures.

Simple procedures to maintain security

Staff using networks should follow a number of simple procedures to help avoid breaches of network security, such as:

1. Only acceptable passwords should be used. Obvious choices such as 'SECRET', 'COMPUTER' and the user's name should be avoided. Ideally, the password should consist of a mixture of letters and numbers and should not spell out a meaningful word. The system can be set up so that only certain types of passwords can be used, e.g. a minimum length can be specified and that the password contains letters and numbers.
2. A password should always be kept secret. It should never be shared with others nor left written down on paper, or even worse, on a post-it note attached to the computer screen!
3. A password should be changed frequently. Many systems are set up to require that a user changes their password on a regular basis, perhaps every month. Usually, the user is given a number (typically three) of login attempts, called **grace logins**, to access the system by entering the correct password. If all three attempts fail then the network manager is alerted and the user account is disabled for a period of time.
4. Logged on computers should not be left unattended without the use of keyboard locks or password protection. The network may also be set up so that a user may be able to log on to only one station at a time.

Other problems with networks

Viruses are also easier to spread over a network, especially if all the machines have their floppy disk drives active and the employees all have access to the Internet and e-mail.

The risk of unauthorised access increases when data is transferred over a WAN using public communication links.

Protecting networks against illegal access through a wide area network

Physical security, such as locks on doors to sensitive areas, is suitable for a local area network. But as so many networks are wide area networks, often linked to the Internet, physical security is not an option as the network can be accessed remotely.

Nearly every company will be subject to some illegal attempt to gain access to their computer material. As well as using passwords and sensible procedures, there are a number of other measures that can be taken to reduce the risk.

1. The danger of break-in can be guarded against by the use of a **firewall**. A firewall is a system placed between an internal network and a public network which ensures that all traffic passing from the inside to the outside, or the outside to the inside, must pass through it. Only traffic which is authorised by the organisation's security policy is allowed to pass. A firewall is designed to protect a safe and trusted system (the internal network) from a risky and untrusted system (the public network). The firewall software will stop access to unauthorised websites, or sites containing certain specified key words; stop e-mails and incoming data from certain specified sites and scan incoming data for viruses.
2. Impostor hackers sometimes use 'packet sniffer' programs to intercept identification numbers and passwords, which they then store for later use. A widely used way of countering the effectiveness of sniffer programs is the use of **data encryption**. This is the process of 'scrambling' or coding data so that it can only be recovered by people authorised to see it. It is used when data is transmitted or stored to ensure that the data does not fall into the wrong hands. When the data is to be used, it needs to be 'unscrambled' or decrypted using a key that only the appropriate people possess. The use of a callback modem can also increase security.
3. **Spyware** is another threat. It is software that is secretly installed on your computer, often as a hidden side effect of using a program. It then transmits information without your knowledge. This information may be used for advertising purposes or, even worse, to steal secure information such as passwords or credit card details. You can install software such as Spy Sweeper to detect and remove spyware.

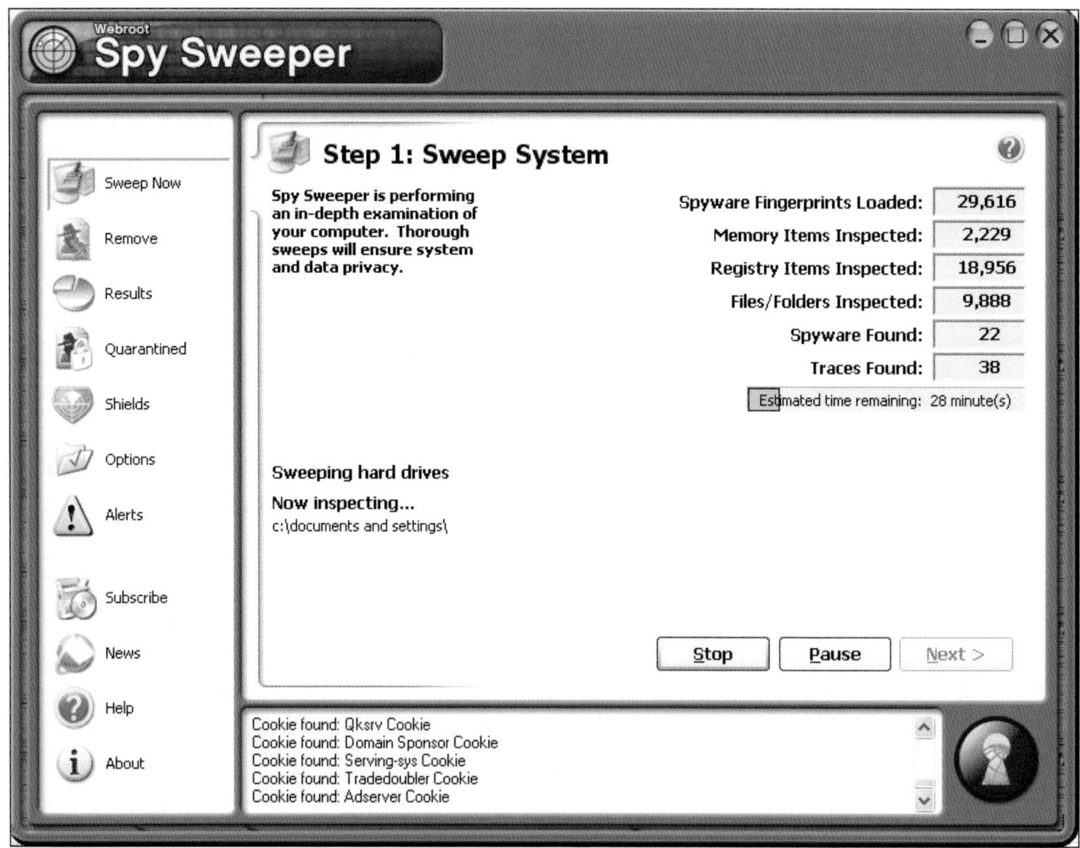

Figure 19.1 Spy Sweeper finds some spyware

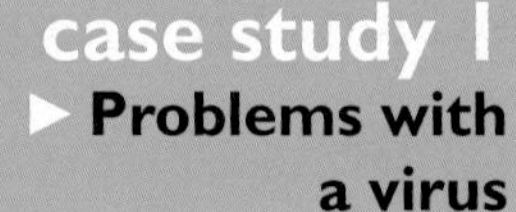

case study 1
▶ Problems with a virus

The publicity officer of a university was caused considerable inconvenience by a virus. Over a period of several weeks, she had put together the proofs of the prospectus for postgraduate courses. This involved considerable effort as entries had to be gathered from a range of contributors in different departments. A number of edits were made and the final versions were recalled from disk and visually checked on the screen with great care. The files were copied to floppy disk and transferred to the printers, who were located on the other side of town, by motorcycle courier. When the files were loaded into the computer at the printers they no longer incorporated the latest edits. The disks were returned. This process was repeated several times as the final deadline got closer and closer. Finally the problem was pinpointed to a virus which affected the copying of files.

1. How could the virus have got on to the system?
2. Outline precautions that the publicity officer should have taken to prevent this problem from occurring.
3. Research some of the effects caused by the latest viruses.

Network management

An organisation with a network will need to appoint a network manager or network administrator who is responsible for maintaining the network. Their duties include:

Installing software

Much software will be installed on central file servers. Some frequently used applications, such as Microsoft Office, may be installed on each individual computer. Modern network operating systems allow this installation to be done centrally. The network manager will have the responsibility of ensuring that all the appropriate software licences are held.

Allocating user accounts

When new personnel join an organisation they will need to be allocated accounts with appropriate access rights and levels of resource usage set up. Each new user will be assigned an initial password. Whenever a member of staff leaves, their network account must be removed.

Taking regular backups

All the data stored on the network will need to be backed up regularly. This is much easier if all the data is stored centrally on a file server. A case study that investigates the backing up of network files is to be found in Case Study 1 in Chapter 15.

Running and updating antivirus software

Antivirus software detects and removes viruses. The network manager must ensure that the latest version of antivirus software is used. He is likely to be able to update the virus software automatically online. The network manager will also manage the firewall to ensure that no unauthorised access is made.

Auditing network use

This involves tracking the use of a network and software by individual users. Software that provides suitable audit information is discussed in detail below.

Network auditing

Audit software enables the network manager to keep track of who has been doing what on the network. This is very powerful and will help in maintaining security and can also be used to monitor staff. The software will record:

- all logins and attempted logins – any illegal attempts to login at a particular workstation can be highlighted.

- attempts to access restricted files
- the identity of the user
- the identity of their computer, normally a unique address held on the network card
- the date and time of access
- what software they have used
- what files have been opened, modified and deleted
- how many reads and writes have been executed
- how many times a server has been accessed
- websites accessed or attempted access including filtered websites
- length of time at sites.

Audit software is very useful in detecting fraud and misuse of the system. It will help to ensure that users follow the company's network security policy and Internet use policy. For example if a network user visits a website and downloads some music files in breach of the copyright laws, this can be detected with audit software.

When a software licence has been purchased that allows for a number of concurrent users, audit software can be used to keep a track of the number of users at any time so that steps can be taken to prevent access to more than the allowed number of users.

Network accounting software

Network accounting software provides statistics about network use to the network manager. These statistics are used in managing the network.

Accounting log

The network accounting software will produce an accounting log for the manager. The log is a report that includes for each department items such as:

- a list of facilities used including processor time
- number of pages printed
- amount of disk space used
- details of e-mail usage
- numbers of logged-on users
- details of applications
- time of day when facilities are used
- details of network traffic.

Use of the accounting log

One use of an accounting log is to charge the different departments of a company for using the computer network.

Traditionally departments have been billed for consumables such as paper. By using the network accounting software, the manager can calculate the exact network use for each department, including the departmental bandwidth use. She can also get accurate information on printer use, disk space used and e-mail usage. This information can be used to divide up the costs accurately between the various departments.

Another use of the accounting log statistics is to plan future network developments. Trends can be examined to see if current network capacity will be adequate in the future. Expansion can be planned in the areas of most use.

The manager can also use the accounting log statistics to observe usage patterns of users and find peak times. The manager may use this to try to reduce traffic at peak times and smooth out demand so that important information is not delayed.

Activity 1

A college of 1500 students and 200 members of staff has decided to adopt an accounting policy for its network.

- Suggest five issues that they will need to consider when writing this policy.

case study 2
▶ IP Sentry

IP Sentry is a Windows-based network monitoring software package used by thousands of ICT specialists around the world. Amongst the features it offers are:

- web server monitoring
- mail server monitoring
- event log monitoring
- file/directory monitoring.

Find out more at http://www.ipsentry.com/

Activity 2

It is likely that your school or college has a network and that you have a user account. If so, answer the following questions.

- What is your user ID?
- How are these IDs allocated?
- What rules govern your choice of password?
- How frequently do you have to change your password?
- Can you log in at more than one workstation at the same time?
- How many login attempts are you allowed?
- What happens if you exceed these attempts?
- List the directories/folders/drives that you have full access rights to.

- List the directories/folders/drives that you have no access rights to.
- List the directories/folders/drives that you have read-only rights to.
- What categories of people have different rights from you, and how do they differ?
- Is printing monitored?
- If so, explain how this is done.
- What disk space allocation do students have?

The network environment

Although the application software used by a networked computer may be exactly the same as that on a stand-alone machine at home, the network environment is very different. Some ways in which it is different are:

- Hardware
- User interface
- Security
- Control of software
- Control of files
- Access rights.

Hardware

You will have learned in ICT2 that the following items of hardware are normally required for a network:

- One or more network **file servers** to store and distribute files over the network.
- A **network adapter card** inside the computer that physically connects your computer to the network.
- **Cabling** or a wireless connection to connect each network computer and printer to the file server.
- A **hub** that takes in data from one network cable then forwards it on to many network cables.
- A **switch** that forwards incoming data to its intended destination.

User interface

The user interface provided on a network will differ from a stand-alone machine in a number of ways. Security will be enforced centrally so the user will always have to log on to the network before they can start to use their machine. When a computer that is attached to a network is switched on, it can 'boot up' from the network file server. The user will then be presented with a log on screen and will need to enter their ID number and correct password before being able to access any files or software.

Software is likely to be restricted to what has been authorised and is available on the network. The user will probably not be able to install additional software.

The GUI might be controlled centrally to stop individuals customising their environment. This will create a consistent corporate image and will also ensure that anyone can use any machine.

The user will have more drives available. Conventionally, on a PC-based system, **a**: to **h**: are reserved for the local floppy, hard disk CD drives and memory sticks while **i**: to **z**: are network drives. Typically, the **n**: drive might be the user's own private storage area on the file server and other drives such as **p**: could be used to store shared files and software.

Once a user has opened a program, their view will be little different from that of a user of the same package on a stand-alone machine. Certain activities are more complicated for a user on a network than on a stand-alone computer. The use of shared printers is one such example. All documents for printing are sent to the appropriate job queue and printed when the printer is free. The user needs to ensure that they select the correct print queue from their software; otherwise they could find it hard to track down their document!

Security

Password protection gives networks greater security than stand-alone machines. However there are additional security hazards associated with networks. One such hazard comes from viruses. A virus on one workstation can quickly spread to the rest of the network and destroy the files of a whole business.

Viruses are transferred to systems from floppy disks that have themselves been infected from another computer system. Some CD-ROMs have been distributed containing a virus. Access to public networks such as the Internet also poses a threat as files downloaded can contain viruses. E-mail attachments may also contain viruses.

A number of measures can be put in place to help prevent a network becoming infected by a virus. Antivirus software

Figure 19.2 Scanning for antivirus updates

should be installed so that it will check all new files for viruses and clean or delete infected files.

The antivirus software needs to be updated on a regular basis as new viruses are being developed all the time. Antivirus software companies produce updates often on a daily basis. These updates are normally installed automatically via the Internet.

Preventing viruses is better than trying to cure them. It is important to follow good practice to avoid infection. Users can be forbidden from using floppy disks or memory sticks in a networked computer without first checking it for viruses. Antivirus software can be customised so that it checks all e-mail attachments before they can be opened.

Another hazard is hardware failure. The need for backup becomes crucial when a network is in use as the implications of data loss could be enormous. Good practice is important. For example, backing up should occur regularly and backup copies should be checked as soon as they have been created to ensure that the process has been carried out correctly.

Control of software

The network manager has responsibility for software used on a network. This software must only be used in adherence to the conditions of the licence. If a licence only allows 20 users, the network can be set up so that no more than 20 stations can access this software at once. The licence documentation and original software disks must be stored safely in case they are needed.

Users' access to certain software must be restricted. Password management software and software to add or delete users would not normally be available to ordinary users. The users' accounts must be set up so that access to these programs is not available.

Control of files

Users can normally only access their own data files and not anyone else's. However in some applications users must share data. In a hospital, different doctors, nurses and clerks will need access to parts of the patients' database. In a college, students will need to access shared software and files containing assignments created by their teachers. There needs to be some means of allowing different users different levels of access.

Typically, the **s**: drive on the server will be used for shared data. Users may or may not have read-only or read/write access to folders in this drive, depending on their status and access rights.

Access rights

When a new user account is added to a network, it is necessary to decide on more than the username and password. A networked system does not have unlimited disk space and an individual user cannot be allowed to use up more than their fair share of this resource. The network manager can allocate each user a maximum allowance; any requests for more space would need to be justified.

The manager can specify exactly which software the user can use. They can specify whether or not to allow Internet access. Login can be restricted to certain times of the day and an expiry date and time for access set. If necessary, an account can be disabled.

Users can be assigned access rights to shared directories by the network manager. These can be full rights (allowing the user to read, alter or delete files), or limited to read-only or access may be completely forbidden.

It is likely that a user will have different access rights for different drives. Access rights to files will be based on business or security necessity. Different people will have different levels of access based on their job, e.g. human resources staff will be allowed to look at and change everyone's records whereas an individual will be able to look only at their own details. Managers might be able to look at and edit the details for all of their staff but would not be able to delete records or add new employees.

Worked exam question

Part question: The manager of the company feels that some of his employees are misusing the network facilities, as he has noticed an increase in the use of printer consumables. Explain one method the manager can use to monitor and control the usage of the printers on the network. (3)

ICT5 June 2004

EXAMINER'S GUIDANCE

There are three marks so three different points within the answer are wanted such as:

The manager can use network auditing software to see how many copies each user has printed. He can set a printing quota for each user. If users exceed their print quota, they can't print.

SUMMARY

- **The use of networks gives rise to increased problems of security.**
- **WANs are particularly vulnerable to illegal misuse.**
- **A major role of a network manager is to maintain security.**
- **A firewall can be used to reduce the risk of unauthorised access.**
- **Viruses pose a major hazard to network security.**
- **Use of encryption can keep data secure.**
- **Network auditing software is used to monitor access to the network and highlight misuse.**
- **Network accounting software is used to keep track of the use of network resources.**
- **Users of a network are assigned different access rights to data files.**

Chapter 19 Questions

1 A company has a computer network system. Activity on this network is monitored by software, and an accounting log is automatically produced so that departments can be charged for their use of system resources.

a) State **four** items of data that this log might include. (4)

b) Give **four** reasons why such a log is useful. (4)

ICT5 June 2005

2 Describe **three** ways in which a company can make use of computer networked systems. (6)

ICT5 January 2005

3 Users may be aware of differences in the user interface between a stand-alone machine and one that is on a computer network. For each of the following issues, describe **one** possible effect of a network environment on the user interface:

a) security of the system (2)

b) control of software used (2)

c) control of files used (2)

d) access rights to resources. (2)

ICT5 January 2005

4 A small business has twenty-five staff each of whom has their own stand-alone computer. The business is considering networking all these computers but is concerned at problems this may create. As an ICT consultant you have been asked to prepare a report for the company directors, outlining the issues, and the potential benefits that networking the computers could bring. Your report should include:

- the benefits of moving to a networked system
- problems that may arise from using a networked system
- the communications facilities that this network could provide
- how the company can prevent staff misuse of these communications facilities.

Your answer must be written in the form of an essay. (20)

5 Whilst planning to install a network accounting system, a company has become concerned about the security of its local computer network.

a) Explain **two** procedures that the company could adopt to discourage breaches of security. (6)

b) State **two** reasons for using accounting software on a network. (2)

ICT5 January 2003

6 A medical supplies company has a local area network. At present the network is hard-wired but the manager is considering using wireless technology to provide network access in a second office nearby.

a) State **two** issues that might be a problem with a wireless network. (2)

b) State **two** advantages of a wireless network compared with a hard-wired network. (2)

7 A small company is devising its password policy. Suggest, with reasons, **four** rules that should be in this policy. (8)

8 Describe **three** differences that you will notice when using a networked computer compared to using a stand-alone computer running the same software. (6)

20 Human–computer interface 

It is often said that a system fails because of 'user error'. However, the fault does not always lie with the user, but with the computer professionals who failed to foresee the potential error during the analysis, design or implementation of the system. It could be possible that greater attention to the human–computer interaction, the way in which communication takes place between user and the computer, would have prevented such an error from taking place.

A recent BCS (British Computer Society) conference on human–computer interface (HCI) research and practice focused on the theme 'Memorable yet invisible'. Making systems memorable is one way to make them easier to operate and thus reduce errors, but users also want systems to make the technology in use invisible to them.

Human–computer interface is a term used to describe the communication between people and communication systems. Considerable attention needs to be given to the human–computer interface when a new system is being designed and developed; a poor design will give rise to user frustration and a high error rate. A good design will allow the user to work quickly, making few errors, thus operating more productively. A bad design that does not address the user's needs can reduce job satisfaction and increase unnecessary stress.

Psychological factors

Computer systems are used most effectively if they take into account the psychological factors which affect human–computer interaction.

User-friendliness and help

The interface should be **user-friendly**. This means that the software should be easy to use and new features easily learned. It should have a consistent 'look and feel': wherever users are in the software they should be presented with things in the same way. For example, the date might always appear in the top right hand corner or messages pointing out when data has been incorrectly entered should be given in a standard way. If common functions are accessed in a similar way across a range of software packages, a user can transfer already acquired skills when using new software for the first time.

An interface should be designed to be accessible to the widest audience and should be as obvious to use as possible with an easily navigable screen layout so that users do not become frustrated. Screen navigation is the way in which a user moves between options and functions. It can be achieved through the use of menus, icons or by keying in commands.

Figure 20.1 Microsoft Word Help Assistant

Of course, not all users are the same and some features may appeal to one user and irritate another. An example of this is the Microsoft Word Help Assistant shown in figure 20.1. While many users find this to be a helpful facility, others consider it to be an annoying distraction to their work. The software offers the facility to switch off the Assistant so that it does not appear.

Many packages provide a range of options that the user can choose so that his or her own preferences are met as far as possible. Figure 20.2, shows a dialogue box from Microsoft Word that allows a user to make some choices about the look and feel of the HCI.

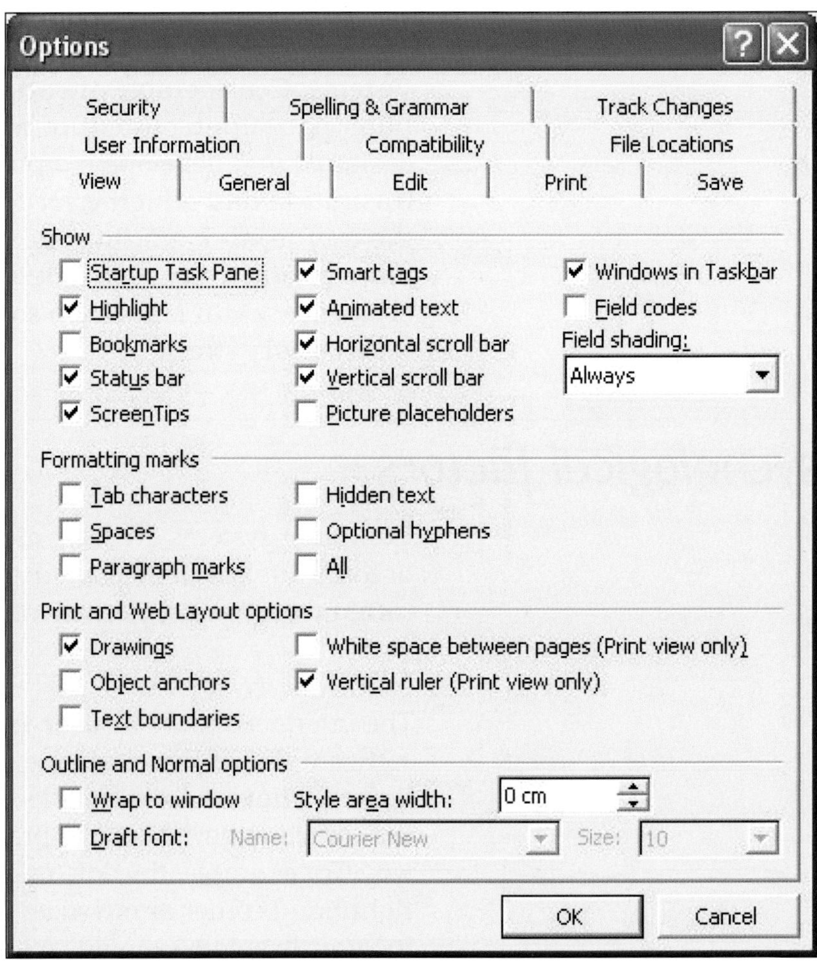

Figure 20.2 Dialogue box for choosing HCI options in Microsoft Word

As a general rule, screens should be clear and, whenever possible, self-explanatory, so that a user has all the required information on the screen. It is very important that the screen is not too cluttered as this can lead to confusion. Maintaining a standard '**look and feel**' will allow the user to build up confidence. The use of **prompts**, which guide the user through a dialogue box, reduces the amount of prior learning that is required.

In many packages the size of the standard font displayed on the screen can be adjusted to meet the needs of the user. An A4 page can be displayed at 75 per cent or 100 per cent of full size for normal work, 200 per cent when details are to be checked or whole page view for checking layout. Sounds can be incorporated to help the user, bringing errors to their attention.

Help facilities

Nearly all recent software includes help facilities for the user to help them to use unfamiliar features. Even an experienced user will need help when wishing to use a feature of the package for the first time. The help screens should be written in clear English, avoiding jargon whenever possible.

Adequate and consistent help should be given to novices. Many software applications include **wizards** which provide a novice with prompts that take them through a particular task. The use of a wizard can allow a user to complete most parts of a complex task by guiding them step by step through the required stages; an example can be seen in figure 20.3.

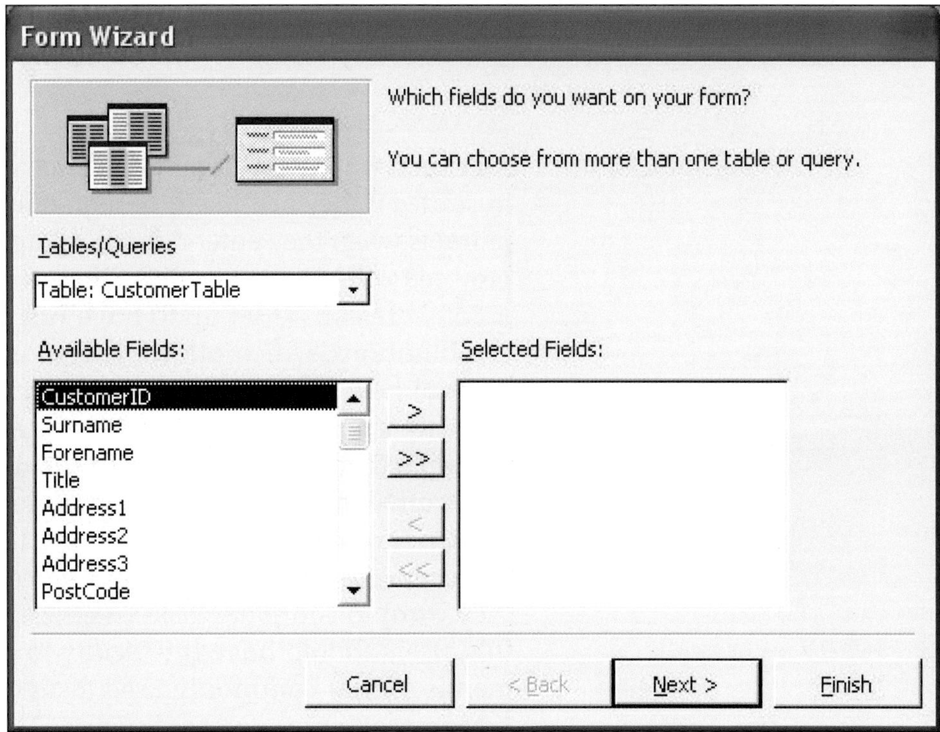

Figure 20.3 A wizard in use in Microsoft Access

Some software also offers **tips** or **assistants** that are displayed when the user is carrying out a particular task. Such tips can provide the user with an alternate way of carrying out the task.

Built-in **demonstrations** that take the user through an example of a particular task being carried out with sample data, can show users how to complete complex or unfamiliar tasks.

Help can be **context sensitive**. This means that when help is requested (via a key press or a menu choice) information is given which relates to the current function being displayed. It is standard for the F1 key to load the help screen and for users to be able to search for help on a key word. Context sensitive help provides the user with a consistent method of gaining help.

Activity 1

Help facilities should be accessible to users. Using a software package which you have used before, examine the help facilities. You should choose a software package that has a large range of features, such as a word processor or a spreadsheet.

For each of the following types of help, state whether or not they are available, how they are accessed and how useful you find them.

- context sensitive
- wizards
- demonstrations
- tips
- other (specify).

1. Comment on the appropriateness of the language used.
2. Use the help facilities to learn how to use a function of the software that you have not used before.

Shortcuts for experts

An expert who uses the same package very frequently can become frustrated if they are taken through a number of menus and prompts when they enter data. It is important that they are provided with shortcuts which allow them to avoid wasting time.

Software can be set up to have **hot keys**, special key press combinations, which allow pre-set tasks to be carried out without having to make lengthy menu choices. A commonly used hot key combination is CTRL + P used to print, in place of having to choose Print from a menu option. The ability to use alternative input methods for commands such as this can aid efficiency and reduce frustration for the user.

Once a user is familiar with a process or piece of software, they want to complete tasks as efficiently as possible. To allow this, users should have the facility to **customise** toolbars and menus so that commonly used tasks are easily available.

Many software packages such as Microsoft's Access, Word and Excel allow the user to customise software. In these packages buttons can be added to run **macros**, automatically load a customised front-end screen interface and set up **templates** which provide a skeleton for types of documents.

Make use of long-term memory

Humans remember different things in different ways. Two types of memory have been identified: short-term and long-term. We use short-term memory to recall things for temporary use. For example, when you look up the page reference for a word in an index you are able to remember it for the seconds that it takes to turn to that page. Try remembering the page reference a day or even an hour later and you are unlikely to be able to.

When we remember things more permanently we have transferred them to long-term memory. Sometimes we do this consciously by purposely 'learning', at other times repeated use results in our remembering something: a friend's phone number for example. It is easier to commit something to long-term memory if it has a meaning for us, if we understand it. Once we have stored something in our long-term memory we are slow to forget it.

It is good practice to make use of human long-term memory when designing an HCI for a user as it will maximise efficiency. If the on-screen environment is familiar and makes sense to the user then he or she will quickly be able to use the interface intuitively. The development of 'desktop' interfaces that attempt to model an actual desk have been designed to make a user mimic normal actions. Hence the 'trash can' icon is used in some systems for users to dispose of unwanted documents – just as they might throw away paper documents into a waste paper-bin in the real world. In Windows programs the same icon is used to represent a particular action. This reduces the amount of learning needed when a particular Windows program is used for the first time.

However, an icon can be confusing when first encountered. An inexperienced user, when first being introduced to Word wondered why there was an image of a tank. It became clear that she was referring to the print icon!

The use of standard menu items and key strokes reduces the time taken to learn to use new software.

Activity 2

Many software packages have a menu bar at the top of the screen. It is common to find the Print function as a choice from a drop down menu from the File option on the main menu bar. The File option is usually located on the left hand side of the menu bar. Someone using a software package for the first time will not have to learn how to print as they already know how to do it from prior experience.

List ten other features that are common across a number of different packages.

Screen design

It is important to choose a screen design that is appropriate for the likely users. Features such as the size, typeface and amount of text, the use of colour and the incorporation of graphics, icons, buttons and moving images need to be chosen carefully. Consistency of headings, menus and layout are very important.

Error messages

The error message is a key feature of an interface. Such messages alert the user whenever a possible mistake is being made, for example, closing a file without saving it. They should be displayed clearly and be consistent in form and positioning. An error message is of little use if the user is not clear how the error can be corrected.

Error messages provided by the system should provide the end-user with information so that they can put right the error. The message should tell the end-user what is going wrong and why.

Many modern packages can be configured to modify the number of error messages that appear. Warning sounds can be used to inform the user when an error occurs.

Figure 20.4 An example of an error message

Different types of interface

A range of different types of interface were studied in ICT2 (AS).

A **command line interface** (see figure 20.5) requires the user to key in individual commands. The input is in text form and requires the user to know exactly what the command is they wish to execute. A command line interface is most suited to experienced, regular users who can take advantage of

```
Command Prompt
Microsoft Windows XP [Version 5.1.2600]
(C) Copyright 1985-2001 Microsoft Corp.

C:\>dir f:\wp/w
 Volume in drive F is STAFF
 Volume Serial Number is C0A8-44C9

 Directory of f:\wp

[.]             [..]            LPYYY>.SET      PR<PR>.SET      SSYYY<.CHK
SSYYY<.DI0      SS>SS<.Q1       SS>SS<.Q2       STANDARD.PRQ    STANDARD.PRT
temp.txt        WINWORD.OPT     WP___<.BV1      WP___<.CHK      WP___<.SPC
WP___<.TV1      WPAQS>.SET      WPASL>.SET      WPB__>.SET      WPLIB<.BV1
WPLIB<.CHK      WPLIB<.SPC      WPLIB<.TV1      WPMEE>.SET      WPSAL>.SET
YYYSHELL.FIL    [A2 Computing] [as computing] [BITS]          [EQR]
[FACULTY]       [PASCAL]        [Smart]         [SYSTEM]        [tutorial]
              24 File(s)        136,948 bytes
              11 Dir(s)  30,261,420,032 bytes free

C:\>
```

Figure 20.5 A command line interface

keyboard shortcuts. The interface only requires a keyboard and a screen as peripheral devices. It allows faster execution as the processor has less to do to support the interface. A command line interface is also more efficient in that one line can give as much information to the system as a number of menu choices. However, command formats need to be memorised by the user.

A command line interface is used when setting up a system when limited hardware may be available and the task is to be carried out by experienced professionals. Configuring hardware is another activity when the use of a command line interface is most appropriate.

A **menu based interface** (see figure 20.6) provides the user with a restricted number of choices from which to select. A menu choice can lead to the display of a further menu and so on. Menu formats can be full screen, pull down or pop up. Menus provide an easy way for inexperienced and infrequent users to interface with a system as they provide the user with a limited range of choices and do not require any prior memorising of key strokes. Menus should be structured in a logical hierarchical fashion so that users can make intelligent guesses to find a particular function. The inexperienced user with few ICT skills can be guided through the system; as the user is presented with fewer options they are less likely to make mistakes.

Because menu systems are hierarchical in nature, a user must go through a number of choices every time before reaching the required function. For frequent, experienced users this can prove time consuming and frustrating.

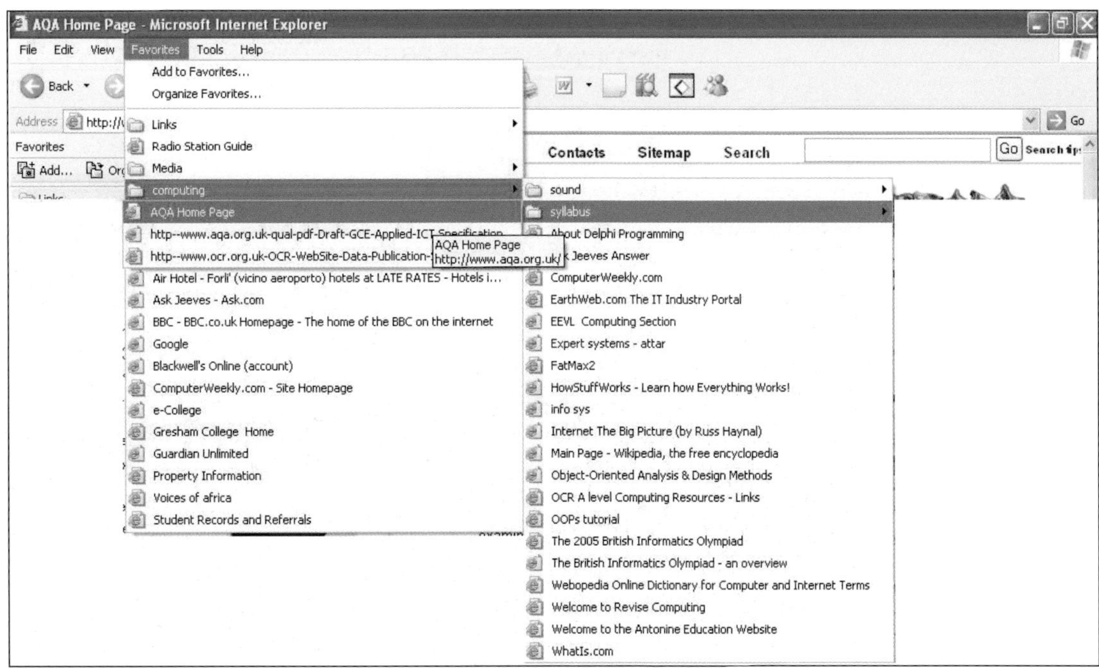

Figure 20.6 An example of a menu based interface

Menu systems are not demanding on resources. As the options are displayed in text they do not require large amounts of main or backing storage or high processing speeds.

A menu system only requires a simple input device, such as a set of buttons; they are often used with systems using touch screens. An example of the use of a menu based interface is a bank's Automatic Teller Machine where the user is presented with a number of options (choosing cash, requesting statement, printing cash balance) each of which may lead to a further choice of options. Keys on the device are used to make a choice. A menu interface is appropriate because only a restricted number of tasks can be performed using an ATM.

A **graphical user interface (GUI)** uses features such as windows, icons, dialogue boxes and menus to provide an interface that is easy to use. (See figure 20.7). A pointing device is used to make selections and the user has the facility to drag and drop components around the screen. All these features make operations simple to perform. The input device that acts as a pointer can be chosen from a range of devices; the user can choose the one that meets their special needs.

The interface is not based on language use so it is suited to different native tongues and the same interface can be used in different countries. The screen designs are similar across a range of packages and users can set up their own desktop menus. Data can be taken from one application to another very easily.

Unlike a menu based system where, typically, a number of choices have to be made to reach a required function, the use of a graphical user interface allows shortcuts to frequently used functions to be provided. Thus certain tasks can be carried out more efficiently.

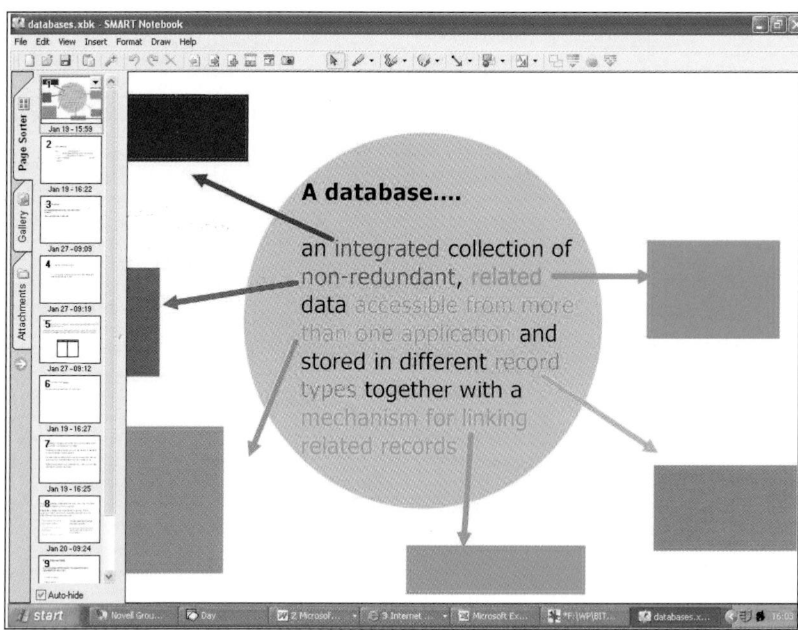

Figure 20.7 An example of a graphical user interface

Many software packages for use on personal computers use a graphical user interface. Application packages such as word processors, spreadsheets and drawing packages all provide an easy to use, versatile graphical user interface.

Activity 3

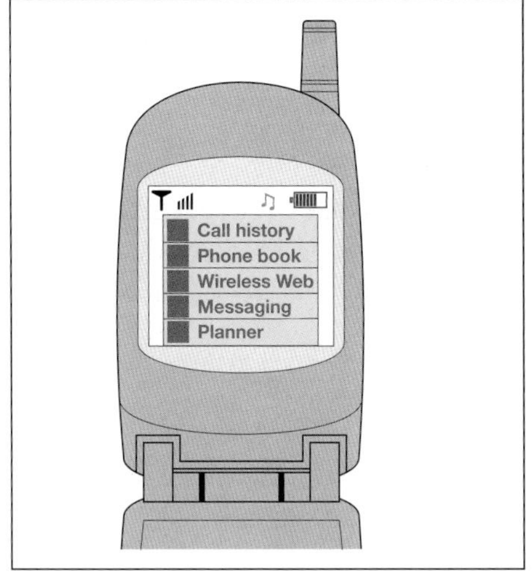

Figure 20.8

A good example of an HCI that makes use of menus as a system of navigation is used on mobile phones. The user is taken through a number of options to get to the desired feature. The diagram in figure 20.8 shows an outline for a simplified mobile phone menu system.

- Draw out a similar diagram for an actual mobile phone.
- Why is a menu-based HCI more suitable for use with a mobile phone than a command line interface?
- Why is a graphical user interface not the most appropriate in this application?

Worked exam question

One method of providing a human-computer interface (HCI) is to make extensive use of menus. An example of where menus are used in this way is with mobile telephones.

Name one other situation where menus are used as the main feature of an HCI. (1)

Describe four reasons why menus are appropriate in situations such as these. (8)

ICT5 June 2004

▶ **SAMPLE ANSWER**

a) An appropriate situation would be a bank cashpoint machine. (Another situation would be an MP3 player.)

b) Reasons why menu are appropriate:

- A menu system can be used very quickly
- Can be used whatever the IT skills of the user
- Prevents errors
- Uses less hardware resource.

Input and output devices

Very often consideration of input and/or output devices is an important part of designing an interface. The age and ICT experience of the user, the physical environment and the characteristics of the application will all be factors in choosing the devices.

Activity 4

Copy and complete the table below – for each application:

Choose the appropriate input and output devices and justify your reason.
Choose the appropriate interface type and justify your reason.

Application	Input / output device(s)	Reason	Interface needs
Automated rail ticketing system	Touch screen	Robust for use in a public place; easy for public use	Uncluttered, easy to use interface that has minimum of text as not all users will be English speakers. Must be usable by people with few ICT skills. Must provide simple to follow help using clear message if a user makes an incorrect entry.
Mobile phone			
ATM			
MP3 player			
A drawing package to be used by children under the age of eight			
Configuring a new server on a network to be carried out by ICT technician			

Worked exam question

A mail order music company has decided to expand and has established a retail outlet in a busy shopping centre.

a) An important feature of the mail order system is the interface for the staff who use it.
State three features you would expect the human-computer interface to have in such a system and give a different reason for each one. (6)

b) i) Name an appropriate device for capturing data on each item that is sold via the retail outlet. (1)

ii) Describe one advantage for the company of using this device. (2)

▶ **EXAMINER'S GUIDANCE**

The examiner is asking for features of the human-computer interface that are relevant to this specific interface. To answer this question, it is necessary to spend a bit of time getting a picture in your head of what the system in question is all about.

The system is essentially one of recording the sale of goods both by people taking orders from forms filled in by the customer (the original mail order business) and in a shop when a customer has selected the product he wishes to buy. The people using the system in the retail outlet (shop) may not be very ICT literate, whilst those dealing with mail order will be using the system all day and so will want a system that allows for short cuts. So you could say:

The interface should cater for different levels of user expertise as some workers may not be very ICT literate whilst those dealing with mail order will be very competent

Another factor that is specific to this example is that it would be important to have consistency at both sites so staff do not have to learn two systems if they are moved between roles.

Note that each of these points have a feature (underlined) supported by a reason (the rest of the sentence).

Other, more general features could be given.

From the table below, construct five sentences each consisting of feature and reason. You will have to think of the appropriate feature.

Feature	Reason
Sensible use of colour	as the system will be used fairly intensively
	so that users are able to assist themselves when they need to
	so that the input choices are restricted to items sold by the company
	to build on the user's previous experience
	to reduce errors

b) i) The two most likely devices are the barcode scanner or the keyboard. Choose the one for which you can write the best advantage in part (ii). Remember that there are two marks available for the advantage so you ***need to expand your point****.*

ii) A possible answer for a keyboard could be: it is a cheap method compared with a barcode scanner so it would be less costly for the company to install.

Four reasons for using a barcode scanner are:

1. *It is a simple method.*
2. *The music stock is already provided with bar code from supplier.*
3. *It is a relatively fast method of data capture.*
4. *There will be few data entry errors.*

Expand each of these reasons into a two mark answer.

Resource implications

The use of a user-friendly, sophisticated interface such as a GUI will make heavy demands on the computer's resources. They require a processor with a **high clock speed**, large amounts of **main memory** (RAM) to run, will take time to load and need large amounts of **backing storage** in the form of magnetic disk space. An input device, such as a mouse, that allows '**point and click**' will be needed to use the interface.

If a software application is being transmitted over a network, the use of larger files, for graphics for example, will increase network traffic and could impair performance.

Large amounts of programming code are required to process complex graphics. The processor must have a high clock speed so that it can carry out instructions fast enough to cope with the transferring of the images to the screen at a high enough speed. If the processor is slow, the graphics will not be produced smoothly. The use of a graphics card will allow the processor to be dedicated to other programming tasks while the graphics card carries out the transfer of image data.

A high main memory capacity is needed to store the graphics and the programming code needed to manipulate the graphics whilst the program is running. Complex graphics will take up a lot of space in main memory when they are being used, due to the bitmapped nature of graphics. The use of bitmaps for high resolution screens displaying a large number of colours requires a large amount of memory. A high speed, high-resolution monitor will be needed to display the graphics clearly.

Programs that operate in an environment such as a GUI will tend to be complex in terms of how they have been programmed, and so tend to be large and therefore take up a considerable amount of disk space. The operating system will consist of large graphics files that require storing. Comprehensive help systems will have a large number of files to be stored. The size of programs has grown enormously as interfaces have become more sophisticated.

To run Windows XP it is recommended that you have a PC with at least a 300 MHz processor with 128 Mb RAM, 1.5 Gbyte hard disk space and a super VGA monitor. This would be the minimum. Performance may be poor with such a specification and a user is likely to demand at least 600 MHz with 256 Mb RAM and a 10 Gbyte hard disk. The following features of a sophisticated HCI make considerable demands on resources:

- **On-screen help**. Context-sensitive searching on different topics, tutorials and wizards all require considerable storage (hard disk) space. When help facilities are being accessed they need to be stored alongside the operating system, application program and data in immediate access store in order to be of use. On-screen help makes considerable demands on system resources, including extra hard disk space to store help files which can be very large if a wide range of help facilities, such as wizards and demonstrations, are used. Use of **colour** enhances user-friendliness, but results in a high use of immediate access store. The more colours used in display, the more bits that are required to store each pixel.

- The use of **graphics** and **animation** add much to the user-friendliness of software. However, complex graphics require a fast processor if the changing images are to be displayed smoothly. Complex graphics, high-resolution screens with many colours require large amounts of immediate access to store bitmap images. Large amounts of disk space are needed to store graphics files and the complex programs needed to manipulate the graphics.
- The use of **GUI features** such as icons, scroll bars and dialogue boxes require considerable amounts of disk space to hold both the graphical images and the many lines of program code needed to display the graphics on screen. High capacity immediate access store is needed to hold the graphical data and the program while it is running. The complex programming needed to run the interface requires a processor with a high clock speed. The complexity of the interface will mean that considerable time will need to be dedicated to it.
- Many sophisticated interfaces allow for **multitasking**, where several tasks can be run concurrently. For example, a document can be repaginating whilst other tasks are being carried out. A spreadsheet can be recalculating whilst a user is word processing a letter. Multitasking involves the sharing of the processor between tasks and demands that a processor runs at a high rate. Such activity requires a fast processor as well as adequate immediate access store otherwise the user will suffer frustration having to wait for task and window swapping to complete. Large amounts of main memory will be required in order for multitasking to take place, as when a task is not being accessed it has to be stored in main memory where it can be accessed immediately.
- Many current developments that attempt to improve the HCI for a user make high resource demands. The use of **voice recognition** to replace keyboard entry uses complex programming that requires a fast processor and large amounts of immediate access store.

Activity 5

Draw up a table like the one below and enter details for eight major application packages used in your school or college. Use manuals, the Internet and magazines to gather the required data.

Package	Minimum processor speed	RAM needed	Disk space required for full implementation	Disk space required for help files

Customisation of software

Certain software packages can be customised to meet an individual user's specific needs.

In a word processing package a user can choose their own default settings for many things such as margins, tabs, font and language used.

Many packages allow the user to choose the toolbars and icons to be used. The contents of menus can be altered to meet specific needs. A personal, supplementary dictionary can be set up so that commonly used names and words specific to the business can be added. A package such as a spreadsheet can be customised to hide unwanted functions from an inexperienced user and add a user-friendly, task-specific interface.

Features such as **macros** and **templates** are common in general-purpose applications packages. Macros allow the keystrokes of frequently used tasks to be automated so that time can be saved. Macros can be set up to allow novice users to carry out more complicated tasks than they would otherwise be capable of. Templates allow users to pre-set and save their own document styles.

Implications of customisation

Customisation of software can allow a user to make the best possible use of it. An inexperienced user can be provided with a simplified set of choices, maximum help and hints and a range of pre-set options, for example, through the use of macros. An experienced user will customise the same package in a completely different way that will allow them to save time and remove unnecessary and intrusive help.

However, the customisation of software can lead to complications. ICT support staff within an organisation might have greater difficulty troubleshooting when every installation of a particular piece of software is customised in a different way. Identifying a source of error or guiding a user through a new task will be much more complicated when many option settings differ from the norm. More time may be taken up in support as staff will have to identify which icons perform which task and the position of the icons on the screen. Changes made by the users may have other consequences that may be difficult for the support staff to assess without access to the user's system so that assistance cannot be given over the telephone.

If the software has to be reinstalled for any reason, the customisation process will have to be carried out again to re-establish the user's own requirements.

If users move between workstations, as they do in a school or college environment, finding differently customised software will complicate access; users will be unfamiliar with the layout and options.

Activity 6

Using a word processing or spreadsheet software package that you are familiar with, explore the ways that the package can be customised. List 15 different features that can be customised, explaining why a user might wish to make each customisation. Try to choose a variety of features.

SUMMARY

Psychological factors affect human–computer interactions. It is important when designing an interface for new software to take the following factors into consideration:

- **ensure that the software is user-friendly**
- **provide a range of help facilities for novices**
- **provide shortcuts for experts**
- **use long-term memory to maximise efficiency.**

Sophisticated HCIs are demanding on system resources. These resources include:

- **processor speed**
- **main memory**
- **hard disk space.**

The high demands are made by:

- **on screen help**
- **the GUI nature of an interface**
- **use of graphics**
- **use of many colours**
- **multitasking.**

Certain software packages can be customised to meet an individual user's specific needs. This can save time for the user and make the software easier to use.

The customisation of software can lead to complications within an organisation. Support staff might have greater difficulty troubleshooting when different computers have the same software configured in a different way.

Chapter 20 Questions

1 A technical author purchases a new word processing package which he customises to fit his specific needs. Explain the term customise in this context. Describe what such customisation would involve. (6)

2 A supermarket chain has recently implemented a new stock control system in each of its branches. Many of the staff have described the system as being 'user-friendly'. Give **four** features of software packages that would merit the description 'user-friendly'. (4)

3 A composer has decided to invest in a music software package to aid his productivity. He already uses a generic office package and is competent in its use. Both software packages operate with a graphical user interface (GUI).

Describe **two** features of his PC hardware that will be necessary in order for the GUI to operate efficiently. (4)

ICT5 June 2001

4 a) Describe **two** factors that need to be considered when designing for human-computer interaction. (4)

b) Describe **two** resource implications of providing an effective interface. (4)

c) Some users may customise their interface. Describe **one** consequence this may have for support staff when providing technical assistance. (2)

ICT5 June 2002

5 There are several types of human-computer interface.

a) i. Describe **one** feature of a command line interface. (2)

ii. Name, giving **one** reason, one application where this interface would be appropriate. (2)

b) i. Describe **one** feature of a menu driven interface. (2)

ii. Name, giving **one** reason, one application where this interface would be appropriate. (2)

c) i. Describe **one** feature of a graphical user interface. (2)

ii. Name, giving **one** reason, one application where this interface would be appropriate. (2)

ICT5 June 2003

6 A Graphical User Interface (GUI) is one form of interface that is commonly used with modern computer systems.

a) State the meaning of the term *Graphical User Interface.* (1)

b) Describe **three** features of such an interface. (6)

c) Name **one** other form of interface. (1)

d) Describe **two** features of the form of interface named in **c)**. (4)

e) A Graphical User Interface makes high use of system resources. State **two** such resources and, for each one, explain why high use is required. (4)

7 ICT systems are used most effectively if they take into consideration the psychological factors that affect human-computer interaction.

Describe **three** such psychological factors and state how they affect human-computer interaction. (9)

8 A city's tourist board has decided to install computer systems that provide information on the city's facilities to the general public. Devices will be installed at various locations in the city including the railway and bus stations.

a) State the input and output devices that would be required, giving reasons for your choice. (6)

b) Name the most appropriate interface for this application. (1)

c) Describe **three** relevant features of this type of interface. (6)

21 Software development

Off-the-shelf software

Suppose that a small business wishes to install a new payroll system to pay its staff. Many companies use computer systems to pay their staff salaries, so there are many payroll system products already available.

Just go to any search engine and type in *payroll system* and you will see links to dozens of software companies who supply such software.

Pre-written software like this is called 'off-the-shelf software.' It is available for common software applications such as payroll or stock control and can be purchased from computer stores, office supply stores and, of course, over the Internet.

For a very common application such as payroll, it is highly likely that the business will find a suitable package to meet their needs. The business should use the criteria described in Chapter 16 to decide which package to buy.

However, off-the-shelf software does not meet all potential needs. Very often it is not possible to purchase an off-the-shelf package as the software simply does not exist.

In this case, specialist software has to be developed to meet the company's needs. For example, many public sector organisations, such as HM Revenue and Customs, the Passport Office and the London Underground have had software developed specifically for their own needs.

Bespoke software

Software that is developed specifically for a particular system is known as bespoke software. An organisation will choose to develop bespoke software when they wish to implement a new system that performs things that no other system has done. For commercial organisations this might be seen as a way of keeping ahead of the competition.

Bespoke software has the advantage that it can be designed precisely to meet the user's requirements and that a solution can be produced in such a way that the system will be able to grow and adapt to changing business circumstances.

The development of the new system can be phased so that costs can be distributed. In some cases, bespoke software that is developed for a particular organisation may then be sold to other organisations in the same sector.

The main disadvantage of commissioning bespoke software is that it is likely to be costly and will take much longer to implement than if an off-the-shelf package had been used. When something new is being done, perhaps incorporating new technology, there can be a high level of risk; it might turn out that the new system cannot be made to work as intended. Many such systems go substantially over budget and are not implemented on time, indeed some have to be abandoned.

Activity 1

Find a specialist software application that has recently been developed. Using information from specialist ICT magazines and websites, prepare a report for your class using presentation software.

You should include details of:

- the purpose and nature of the application
- why specialist software is needed
- any problems that were encountered in its development.

Customising a generic software package

In many systems, there is often a combination of bespoke and off-the-shelf software in use. Very many specialist application systems are built by customising generic software packages.

Databases such as Oracle form the basis for many such systems: the functionality of the DBMS is incorporated into the specific application. An alternative generic solution which has become increasingly common is to use a web-based format. This solution would store the data as active server pages – a database format that could be accessed by a browser such as Microsoft Internet Explorer.

When customising a generic package, large sections of the programming code are already written, so the volume of programming is much less. This should mean that both the development time and implementation costs will be less than if a fully bespoke system were to be produced.

case study 1
Adapting existing software

A large multinational organisation recently needed to replace a 15-year-old system. This system had been programmed from scratch as at that time there was no other option as no software in the field was on the market. When considering the replacement options, the analysts rejected the idea of producing bespoke software as it would take too long; the scope of the project was huge and would require many thousands of man-hours to develop.

One software package available on the market met approximately 90 per cent of the organisation's requirements. The team negotiated with the manufacturers to buy the product, together with the right to modify it to meet their specific needs. This core product provided the basic functionality; programmers then had the flexibility to build on this so that the extra features could be added and the software made to integrate with other existing software in use within the corporation.

Choosing a suitable way of producing specialist software

When an organisation decides that bespoke software is required or existing software is to be modified, a decision will need to be made as to how the development is to be undertaken. There are three options:

- The users could write their own software.
- A team within the organisation, perhaps part of an ICT development department could write the software.
- An external company could write the software.

User written

This is not a commonly-used approach. Few users will have the skills or the time to design, write, test and implement their own software.

They may have the ability to customise a generic package. For example, within your school or college it is possible that enthusiastic members of staff have customised a spreadsheet or database package to store students' marks. You will have experience of this kind of customisation in your AS level coursework and are probably working on another project at the moment.

The main advantage of a user developing a software solution is that the requirements of the system will be fully known and understood. No one else will need to be involved, so there would be no chance of a misunderstanding. However, it is rare that a user would have the required skills to develop a system, and even if they did have, it might not be an appropriate use of their time.

Internal development team

Large organisations may employ a team of ICT staff. Very large organisations may have a complete ICT department that consists of analysts and programmers who will produce bespoke software solutions. An advantage of maintaining a dedicated team is that the people developing the software will have a thorough knowledge of the work done by the organisation, its current systems and its procedures. Continuity will be provided as the team that produced the software will be on hand to maintain and modify it.

External company

Getting an outside software company (sometimes called a software house) to produce a bespoke or tailor-made program to meet the specific user needs is an alternative way of producing specialist software. A software house is a company that employs a number of analysts and programmers with a range of skills, usually in a number of programming languages. Good software houses will employ professionals who are well qualified, reliable and adaptable.

Many software houses specialise in different types of work. Some may specialise in Internet-based systems, others may work mainly within a particular business sector such as retail or banking. Many offer a wide range of services. Analysts from the software house will work closely with the client organisation to ensure that they have a clear understanding of the system requirements.

As the programs developed by a team from a software house are written especially for the user, they should fit all their needs. However, getting a company to develop the solution for a user is likely to be expensive and take time. It is important for a client company to choose a software house that has a good reputation in the given field of work. This can be found out by talking with previous clients of the software house.

The range of skills available within the software house should be appropriate. The client will also need to be assured that any system that is produced for them will be adequately supported so that if things go wrong they will be sorted out quickly. There will also be a need for system maintenance so that when minor program modifications are needed to reflect changes in the organisation, the software company will be able to carry them out.

case study 2
▶ International banking

David works in the ICT department of a large multinational bank. The department is made up of several hundred people. He works in a section that develops and supports the systems used by the bank traders in the cities that house the main international money markets.

He is working on a project that will produce a back office system to replace the current, rather outdated system that will soon not be able to cope with the demands placed on it. The system involves sending out payments and confirmation of deals done. The requirements of the system are wide ranging but very specific to the organisation. There is no one piece of software on the market that will carry out the required tasks.

An estimated 150 analysts and developers will be needed to work on the project over the next three years.

1. David could have chosen to use a software house to develop the software instead of producing it in house. What factors do you think influenced the decision?
2. Why might it be appropriate for such a large organisation to develop an in-house solution whilst it would not be appropriate for a small business?
3. What are the dangers of choosing to develop an in-house solution?

case study 3

▶ IPL create a system for Teachers Provident Society

Teachers Provident Society (TPS) provides a range of financial services that include advice on mortgages, investment management and unit trusts as well as a large range of other financial investments and products.

Facing fierce competition, TPS called in the software house IPL because they wanted to develop a system that would take advantage of new technological developments and cut costs within the organisation. They previously had an assortment of business applications that could not communicate with each other effectively.

The new system would enable TPS to reduce the costs of launching new products, respond to customers' queries immediately and analyse the preferences and profiles of individual customers. TPS had to decide whether to upgrade their previous system, replace it with an off-the-shelf solution or to develop a bespoke replacement.

TPS decided to use IPL, one of the UK's leading independent software and systems houses (http://www.ipl.com). Together, IPL and TPS produced a radically new system. Not only is the system extremely flexible, but it can also support hundreds of simultaneous users across multiple sites, and store details of millions of customers.

The system is also reliable. In the first three years of operation, less than 20 man days were spent fixing software errors.

1. Explain why you think TPS chose a bespoke development of their new systems.
2. Why do you think that TPS did not develop the new software in house?
3. How do you think TPS went about choosing an appropriate software house? List the criteria that they should have used to make their decision.

Activity 2

Specialist software houses are companies that can be commissioned to write software for a user.

In recent years these companies have offered a larger range of services to users and are often called computer bureaux, software consultancies or software houses. The services offered may include:

- selling and installing standard, off-the-shelf software
- tailor-made software
- customising generic software
- computer consultancy and advice
- networking advice
- Internet advice
- website design
- web hosting and maintenance
- selling and installing hardware
- hardware and software rental or leasing
- help in data preparation.

Use the Internet to find two examples of software houses. What services do they each provide? Can you add other services to the list above?

Prepare a presentation for your class describing the differing services provided by software houses.

Choosing the right solution – software selection criteria

If no suitable software already exists to meet a user's needs, a decision will have to be made to decide upon the method of development.

The following criteria are likely to be among those considered.

Development time

The time that it will take to develop and implement the system will be most important when deciding which approach to use. The timescale within which the system must be completed is likely to be determined by factors within the organisation. New organisational functions that are needed by a certain date may depend upon the new system, for example, the start of another project that has already been planned might require this system to be up and running.

As well as producing all the new program code, the new system will need extensive and time-consuming testing. Customising a generic package will usually take less time compared with other methods. The generic package will already have been coded and tested.

Cost

Cost is likely to be a major factor. The cost of producing bespoke software will be high as programmers will have to be paid for all the time that it takes to develop the software. The costs incurred when customising a generic package will consist of the cost of the package together with payment for the time taken to customise it for the specific needs.

The amount a client pays for generic software is considerably less than the amount that it costs to create it. The development cost for generic software is spread as such software will be sold to a number, in some cases a very large number, of users.

Costs of developing bespoke software can sometimes be partially recouped by selling the software to other, similar organisations who may be able to adapt it to their needs. However a business probably wouldn't want to sell software to a competitor.

Flexibility to extend

In some situations it is very important that the new software that is created is able to be extended in the future to meet changing needs within the organisation. When developing bespoke software in-house, the developers are likely to have a very clear understanding of what the future requirements of the system could be.

Appropriateness of solution

It is important that the chosen solution will adequately meet the needs of the users. A bespoke system should be able to meet these needs exactly. A generic package might need very extensive customisation which even then might only partially meet the requirements.

Compatibility with existing hardware and software

When a solution is being chosen, considerations of compatibility must be made. It may be that extra memory or a faster processor will be required to run the new software. Data files from the old system will need to be read by the new system.

Skills within the organisation

If an organisation does not employ its own ICT developers, it will not be able to develop bespoke software in-house. If bespoke software is required, the organisation will have to use the services of a software house. Even if the organisation does employ its own developers, they may not be familiar with the programming language or languages required to implement a particular system and the best option in this case may be to use a software house rather than retrain staff or employ new extra programmers.

Do other, similar systems exist?

Very often, similar systems already exist in other organisations that can be adapted to meet the needs of the new system. Whether this is a feasible option will depend upon the degree of competition between the organisations and whether such systems are compatible with current hardware and software.

Corporate strategy

An organisation's senior management will produce a corporate strategy that will include plans for future developments within the organisation. These will include the development of new ICT solutions and will lay down the scope and timescale for each such project.

Decisions to purchase new software cannot be taken in isolation. Although only one department in a company may use the software, other departments may use the data generated. A sales system might record sales, but the data is needed to reorder stock, to send invoices, to pay staff commission, to plan future services, etc.

The company's ICT technicians and help desk staff may be familiar only with one hardware platform. Purchasing software that requires different hardware may mean that the same level of technical support is not available.

In a rapidly changing environment where hardware and software become out of date very quickly, it is vital to plan ahead and have a corporate ICT strategy. This strategy will cover the whole company and not just individual departments. Any software development must be in line with the corporate ICT strategy.

Worked exam question

Software solutions to specialist problems can be supplied in several ways.

For each of the following ways:

- give one situation where it would be appropriate
- describe one advantage of this approach
- describe one limitation of this approach.

a) Software created by the user. (5)
b) Software created by an internal development team. (5)
c) Software created by an external development team. (5)

ICT5 January 2004

EXAMINER'S GUIDANCE

For each part there is one mark for stating an appropriate situation, two for describing an advantage and two for describing a limitation.

This is a 15 mark question.Your must say why it is an advantage or a limitation. If you have only written eight lines, either your answer is too brief or you have tiny hand-writing!

▶ **SAMPLE ANSWER** Possible answers for part (a)

An appropriate situation for the user to create their own software would be if the user was familiar with programming and required specialist software that was not available elsewhere, for example a statistician might wish to use random number generation in an experiment.

An advantage would be that the solution will be exactly what the user wants as it has been generated by the user and not a third party.

A limitation would be that there may be a lack of documentation for the software as the user will know the software well and so is unlikely to produce a manual.

Now produce answers for parts (b) and (c)

SUMMARY

- **Specialist software cannot always be bought off the shelf.**
- **The main ways a business can provide software solutions to specialist applications are:**
  - **Getting the user to write the software themselves.**
  - **A team within the organisation, perhaps part of a dedicated ICT development department could write the software.**
  - **An external software house could be commissioned to write the software.**
  - **Customising a generic software package.**

When choosing between different software solutions to specialist applications the following criteria need to be used:

- **development time**
- **cost**
- **flexibility to extend**
- **appropriateness of solution**
- **compatibility with existing hardware and software**
- **skills within the organisation**
- **do other, similar systems exist?**

Software purchases must comply with the corporate ICT strategy.

Chapter 21 Questions

1 Software solutions to specialist problems can be supplied in several ways.
For each of the following ways:

- give **one** situation where it would be appropriate;
- describe **one** advantage of this approach;
- describe **one** limitation of this approach.

a) Software created by the user. (5)
b) Software created by an internal development team. (5)
c) Software created by an external development team. (5)

ICT5 January 2004

(The answer to part (a) is shown in the worked exam question.)

2 A lighting manufacturer is considering using off-the-shelf software to store details of customers' orders. Describe **one** advantage and **one** disadvantage of buying off-the-shelf software. (4)

3 A manager of a company who describes himself as computer literate wants to write his own software package to store customer details.

a) Give **one** reason why this decision may be the most sensible option. (1)
b) Give **three** other ways of acquiring this software package. (3)

4 A large retail company is considering a new computerised help desk system for recording and supporting ICT-related problems.

a) Name **two** ways in which this software could be obtained. (2)
b) Describe **three** factors that might affect the company's decision on how to obtain this software. (6)

ICT5 June 2005

5 A record company wishes to use a database management system to store details of all their suppliers. As an ICT consultant, you have been asked for advice.

Discuss the various options that the company has.
Your discussion should include:

- the various ways in which the software could be provided
- why data portability is an important criterion in the selection of software
- other evaluation criteria that the company should use
- the contents of the evaluation report.

Your answer must be written in the form of an essay. (20)

6 One method of providing a software solution is to write your own software.

a) Explain why this method may not be the most reliable. (2)
b) Explain why this method has been used less in recent years. (2)

7 A business manager is told that a good way of providing a software solution is to customise a generic package.

a) What is meant by a generic package? (1)
b) Using an example, explain what is meant by customisation in this instance. (3)

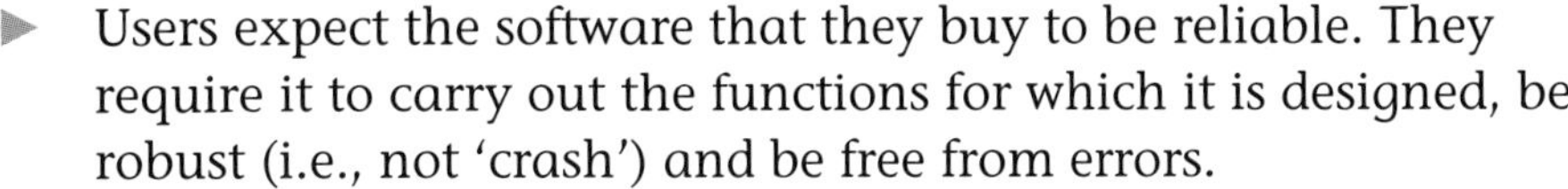

22 Software reliability

Users expect the software that they buy to be reliable. They require it to carry out the functions for which it is designed, be robust (i.e., not 'crash') and be free from errors.

To make sure that software is reliable a process of rigorous **testing** needs to be carried out. Testing is a process of running a program with pre-selected data to make sure that it performs in exactly the way that the specification lays down. The choice of data is not a random thing: every test will have a specific purpose and the output that is produced will be checked against the expected output.

Testing may also highlight other desirable changes to software. For example, the user interface may prove unwieldy or inappropriate or default values for some fields may need to be changed.

When testing highlights an error, a process of **debugging** will need to be followed. This involves studying the program code to find the source of the problem (the bug). This can prove to be a time-consuming activity.

A **test plan** is needed to ensure that the software is tested rigorously. The test plan provides a structured approach to testing and should ensure that all the required options are included. When the plan has been prepared, it can be carried out by anyone as the testing will consist of entering the specified data and recording the outcome. The results of the tests can then be compared with the expected outcomes. If the actual outcome does not match the expected outcome, the tester can report the occurrence and the software solution will need to be modified.

The process of rigorous testing must take place before the software is released on the market. If new software contains many errors, it will, at best, be embarrassing for the software company. At worst, it will lead to a loss of confidence in the company's products and affect sales.

Software is tested in stages.

Alpha testing

Alpha testing is performed in-house by the developers of the software, using a fixed set of data to generate predicted results. The test data used is carefully chosen to test all parts of the system. Alpha testing is designed to show that all parts of the solution work as the developer expects. When alpha testing is completed, the developing company can be satisfied that the software generally works before it is released outside the company.

The people carrying out the testing process are unlikely to be the same people who developed the software as it is very hard for programmers to look objectively at a program that they have written themselves.

Alpha testing could involve testing with different hardware platforms and different operating systems.

When alpha testing is complete and any changes made in the light of the results of the testing, beta testing can be undertaken.

Beta testing

Beta testing is performed by a selected set of potential end-users outside the developing organisation to ensure that the solution works in real situations.

The software will be tested using real data in a real situation, using different platforms (different processors, different memory sizes, and so on). Beta testers may have many different types of software installed and running on their computers, so any problems caused can be highlighted.

The particular situations may not have been considered by the developers; testers are likely to use the system in unpredicted ways. This may detect errors not previously found. Thus beta testing provides a more extensive method of testing and a wider variety of issues with the system are likely to be highlighted.

With the growth of the Internet, beta software is often distributed freely over the web to enable a wider audience to test it. For example, Microsoft distribute beta software over the Internet and often release their operating systems in different beta stages.

When Microsoft developed Windows XP, they had over 3,000 alpha testers. They then distributed the beta version to nearly half a million beta testers!

Why is beta testing used?

There are a number of advantages of getting real users involved in the testing of newly-developed software.

The testers are independent of the producers and therefore impartial. They are interested in finding out whether the software actually does the job they want it to do.

The product is tested in the 'real world' under realistic conditions. There are many modes of use of software that reveal errors only when real users use it. Users can sometimes try to do things that have not been thought of by the designers and programmers. Sometimes a particular, unusual, sequence of key presses or option choices can lead to an unexpected error. The volume of data and frequency of access may far exceed that used in alpha testing. More platforms can be used for testing than the software company is likely to possess.

The users can provide valuable feedback to the developers so that problems can be put right before the software is distributed more widely.

Beta testers are able to try out new software before most people. For many people it is rewarding to be involved in an important part of the production of new software.

Beta testers may enter into an agreement with the software house to test the software in certain situations. They must not distribute the software to any other users. The agreement might state that they will be entitled to a discount when the software is eventually marketed.

Some beta testers may even pay for the privilege so they can get early copies of the software. Beta testing is a vital part of software development. A company needs a sufficient number of beta testers to test the product fully but not too many so that the product becomes too public before it is fully released.

Only if both types of testing are successful will the software be released for sale. Windows XP took several years to develop. Firstly, faults had to be ironed out in house. Eventually, six months before the program went on sale, beta copies were sent out to testers. Several bugs still remained which had to be corrected before distribution. Of course, distribution outside the company reduces security. By the time Windows XP was released, the press knew exactly what it would do.

Activity 1

Use a search engine such as Google.co.uk to search for sites that recruit beta testers. Find three different software developers who are recruiting beta testers. Copy the table below and answer the questions for each site.

	Site 1	Site 2	Site 3
Name of software developer			
Who can be a beta tester?			
What are the benefits to the tester?			
What does beta testing involve?			

case study 1
A beta tester

Julian is a computer consultant who volunteers to beta test software. He first got involved with beta testing after being approached to look into an early version of Windows. 'I was disappointed about a number of things in the beta version not getting into the final release, so I vented my anger by writing to Mr B Gates at Microsoft,' he said.

Not expecting an answer, he was surprised when a personal reply arrived. The upshot was that he was invited to join a group of beta testers called Club Internet Explorer.

Julian gives many reasons for being a beta tester. He gets to know the software. As a computer consultant, customers with a problem expect him to know their package inside out. He gets the chance to use software before it is released on the market. He had a new version of Windows up and running a year before it went public.
'You get a lot of free software,' he says. 'There are always goodies from the computer firms.'

Julian's real satisfaction comes when his suggestions are incorporated in the final released version of the product.

The group of beta testers are not paid and as the beta software is not fully tested there is a relatively high risk. 'I've never lost any data through using beta software,' Julian says. 'But frankly, if you use beta test software to run your business you are daft.'

- What advantages does the beta testing process bring to a) Julian and b) Microsoft?
- Julian detected some bugs in a version of Windows that had not been picked up during alpha testing. Why did this happen?

Sample questions

1. Differentiate between *alpha-testing* and *beta-testing*. (4)
   ICT5 June 2003
2. Describe two benefits that a software manufacturer gets from customers trialling a new operating system before it is made generally available. (4)
   ICT5 June 2001

Testing bespoke software

When software has been specially written for an organisation by a software house, a programme of testing will have to be agreed between the two parties. It is likely that the client organisation will provide the software house with realistic test data.

Once the software house has completed testing and put right any errors that have come to light during the testing process, the software will be handed over to the organisation to carry out its own testing. This phase is known as **acceptance testing**. Users will run the software with real life data under normal working conditions. Only once they are happy that the software fully meets the original requirements will the software be accepted.

Software errors

However well they are tested, programs can still be sold with faults in them. The commercial demands to get software into the shops, the many different platforms and operating systems that are now available and the huge number of possible paths in a program means that making software bug-free is almost impossible. The errors may only come to light when the program has been marketed.

In September 1999, a NASA spaceship costing around $125 million crash-landed on Mars after a voyage of 122 million miles taking nine months. The craft was destroyed and the crash blamed on software error.

Errors in personal finance software, QuickTax, which was designed to help income tax payers fill in a new self-assessment form, led taxpayers to fill in their self-assessment forms wrongly. Several errors were reported by users, which the company said were the result of inadequate testing.

Maintenance releases

Software developers usually produce later versions of a software package some time after the original is distributed. These are called maintenance releases and they include changes to the original version of the software. There are a number of reasons for changing the software.

The changes could be made to put right errors in the original software that come to light after it has originally been released. These errors are usually reported by end–users. Microsoft Office has a feature that allows the user to inform the company directly if a fault occurs that has not been met before. Modifying software to correct errors is often known as **corrective** maintenance.

Changes could be made to improve performance of the software in some way, for example the speed taken to carry out a particular function. This is often known as **perfective** maintenance.

Adaptive maintenance is a name given to modifications that are made to meet changing needs, for example, the introduction of the euro or to interface with a new operating system.

If major, extensive changes are made then a new, upgraded version of the software will be produced. This will involve extensive rewriting of the software and will go through all the normal development changes, including alpha and beta testing.

The software producer must ensure that all existing licensed users are given details of any maintenance changes. Very often a **software patch** is produced. A software patch is a mini program, a brief piece of code that will make the correct changes to overcome the specific problem in the software.

Maintenance is provided for customers in a variety of ways:

- by carrying out a **mail shot to all licensed users** who have registered for support, including a floppy disk or CD-ROM containing the software patch or patches of the changes which need to be made. It is therefore important that users register with the software producer by completing and returning licence agreements.
- Increasingly, users can **access a software developer's website** where technical staff can obtain details of known errors and ways to deal with them, as well as download a software patch that they can then install on their system to overcome the error.
- If the problem is extensive the software house may **recall all the current licensed copies** of the software and provide the users with a new, corrected, version of the software. The new, amended, version of the software would then be available to new purchasers.

Software numbering

Software is often given a version number or a number representing the year it was introduced, for example, CorelDraw 10 or Microsoft Office 2000. When an upgrade version of CorelDraw 9 was produced with more features it was called CorelDraw 10.

A corrected version of software is not an upgrade. It will usually be given a .1 number, for example, Netscape 6.1.

Maintenance updates of these products may be numbered .11, for example, 6.11.

Why things can still go wrong

Even when rigorous testing has taken place software may fail to operate successfully as part of an information system.

This could be because the software was not designed for the situation in which it is being used. Perhaps the volume of the data and the size of the resulting files are much greater than the software was designed for. A user might use the software in ways that had never been considered causing software to behave in unexpected ways.

It could be that the software is being used in a different environment (see the Air Traffic Control case study on page 274).

New software cannot be tested for use with every combination of hardware and other software. Installing and using new software may cause an established system to fail.

It is not uncommon for a software house to release a product when inadequate time has been given to the testing process. This may be because the requirement to keep development costs to defined limits or the need to keep development time to tight deadlines means that not enough time can be allocated to testing.

It may be urgent to release the software as soon as possible in order to get the product to the market first, before other companies, thus gaining an edge over the competition.

Much software produced today is very complex and contains many features; it is simply not possible to test every part of the system with every other part. A particular combination may only be first used some considerable time after the software has been released, thus highlighting the error in the software for the first time.

Another reason could be incompatibility. The software might need to interface with parts of an information system and compatibility problems might arise.

The hardware resources provided to run the software may not be sufficient for it to run at its optimum. This could cause systems to run unacceptably slowly or even to crash frequently. New hardware could be released that the software will not work with and the developing company would not have been aware of these changes when the software was developed.

Of course, the problem could be that the test plan and the data used were inadequate and that the software had not in fact been adequately tested.

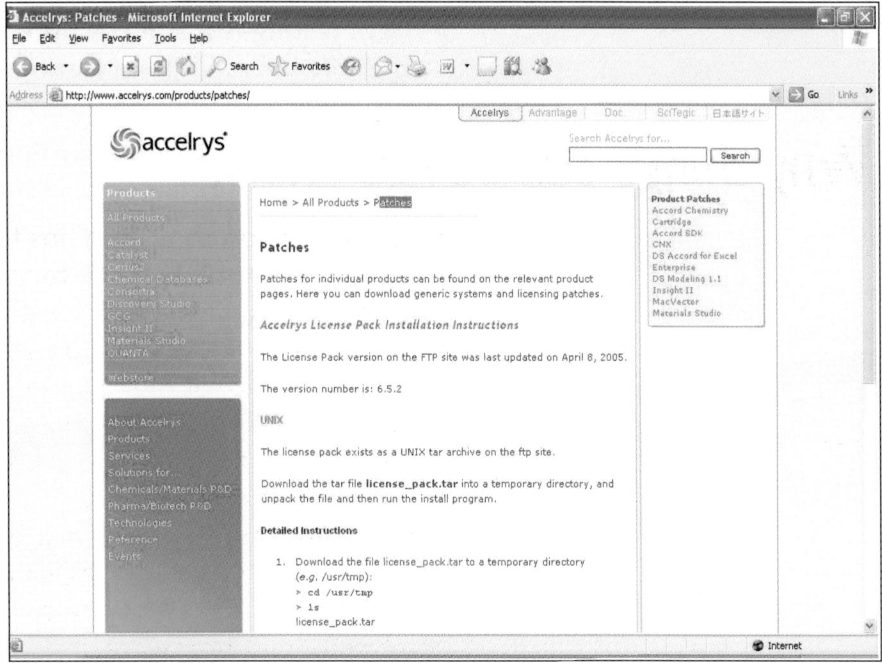

Figure 22.1 Getting hold of software patches

case study 2

Air Traffic Control problems at Heathrow

Several years ago a new computerised air traffic control system was installed at Heathrow airport. The software was tried and tested, having been in use for a number of years at several airports in the USA.

The original system took 1600 programmer years to write and a further 500 programmer years for developers to modify it for the more crowded skies of southern England.

When the system was put into action at Heathrow, there were a number of serious errors still remaining. One problem concerned the way in which the program dealt with the Greenwich meridian. The program contained a model of the airspace it was controlling, that is, a map of the air lanes and beacons in the area.

As the program was designed for use in the USA, the designers had not taken into account the possibility of a zero longitude, consequently the need to consider negative values was ignored. The software caused the computer to, in effect, fold the map of Britain in two at the Greenwich meridian, placing Norwich on top of Birmingham.

1. Describe, in your own words, the nature of the error and how it arose.
2. How could the problem have been avoided?

SUMMARY

- **Testing is a process of running a program with pre-selected data to make sure that it performs in exactly the way that the specification lays down.**
- **Alpha testing is in-house testing by a software company.**
- **Beta testing is testing by potential end users from outside the software company, testing the software in realistic situations.**
- **Maintenance releases are minor changes to existing software. Small changes can be made through the use of software patches that are supplied free to registered users.**
- **Maintenance releases can be issued for three reasons:**
  - **corrective**
  - **perfective**
  - **adaptive.**

Chapter 22 Questions

1. Software houses often produce maintenance releases during the life of a product.
Describe **three** different types of circumstance for which a maintenance release is required. (6)
ICT5 June 2001

2 A software manufacturer is developing a new program to enable people to keep track of their household expenses. Testing is an essential stage in the development of the new system.

Discuss the testing programme that the manufacturer should undertake, paying particular attention to the following:

- the need for, and content of, a test plan
- the different types of testing that should be used in a testing programme
- the reasons why errors might still occur when software is released after a testing programme has taken place
- how solutions to the problems causing such errors might be distributed from the manufacturers to the customers. (20)

The quality of Written Communication will be assessed in your answer.

3. Describe **three** reasons why newly purchased software may fail to operate successfully, even if the developer has followed an extensive testing programme. (6)
ICT5 January 2004

4. A software development company has created an image manipulation package.

a) Describe the process of testing you would expect to happen before this package is released to the general public. (4)

b) After it has been released users find that the software 'crashes'. Explain why this may be the case. (2)

c) During the lifetime of the software the company produces several maintenance releases.

i. Describe **three** reasons why maintenance releases may be required. (6)

ii. Describe **one** way that the maintenance releases may be distributed. (2)

ICT5 June 2005

23 Portability of data

What is portability?

The ability to transfer data to or from another package or hardware platform is a feature that is a very important requirement for users. This means data does not have to be typed in again, which would waste time and could lead to errors.

Data is said to be **portable** if it can be transferred from one application to another in electronic form. Portability has a specialist meaning here – it doesn't mean 'you can put a floppy disk in your pocket and carry it around'!

Why is portability important?

It is vital that different applications can share data. This might mean two different pieces of software on the same PC, two different PCs sharing the same software, two different platforms running different software or even transferring data from an external device such as a digital camera to a PC.

The growth in the use of networks has increased the need for portable data files. Portability ensures that data files produced on one application can be accessed by other applications, or by the same application on different hardware platforms.

Examples of portability

1. Web pages written in HTML are portable. They can be accessed from different platforms with different browser software. Not only should text be transferable but also the layout of the page and any graphics, sound and video files.
2. Data can be transferred between different versions of the same application such as Microsoft Office XP and Microsoft Office 2003. A user may have different versions of the software available at home and at work and will need to be able to transfer data between the two computer systems.
3. Data can also be transferred between different software packages such as between Microsoft Office and the open source package Star Office.
4. Microsoft Office is available for both the PC and the Apple Mac. Files can be created and accessed on either platform. A freelance journalist carrying out much of his work at home using a PC but sending articles to a magazine he works for that uses a network of Apple Macs will need such portability.

5. Music files from a CD can be loaded into a PC, compressed and then transferred to an MP3 player that is light and can be taken anywhere.
6. A sales manager needs to write a report on the performance of her sales representatives during the past year. She produces the report using word processing software. Details of sales throughout the year are maintained on a spreadsheet that has graphing capabilities. The sales manager would like to include graphics and tables into her report. Ideally this data can be **imported** into the word processor from the spreadsheet.

The need for standards

Portability can only exist if different manufacturers agree to adopt standards – agreed rules for the interchange of text, numeric data and graphics and common operating systems.

Without these standards it would not be possible to transfer data between different computers or between other devices such as palmtops, mobile phones, digital cameras, video cameras and MP3 players.

Early microcomputers had no common standard for storing data. As a result it was very difficult to transfer data between computers made by different manufacturers. Today manufacturers have adopted a standard set of formats.

Portability is an important sales feature for hardware and software companies. If you bought a new computer system, you would expect to be able to transfer data from your old machine. If you bought a more recent software version, you would expect it to be able to read data from the previous version. If you bought a digital camera, you would expect to be able to transfer the images to your PC.

Hardware standards. Today most computers have a number of USB ports, which are used to connect a wide range of peripherals such as digital cameras, hard disks, modems, scanners, printers and mice. This equipment must also conform to standards, which means that buyers are no longer restricted to one company. Competition means cheaper prices for the buyer.

Software standards. The use of software standards should make applications easier to use by having a common feel. It is standard that the F1 key is used for Help. The names of menus and their positions are consistent. Software can usually save work in a variety of different formats which enable portability and compatibility. Information can be viewed on the web if it is saved as an HTML file. Most modern packages have this feature.

Common operating systems There are very few operating systems in common use for PCs, normally only Linux, Apple and Windows. As a result, software manufacturers only have to develop their software for a limited range of operating systems. This means that they can produce a wider range of software.

Examples of common file standards
ASCII code, developed by the American Standard Code for Information Interchange, is an internationally-agreed binary code used in computer systems to store alphanumeric characters. It is an 8-bit code, that is each character is represented by a unique eight bit binary code. It is used by virtually all small computer systems.

Unicode is a newer international standard code. It uses a 16-bit code for each character, and therefore is able to include more characters than ASCII. Whereas ASCII code can be used for only 256 characters, Unicode can have 65,536 different characters – enough for nearly all the languages in the world. Unicode includes the ASCII character set within it.

CSV (Comma Separated Variable) format is used for transferring data to and from databases and spreadsheets. Each field or cell is separated from the next by a comma.

Graphics can be stored in a number of formats and most programs can import images in a number of forms, such as **BMP** (a Bitmap picture). They can also import images in compressed formats used for storing Internet pictures such as **GIF** (Graphics Interchange Format) and **JPG** (Joint Photographic Expert Group).

Protocols

Protocols are sets of formal rules and procedures that define how devices can communicate. Without protocols there would be no agreed way in which a computer could transfer data to and from another computer.

Protocols enable the use of open systems - computer systems that can communicate regardless of the manufacturer and the platform. This is very important for the Internet which can be accessed by a wide variety of hardware devices such as digital TV, mobile phones and PDAs.

Internet protocols, standards and address mechanisms

The Internet uses a number of internationally-agreed standards and protocols which mean that it can be accessed by a variety of hardware platforms. These standards also mean that it is possible to access the net with digital TV, mobile phones and PDAs.

The standards ensure that there is a reliable connection between devices and provide error detection and correction mechanisms.

Examples of Internet protocols include:

File Transfer Protocol (FTP)	FTP allows a file to be transferred from one computer to another. Often used to upload files onto the World Wide Web
HyperText Transfer Protocol (HTTP)	A standard for transferring web pages
Post Office Protocol (POP)	A protocol that defines standards for transferring e-mail between computers.
Transmission Control Protocol/Internet Protocol (TCP/IP)	A protocol that allows Internet providers and users to communicate with each other, no matter what hardware is used.
Wireless Application Protocol (WAP)	A standard for wireless communication networks used by mobile phones to access the Internet

Other standards used by the World Wide Web include:

IP (Internet Protocol) address	Every device, such as a computer, connected to the web has to have a unique IP address of the form 192.168.0.233 so that any device on the web can be uniquely identified and data is transferred to the correct device. Find out your PC's IP address at www.whatismyip.com A URL such as www.tesco.com simply maps to an IP address but is more easily understood and more easily remembered.
HyperText Mark-up Language (HTML)	Web pages are stored in a standard format up (HTML) which can be accessed by a variety of browsers and a variety of hardware platforms. You can see the HTML coding of any web pages in Microsoft Internet Explorer by clicking on **View > Source**.

Gif and jpg images	These image formats use compression techniques to store graphics files, meaning they can load in a fraction of the time it would take to load a picture in bitmap format.
Animated gifs and Flash animations	Files that can be embedded in HTML pages allowing eye-catching moving images
JavaScript	A scripting language for the World Wide Web that can be included in HTML pages and gives interactivity to web pages.
Portable Document Format (PDF)	A format for saving a document that can be viewed on the web using freely available software such as Adobe Acrobat Reader. PDF format is used as this sort of software is available for free whereas other software such as Microsoft Word is not. The page formatting, the fonts, images, etc can be included in PDF format. It is possible to copy and paste from PDF files but the document can be password protected to prevent text being copied.

Benefits and limitations of standards

The main advantage of standards is that the user is not restricted to one manufacturer's equipment. Even if one company's computers are all the same make, they may wish to communicate with another company whose hardware is different e.g. for EDI. This would not be possible without protocols.

Being able to choose from a variety of manufacturers means there is competition and prices are likely to be lower.

The main disadvantage of standards and protocols is that they are difficult to change. It is difficult and takes time to get universal agreement on the establishment of new standards. In a fast-changing area, standards may not be able to keep up with technological developments. Open systems based on old standards may be unacceptably slow.

Having to follow standards means that in some cases the full power of the machine might not be available and there might therefore be reduced functionality or performance. Bespoke software, designed specifically for use on a particular platform and ignoring standards, makes better use of the hardware.

Development of protocols and standards

De jure standards

Many standards are formally introduced, often after considerable deliberation by an international committee. These are called *de jure* standards and include:

- ASCII code devised by the American Standard Code for Information Interchange
- The JPG image format was developed by the Joint Photographic Experts Group (JPEG) which represents a wide variety of companies and academic institutions worldwide
- Most Internet protocols such as TCP/IP were drawn up by CERN (the European Organisation for Nuclear Research, an international group of 20 member countries based in Geneva, Switzerland).

De facto standards

Other standards known as *de facto* standards arise through historic precedence or as a result of marketing and sales success of a particular product.

Examples of de facto standards include:

- MS-DOS and Microsoft Windows have become the standard operating system and GUI for PCs
- The GIF image format was created in 1987 by Internet company CompuServe as a format to transmit images over the Internet
- The standard $3\frac{1}{2}$ inch floppy disk was introduced by Sony in 1980. There were many competing formats but over time the industry settled on the $3\frac{1}{2}$ inch format which is now the standard
- The USB 1.1 was developed in 1998, by companies that included DEC, IBM, Intel, Microsoft, and Compaq. USB 1.1 was integrated into Microsoft Windows 98
- PDF format has become the de facto standard for document sharing on the web. PDF is an open standard but was developed by Adobe.

Often de facto standards have evolved, not because they are technically the best but due to commercial or other pressures. In the 1980s there were two types of video recorder: VHS and Betamax. Betamax was widely regarded as being the better quality but VHS became more popular due to better marketing. Betamax flopped while VHS became the standard.

A similar situation is happening in ICT. Microsoft MS-DOS and Windows have such a dominant market share that they have become the standard operating system for a PC. It doesn't mean they are the best. Many people swear by the Apple Macintosh or Linux.

However as Windows has such a large market share, software developers are more likely to be interested in producing new software for Windows than, say, the Linux operating system.

case study 1

▶ Wi-Fi

802.11 standard is a standard used for wireless local area networks (WLANs). It was developed by the IEEE (Institute of Electrical and Electronics Engineers), an international organisation that develops standards for hundreds of electronic and electrical technologies.

Networks using the 802.11 standard are often called Wi-Fi, short for wireless fidelity. As technology has improved, different versions of the standard have been developed using different radio frequencies and offering different speeds of data transfer.

802.11b is a standard for WLANs offering speeds of up to 11 Mbps; 802.11g is a new standard offering speeds of up to 54 Mbps. The latest Wi-Fi standard (802.11n) will bring faster transmission speeds of up to 100 Mbps.

What users will want to know is if increased performance justifies increased cost and if there will be problems on a mixed network.

1. What is a standard?
2. Is Wi-Fi a 'de facto' or a 'de jure' standard?
3. Why is a standard like 802.11 necessary?
4. What is the main disadvantage of standards like 802.11?
5. Use the Internet to research the latest 802.11 standards for WLANs.

Worked exam question

An office worker is having problems connecting to the Internet. A technician fixes this problem, but finds that several websites cannot be viewed correctly, as the page content is not standard.

a) Define the term *protocol* in relation to networking. (2)

b) Explain why standards are important for communication over the Internet. (3)

c) Explain the need for standard data representation in relation to networking and the Internet. (2)

ICT5 January 2005

▶ **SAMPLE ANSWER**

There are two marks in part (a), one for defining a protocol and the other for relating it to networking.

A protocol is a set of formal rules and procedures that define how devices communicate over a network.

There are three marks in part (b) so three different points are wanted such as:

Standards enable open systems so different devices can access the Internet.
Standards allow an IP address so that devices can be uniquely identified.
Standards enable users to share documents in common formats such as PDF.

There are two marks in part (c) so two different points are wanted such as:

Standard data representation allows different browsers to interpret the data.
Standard data representation allows different hardware platforms access to the data.

SUMMARY

- **Data is said to be** portable **if it can be transferred from one computer platform to another or from one software application to another.**
- Standards **have developed for the interchange of text, numeric data and graphics.**
- Protocols **are the formal rules and procedures that need to be followed to allow data to be transferred between devices.**
- **Standards are difficult to change and so may be out of date as technology advances. Open systems based on old standards may be unacceptably slow.**
- **There are a variety of Internet protocols such as TCP/IP and HTTP.**
- **Some standards are developed formally** (de jure standards) **whilst** de facto standards **grow out of historic or commercial precedence.**

Chapter 23 Questions

1 Give **three** examples from everyday life that illustrate the use of standards. (3)

2 Standards in the ICT industry have risen *de facto*.

a) What is meant by the term *de facto*? (1)

b) Give an example of a *de facto* standard. (1)

c) Describe another way in which standards can arise in the ICT industry. (2)

d) Give an example of this standard. (1)

3 Networks of computers are rapidly becoming part of everyday life, both for organisations and individuals.

Communication over networks involves the use of protocols.

a) Define the term protocol. (1)

b) With the aid of an example, describe **one** advantage of using protocols. (3)

c) State **one** consideration that should be taken into account when setting up a network, and explain why it is important. (2)

ICT5 June 2002

4 Using an example, explain what we mean by the term protocol and why protocols are so important to the Internet. (3)

5 Many protocols for the World Wide Web were laid down by CERN, the European Organisation for Nuclear Research based near Geneva.

a) What do we call standards that arise in this way? (1)

b) URLs begin with http. What does this mean? (1)

c) Every computer connected to the Internet has to have a unique IP address. What does IP stand for? (1)

d) Why does this address have to be unique? (1)

6 Most word processing packages can save and open files in Rich Text Format (RTF), a file format that has been developed by Microsoft.

a) Explain why it is an advantage to buy a word processing package that can open and save files in RTF? (2)

b) What sort of standard is RTF? (1)

Exam tips: writing an essay

▶ The last question on A2 exam papers is usually an essay question worth 20 marks.

The question normally includes around 4 bullet points. Writing about each bullet point will gain up to four marks per bullet point. The final four marks are for the quality of language used.

In writing an essay it is important to:

- write in continuous prose i.e. write in sentences. Use paragraphs.
- avoid using bullet points and abbreviations such as 'texting' language
- cover all the points in the question
- have a structure to the essay.

The structure means that the essay must have a beginning, a middle and an end. The beginning is a brief introduction describing the subject, the middle covers all the bullet points in turn. The end is a conclusion.

The best way to ensure that the essay is well structured is to spend five minutes planning the essay. Even though you are likely to come under time pressures in the exams, this is time well spent.

Plan by drawing a mind map, writing down as many points as you can related to the question. Then link them to the bullet points in the question. A spider diagram may help. (An example is shown below.) The plan should ensure that your essay will be in a logical order.

Essay example:

Two building societies have agreed to merge but have discovered that they use completely different computer hardware and software to store their customers' accounts. Neither software application is available on the other hardware.

The board of directors has to decide whether to continue with two computer systems or to have a standard computer system with a common user interface across the whole organisation and have asked you for your advice. Discuss the options available. Include in your discussion:

- the benefits of a standard computer system across the whole organisation
- issues that will need to be addressed if the building society adopts a standard system

- measures that will need to be taken to ensure a smooth change
- the possibility of using emulation.

Your answer must be written in the form of an essay. (20)

The diagram below has four 'spiders' – one for each bullet point in the question. The idea is to write down items to include on that point in your essay. When you have sufficient items for every bullet point, you can start writing your essay.

Keep to a logical order by covering each bullet point in turn. Write at least one sentence on each of the items in your spider diagram.

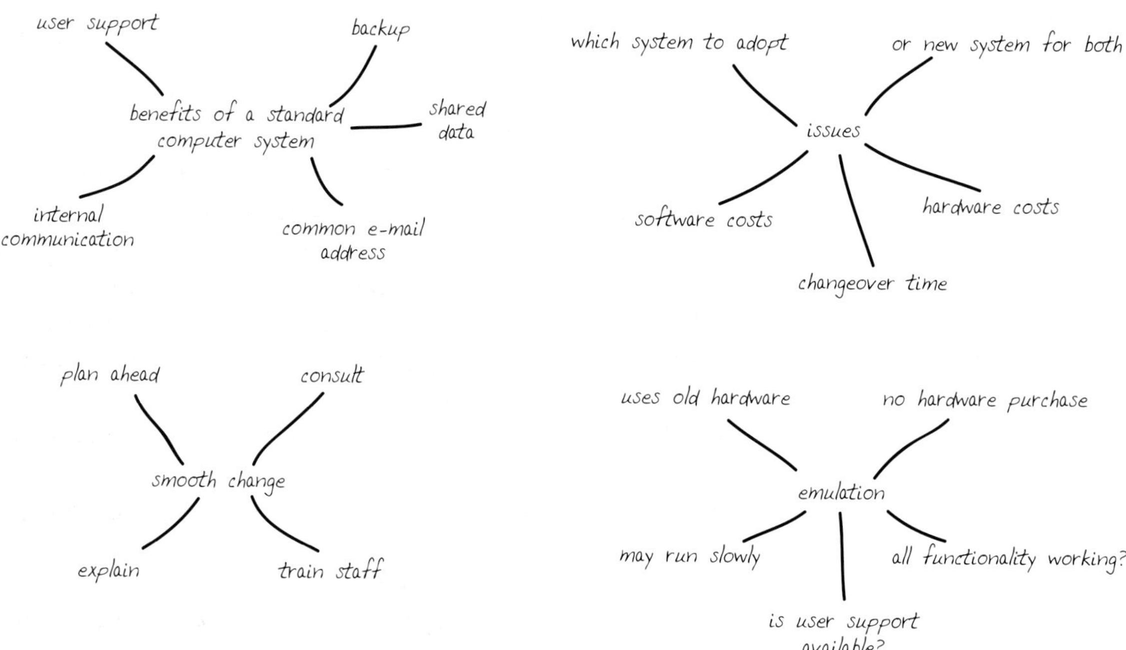

Glossary

Alphanumeric characters	Letters, numbers or other characters, for example punctuation marks.
ASCII	(American Standard Code for Information Interchange). The binary code used in computers to store alphanumeric characters.
ATM	(Automatic Teller Machine). The official name for cash machines outside banks.
Backup	To make an extra copy of stored data in case the original is lost or corrupted.
Bandwidth	Physical limitations of a communication system (usually bits/sec).
Batch processing	A form of processing where all the information is batched together before being processed.
Bit	(Binary digit). A binary number which can only have the value 0 or 1.
Bitmap	An image which stores the colour of every pixel.
Blog	A blog, weblog, or web log is a web page that contains periodic posts. They are often simply individuals' diaries or journals.
Bluetooth	A protocol for the wireless connection of different types of devices – such as a mobile phone with a desktop computer. Bluetooth devices have a short range and do not need a line-of-sight connection.
Broadband	A data transmission method that involves several channels of data and so is faster than older methods.
Browser	A program that allows the user to access a database (typically the Internet).
Buffer	Memory where data is stored while waiting to be processed, typically in a printer.
Bugs	Errors in computer programs.
Byte	A group of eight bits, normally storing one alphanumeric character.
Cache	A very fast but more expensive computer memory.
Caching	Storing Internet files locally – usually on the computer's hard drive – to enable the files to load quickly if revisited.
CAD	Computer Aided Design.
CD-ROM	Compact Disc-Read Only Memory. A small plastic disc used to store data.
Compression	A method of reducing the size of a file, typically to use less disk space.
Configure	To set up a computer system for the appropriate hardware and software. A system will need to be configured for the printers, sound cards and so on.
Crop	To trim part of a picture.
CSS	Cascading Style Sheet. A way of specifying the appearance of pages on a website. The background, font, colour and font size of several pages can be altered simply by altering the CSS.
Cursor	The screen pointer, usually an arrow, which is controlled by the mouse.
Cyber-	A prefix alluding to computer communication often with reference to the Internet as in cybershopping, shopping by computer, cyberspace, everything accessible by computer communications.

Database	A structured set of data stored on a computer.
Data integrity	The reliability of data, that is ensuring it is accurate.
Data security	Keeping data safe from loss.
DBMS	A set of programs allowing the user to access data in a database.
DDE	Dynamic Data Exchange. Shared data in two packages is linked so that when it is updated in one program, it is automatically updated in the other program.
Debug	Remove bugs from a program.
Desktop	An icon-based user interface that enables the user to load software easily. When you load Microsoft Windows, you see the desktop.
Digital	Something that is represented in numerical form typically in binary numbers.
Direct-mail	Advertising a product by sending details directly to potential buyers through the post.
Directory	An area (usually of a disk) where files are stored. A disk may have several directories and sub-directories to make finding files easier and to aid security.
Dongle	A piece of hardware, for example a lead that has to be plugged in to the computer before software will run. Usually used to protect copyright.
DOS	Disk Operating System.
Dot.com	A company usually trading exclusively via the Internet.
DPI	Dots per inch – describes the performance of a printer.
DVD	Digital Versatile Disk. An optical disk which has greater capacity than a CD-ROM.
e-banking	The use of the Internet to communicate with your bank.
e-commerce	The use of computers and electronic communications in business transactions, including websites, EDI, on-line databases and EFTPOS systems.
EDI	Electronic Data Interchange. Transferring information such as orders and invoices electronically between two organisations.
e-tailors	Retailers who do business on the Internet.
e-shopping	Using the Internet to purchase goods and services.
EFTPOS	Electronic Funds Transfer at Point of Sale. The system where customers can pay by debit (Switch) card and the money is taken electronically from their bank account.
Embedding	Including one file (such as an image or a document) in another file. See OLE (Object Linking and Embedding).
Emoticon	Little text-based faces you may see in e-mail and online chat. For example, :-)
Encryption	To scramble data into a secure code to prevent it being read by unauthorised users.
Extranet	The linking of two intranets usually to assist business transaction, for example linking a customer and a supplier.
FAQ	Frequently Asked Questions. A file containing answers to common questions, for example about using a program.
Fax modem	A modem that enables a computer to send and receive faxes.
Fibre optic	A cable made out of glass fibre and used in communications.
Filters	An option in a program enabling the user to import files from or export files to another program.

Firewall	Either hardware or software used to protect a networked computer system from damage by unauthorised users.
Flatbed scanner	A scanner in which the item to be scanned is placed on a flat piece of glass.
Firewire	An interface used to connect devices such as video cameras and MP3 players to a computer system.
Floppy disk	A small removable disk in a hard plastic case, used to store data.
Gif	Graphics Interchange Format. A format used for storing compressed images on World Wide Web pages. These images are usually called a 'gif'.
Gigabyte (GB)	A measure of memory capacity equal to roughly 1 000 000 000 bytes (it is exactly 2 to the power 30 or 1 073 741 824).
GUI	Graphical User Interface, for example Windows. It is sometimes pronounced 'gooey'.
Hacking	Unauthorised access to a computer system, possibly for criminal purposes.
Hand scanner	A small device, held in the hand and dragged over the item to be scanned.
Hard disk	A magnetic disk inside a computer that can store much more data than a floppy disk. Usually it cannot be removed but removable hard disks are becoming more common.
Hardware	The physical parts of the computer, such as the processor, keyboard and printer.
HTML	HyperText Markup Language. The language that web pages are written in.
HTTP	HyperText Transfer Protocol. The standard protocol for sending and receiving data on the Internet.
Integrated package	A package which combines several different applications such as a word processor, a graphics package, database, communications software and spreadsheet.
Interactive	A system where there is communication between the user and the computer.
Internet	An international WAN providing information pages and e-mail facilities for millions of users.
Internet conferencing	Using a PC and the Internet to hold virtual meetings, using for example NetMeeting.
Intranet	A private internal network using Internet software, that can be used for internal e-mail and information.
IRC	Internet Relay Chat. A function of the Internet allowing users to send and receive real-time text messages.
ISDN	Integrated Services Digital Network. A telecommunications digital network which is faster than an analogue network using a modem.
ISP	Internet Service Provider. A company that offers a connection to the Internet.
Java	A programming language used for utilities on web pages.
JPG or JPEG	Joint Photographic Expert Group. An ISO standard for storing images in compressed form. Pronounced jay-peg.
Kilobyte (KB)	A measure of memory capacity equal to 1024 bytes.
Licence agreement	The document which defines how software can be used, particularly how many people can use it.

Macro	A small program routine usually defined by the user.
Magnetic disk	A small disk coated with magnetic material on which data is stored. It can be a floppy disk or a hard disk.
Magnetic tape	A long plastic tape coated with magnetic material on which data is stored.
Mail-merge	A feature of a word processing program that combines details from a file of names and addresses into personal letters.
Master file	The file where the master data is stored. Data from this file is combined with data from the transaction file.
Megabyte (MB)	A measure of memory capacity equal to 1 000 000 bytes (it is exactly 2 to the power 20 or 1 048 576).
MICR	Magnetic Ink Character Recognition. The input method used to read cheques.
Modem	Modulator/demodulator. The device that converts digital computer data into a form that can be sent over the telephone network.
MS-DOS	Microsoft Disk Operating System. The operating system developed for the PC.
Multi-access	A computer system allowing more than one user to access the system at the same time.
Multimedia	A computer system combining text, graphics, sound and video, typically using data stored on CD-ROM.
Multi-tasking	A computer system that can run more than one program simultaneously.
Network	A number of computers connected together.
OLE	(Object Linking and Embedding). A method of taking data from one file (the source file) and placing it in another file (the destination file). Linked data is stored in the source file and updated if you modify the source file. On the other hand, embedded files are part of the destination file.
Online Processing	Processing while the user is in contact with the computer.
Open Source Software	Software where the program source code is openly shared with users who can legally customise programs if they wish.
Operating system	The software that controls the hardware of a computer.
Package	A program or programs for a specific purpose.
Palmtop	A small handheld computer around the size of a pocket calculator.
PDA	Personal Digital Assistant. A handheld portable computer. See also palmtop.
Peer-to-peer	A type of network where there is no server, with each station sharing the tasks.
Pentium™	A processor developed by the Intel Corporation™ for the PC.
Peripheral	Any hardware item that is connected to a computer such as printers, mice or keyboards.
PIN	Personal Identification Number, used to check that the user is the person they claim to be, for example at an ATM.
Platform	Used to describe a hardware or software environment.
Port	A socket usually at the back of the computer.
Portability	The ability to use software, hardware or datafiles on different systems.
Primary Key	A unique identifier in a record in a database.
Protocol	A set of rules for communication between different devices.
QBE	Query By Example. Simple language used to search a database.

RAID	Redundant Array of Inexpensive Disks. A fault tolerant system using two disks to store the same data.
RAM	Random Access Memory. The computer's internal memory used to store the program and data in use. The contents are lost when the power is turned off.
Redundant data	Data that is repeated unnecessarily (in a database).
ROM	Read Only Memory. Part of the computer's memory that is retained even when the power is turned off. Used to store start up program and settings.
Serial access	Accessing data items one after the other until the required one is found. Associated with magnetic tape.
Server	A dedicated computer that controls a network.
Shareware	Software that can legally be distributed freely but users are expected to register with, and pay a fee to, the copyright holder.
Smart card	A plastic card, like a credit card, with an embedded microchip. The information in the chip can be updated, for example when cash has been withdrawn from an ATM.
Software copyright	Laws restricting copying of software.
Software	A computer program or programs.
Systems analyst	A person whose job involves analysing whether a task could be carried out more efficiently by computer.
Toggle switch	A switch or button which if pressed once turns a feature on. If pressed again it turns the feature off. The Caps Lock button is an example.
TCP/IP	Transmission Control Protocol/Internet Protocol. Protocols that enable communication between different types of computers, allowing different types of computers to connect to the Internet.
Transaction file	A file containing new transaction details or changes to old data, which is merged with the master file.
Unicode	A 16-bit code used to store characters in computers.
USB	Universal Serial Bus – a port on the back of a computer used to connect peripherals such as scanners or a palmtop.
USB hub	A device that plugs into the USB port that enables several peripherals to connect to the computer at once.
URL	Uniform Resource Locator – the Internet address, e.g. www.hodderheadline.co.uk
Vector graphics	Image system that stores lines by the length and direction rather than the individual pixels (as in a bitmap).
Webcam	Any video camera whose output is available for viewing via the Internet.
WIMP	Windows, Icon, Mouse, Pointer.
Windows™	A GUI for the PC produced by Microsoft.
Wireless network	A network that uses radio waves to transmit data rather than cables.
WWW	The World Wide Web.
WYSIWYG	What You See Is What You Get.

Index